A Guide to Primary Commodities
in the World Economy

A Guide to Primary Commodities in the World Economy

Marian Radetzki

Basil Blackwell

Copyright © Marian Radetzki 1990

Published by arrangement with SNS Förlag,
Stockholm, Sweden

First published 1990

Basil Blackwell Ltd
108 Cowley Road, Oxford, OX4 1JF, UK

Basil Blackwell, Inc.
3 Cambridge Center
Cambridge, Massachusetts 02142, USA

British Library Cataloguing in Publication Data

A CIP catalogue record for this book is available
from the British Library.

Library of Congress Cataloging in Publication Data

Radetzki, Marian.
  A guide to primary commodities in the world economy / Marian Radetzki
      p.   cm.
  Includes index.
  ISBN 0-631-17112-6
  1. Primary commodities. 2. Commercial policy, 3. Primary commodities—Prices.
  I. Title.
HF1040.7.R33   1990
382'.4—dc20

Typeset in 10 on 12 pt Times
by Setrite Typesetters Limited
Printed in Great Britain by
Billing & Sons Ltd, Worcester

Contents

3.6 Exchange rates and commodity prices   62
3.7 The long-run commodity price trends   65

4   *The Commodity Exchanges*   71
4.1 The commodity exchanges and the commodities traded there   71
4.2 Functions and instruments   76
4.3 Impact on price formation and other influences   87

5   *The Issue of Supply Security*   91
5.1 When will supply disruptions be serious to the importing
     economy?   92
5.2 The nature of problems caused by disrupted commodity
     supply   95
5.3 Measures to alleviate the consequences of supply disruption 97
5.4 The economics of supply security policies   103

6   *Producer Cartels in International Commodity Markets*   107
6.1 The formal preconditions for successful cartel action   107
6.2 Other preconditions for successful cartel action   111
6.3 Actual experiences of commodity cartels   114

7   *Public Ownership of Commodity Production*   129
7.1 How to define and quantify the state enterprise sector   131
7.2 Motivations for public ownership in mineral industries   132
7.3 The distinguishing characteristics of state owned mineral
     firms   134
7.4 The impact of state ownership on the national economy   139
7.5 Implications for the international mineral markets   142

8   *The Problems of Heavy National Dependence on Commodity
     Production and Exports*   146
8.1 Measurement of commodity dependence   146
8.2 Export instability   149
8.3 Extraction of fiscal revenue   159
8.4 The "Dutch disease"   164
8.5 Exchange rate policies in commodity dependent economies 167
8.6 Conclusion: A general case for economic diversification?   170
     Appendix: World Exports of Major Primary Commodities
     1974–1987   173

     Bibliography   175
     Index   182

Acknowledgements

This book would not have been written without the initiatives, encouragement and continuous support of Torgny Wadensjö, Editor in Chief of SNS, the Center for Policy and Business Studies in Stockholm. My academic homes, the Institute for International Economic Studies, University of Stockholm, and the Mineral Economics Department, Colorado School of Mines, provided a congenial and stimulating atmosphere for the work. Ulrik Améen, Rutger Gyllenram and Aake Holmström of the Royal Institute of Technology in Stockholm made substantive inputs to chapter 4 on commodity exchanges. Phillip Crowson, Elke Meldau-Womack, Herman Muegge and Peter Parkinson read the entire draft manuscript; Dean DeRosa, Bo Karlström and Johan Kinberg read selected parts. All of them gave valuable comments which helped me in correcting mistakes, straightening out unclarities and elaborating on incompletely treated issues. Revisions and formatting of the text were skilfully handled by Ann-Charlotte Änggård and Edda Liljenroth.

M. R.

Abbreviations

CBT	Chicago Board of Trade
COMEX	Commodity Exchange
EFTA	European Free Trade Association
EPR	Effective Protection Rate
FAO	Food and Agriculture Organization (of the United Nations)
GATT	General Agreement on Tariffs and Trade
GDP	Gross Domestic Product
GSP	General System of Preferences
IBA	International Bauxite Association
IMF	International Monetary Fund
ISIC	International Standard Industrial Classification
LDC	Less Developed Country
LME	London Metal Exchange
NIC	Newly Industrializing Country
NPC	Nominal Protection Coefficient
NYMEX	New York Mercantile Exchange
OAPEC	Organization of Arab Petroleum Exporting Countries
OECD	Organization for Economic Development and Cooperation
OPEC	Organization of Petroleum Exporting Countries
SDR	Special Drawing Rights (International Monetary Fund currency unit)
SITC	Standard International Trade Classification
STABEX	Stabilization of Export Earnings
UN	United Nations
UNCTAD	United Nations Conference on Trade and Development

Introduction

The purpose of this book is to provide a succinct, but at the same time reasonably complete introduction to the international primary commodity markets. The method of presentation is simple and straightforward. Though the entire analysis is based on economic theory, theoretical constructs are consciously avoided. No particular background is required from the reader, but an understanding of basic economics will be helpful.

The global raw materials markets constitute an important part of the international economy. Trans-border movements of primary commodities account for a significant share of global trade. The economic structure of numerous nations is heavily geared towards the production of exported raw materials. Commodity imports make up sizable components of many countries' food supply. A large part of the world's base industrial activities could not function without foreign raw materials inputs. In the short run, hunger and depression would tend to develop in many places if the international commodity flows were severely disrupted. In the long run, such disruption could be overcome in most cases by expanded local output, but at a very substantial cost caused by the economic loss from tying resources to activities which could be performed cheaper and better elsewhere.

For at least two reasons, primary commodities appear to be "special" and more important than suggested by the figures that indicate their shares in world output and world trade. Both reasons relate to the fact that commodities constitute the initial, basic stage in all production chains.

The first reason why commodities are especially important is that their production and trade continue to constitute the core of the national economy in a great number of poor countries. The inhabitants of these countries comprise a majority of the world's population. Their well-being is crucially dependent on the state and progress of primary commodity markets. In its early stages, the economic development process is seen to hinge importantly on the ability of the raw materials industries either to integrate forward, into processing and manufacturing, or to generate the surpluses needed to finance the economic diversification that regularly characterizes economic progress.

The second reason is the indispensability of commodities for human survival and welfare. This is most clearly evident in the case of food products without which humanity would perish. But the indispensability does not end with food. There could be no shelter without access to structural raw materials; no clothing without the availability of hides and fibres (or the petroleum feedstock from which synthetic fibres are derived). All industrial endeavors which provide for the luxuries of human life beyond the bare needs of food, housing and clothing, are ultimately totally dependent on raw materials. For these reasons, the key categories of primary commodities are much less replaceable than major categories of manufactures, if very substantial welfare losses are to be avoided. In analogy with the argument about the relative utility of a glass of water and a cut diamond in the desert, one can therefore reasonably argue that the ultimate utility, or "intrinsic value" of commodities greatly exceeds the value which they are assigned in market transactions.

Little attention is usually devoted to the international commodity markets when they function normally. Off and on, however, serious disturbances do occur. Examples include (a) the two oil crises of the 1970s, whose severity and durability was magnified and extended by the international petroleum cartel; (b) the cereals price explosion in the early 1970s, resulting from widespread harvest failures; (c) the quintupling of cobalt prices in the late 1970s, in consequence of political upheavals in Central Africa, resulting, with a lag, in wholesale substitution away from this metal; and (d) the profound depression in copper demand in the early 1980s, leading to closures of entire industries and national financial distress in producing countries. On such occasions, the primary commodity markets in crisis receive overwhelming public attention. The institutional forms under which commodities are traded are then put to detailed critical scrutiny. The world is reminded about the intriguing relationships between the developments in commodity markets on the one hand, and the macro- and microeconomic impact of these developments on countries that rely on the exports or imports of raw materials, on the other. The analysis of such institutions and relationships forms an important part of the present book.

A treatise on international commodity markets could adopt one of two basic approaches. The first would be to treat the different commodity groups in turn. The second, more general approach, would organize the subject by looking at specific issues that are of importance in the trade of many commodities. The present book has adopted the second approach. However, to make the analysis more tangible, examples from individual commodity markets are frequently provided, to illustrate the specific issue that is treated.

Chapter 1 presents a geographical and economic overview of international commodity trade. Primary commodities are first defined and categorized into analytically tractable groups. The importance and direction of commodity trade is then analyzed, both in highly aggregate terms, and through more detailed scrutinies of individual countries and commodities. Japan's and Western Europe's great dependence on imported commodity supply is quantified, and the forces that brought this dependence about in the first place are explored.

Comparative advantage implies that it is relatively cheaper to produce a commodity in one country than in another. Such advantage is an important determinant of the location of commodities' production, and of their international trade flows. However, the actual location of raw materials production and processing is also influenced by other considerations, and the outcome often displays a far from economically optimal pattern. Chapter 2 discusses the distortions in this respect caused by protectionism and by the perpetuation of colonial influences on production and trade.

The following two chapters study the institutional arrangements in international commodity markets, and consider the impacts of these arrangements on the way the markets function. Chapter 3 analyzes the mechanisms for price formation under different market forms and trading set-ups. The meaning of different price concepts is clarified in this context. The impact on prices from changes in costs, shifts in exchange rates and "exit barriers" is considered. The instability and the long-run trends in commodity prices are discussed and explained. Chapter 4 is devoted entirely to the analysis of international commodity exchanges, on which trade in commodity futures and options predominates. The major functions of the exchanges and the trading instruments they employ are analyzed in detail. The role of commodity speculators on price stability in different situations is also dealt with.

Chapter 5 considers the importers' concern about international supply security. When the importer is heavily dependent on foreign sources, and when the commodity is not easily substituted in critically important uses, severe damage may be caused by a disturbance in international supply. The nature of the problems caused by disrupted commodity imports is described. The various measures to reduce risks of supply disruption are explored and an attempt is made to relate the costs of these measures to their purported benefits.

The final three chapters look at several issues of concern to the countries that export primary commodities. Chapter 6 analyzes international commodity cartels. The necessary preconditions for launching successful international price-raising measures are first explored. The limits to the durability of such action are then assessed. The chapter ends with analytical accounts of the producers' efforts to cartelize the markets for petroleum, bauxite, phosphate rock, uranium and tin during the 1970s and 1980s. Chapter 7 analyzes the causes and implications, at the national and international level, of the greatly expanded public ownership of commodity production over the past three decades. The emphasis is on the mineral industries of developing countries, since this is where state enterprise has become most common.

Chapter 8, finally, considers the macroeconomic issues that follow from a heavy national dependence on commodity exports. The focus is on developing countries, since such dependence seldom occurs in the diversified economies of industrialized countries. The problems of export revenue instability that often plague commodity dependent economies, are discussed. The major remedies, e.g. price stabilizing commodity agreements and compensatory finance schemes at the international level, but also national stabilization measures, are analyzed. The modes for, and feasible levels of, fiscal revenue extraction from commodity production and trade are explored. The chapter considers the exchange rate policy problems in countries whose exports are dominated by commodities with strong and unpredictable price fluctuations. The issues raised by the "Dutch disease" are also explored.

One of the ambitions in preparing this book has been to provide a reasonably comprehensive coverage of the problems and concerns of international commodity trade, and yet to keep the account very brief. The result is that only cursory attention can be devoted to any one of the many issues that are covered.

The analyses contained in the book lean heavily on the considerable specialized literature that deals with different aspects of international commodity markets. The reader interested in a more detailed treatment of a particular issue will be guided by the notes given in the following chapters.

The existing literature on commodities is usually very selective in its subject treatment. Some works are commodity monographs, dwelling in great detail on a single product. Many treat only one or a few special issues. A string of empirically oriented books has been written about the policies aimed at stabilizing international commodity markets. Others have focused exclusively on areas like commodity cartels, the "Dutch disease", or the problems of supply security. Theoretical treatises have employed sophisticated methods to provide a better understanding of price formation in commodity markets; or to clarify the welfare implications of speculation on commodity exchanges.

Works like these do not respond well to the needs for a brief and simple primer on internationally traded commodities. The present book is intended to meet this deficiency. A majority of its readers will probably be found among undergraduate students in economics, political science, international relations, business administration and economic geography. The book should also provide a useful background perspective to government policy-makers, especially those in developing countries that are raw materials exporters, and to executives in corporations whose business involves primary commodity trade.

1

The Geography of Commodity Production and Trade

The agenda for this chapter consists of four items. The first section defines primary commodities and classifies them into a variety of distinct groups. These distinctions will be employed in the analyses performed in the following chapters. The second section analyzes the values and volumes of international commodity trade, and relates them to the overall trade flows. The third section paints a broad picture of the current geography of traded commodity production and consumption. The import dependence of the major industrial regions on overseas commodity supply is explored and quantified, and the most important commodity exporting countries are identified. Section four, finally, assumes a historical perspective and considers briefly the forces that have led to the increasing dependence of Japan and Western Europe on commodity imports in the course of the present century.

1.1 Commodity groups and their characteristics

The subject matter of this book is the world of raw materials, alternatively referred to as primary commodities, or, for short, commodities. A first important task is therefore to distinguish commodities from other goods. This distinction may sound straightforward and clear, but however one proceeds, substantial ambiguities remain.

The national accounts statistics of individual countries divide the GDP in accordance with the International Standard Industrial Classification (ISIC) of all economic activities,[1] as designed by the United Nations Statistical Office. The GDP is obtained by aggregating the value added from the primary sector − agriculture and mining; the secondary sector − manufacturing; and the tertiary sector − basically public and private services. The outputs from the primary sector can unambiguously be classed as primary commodities, but this definition is far more narrow than the everyday concept of primary commodities. Also, the definition is ill suited for the analyses of commodities in international trade contained in the following chapters. The problem is that the line between the primary and manufacturing sectors drawn by the ISIC is often very early in the production process, before the product has reached its main marketable stage. For instance, meat, paper pulp and refined copper are important primary commodities in international trade, but a significant proportion of their value has been added by the manufacturing sector through the activities of slaughterhouses, pulp mills and copper smelters and refineries. For this reason, the national accounts statistics are of limited use in determining the value − or volume − of commodity production.

The Standard International Trade Classification (SITC), employed to distinguish between different categories of goods in international trade, provides an alternative tool for defining commodities, but similar problems emerge with this approach also. In fact, neither the ISIC nor the SITC constitute adequate bases for distinguishing between primary commodities and manufactures.[2]

Since the focus of this book is on international trade in commodities, I will nevertheless employ the SITC classification to define primary commodities. My definition includes the SITC section 0, live animals and all unprocessed and processed food products; section 1, beverages and tobacco; section 2, inedible crude materials except fuels (edible oil raw materials, division 22, are also included); section 3, mineral fuels, lubricants and related materials; section 4, animal and vegetable oils and fats; division 67, iron and steel; and division 68, non-ferrous metals. This definition is statistically tractable and hence convenient. It is also shared, by and large, by bodies like UNCTAD[3] or GATT.[4] At the same time, it should be noted that the definition is broader than the everyday concept of primary commodities, since it includes products like cheese, spaghetti and chewing gum, or sheets, foils, angles and pipes made of metal.

By itself, the SITC classification is not particularly useful for subdividing commodities into analytical groups. Nevertheless, a major and commonly used categorization at least starts out from the SITC sections and divisions. It classes commodities into:

(a)   food in a broad sense (SITC 0+1+22+4);
(b)   agricultural raw materials (SITC 2−22−27−28);
(c)   minerals and metals (SITC 27+28+67+68); and
(d)   mineral fuels (SITC 3).

Several broad characteristics based on this categorization can be identified.

The distinction between (a), food, on the one hand, and (b), (c) and (d), raw materials used by industry, on the other, is of great practical significance when it comes to demand. A majority of the food items, having a more indispensable character, are likely to experience lesser variations in demand over the business cycle than the other commodity groups. Excepting luxury foods like coffee, chocolate or beef, one can also expect that food has a lesser income elasticity of demand, and hence a lower trend in demand growth in an expanding economy where consumers tend to spend decreasing shares of their income on basic necessities (Engels's Law).

The distinction between (a) and (b), agricultural products, on the one hand, and (c) and (d), mineral products, on the other, is relevant in that the supply of the former is dependent on the vagaries of weather while that of the latter is not. The dependence on weather has a particular relevance for products like rubber or cocoa whose output is geographically heavily concentrated. In general terms, one can say that the price instability of agricultural commodities is more often caused by supply side disturbances, while that of minerals, strikes and cartels notwithstanding, is more related to variations on the demand side.

Though each of the four groups contains many different products, the major substitutes for individual products are likely to be found within the same group. This is probably most evident in (d), the fuels group. An important implication is that prices within each group will have a tendency to move in tandem. For instance, if the price of petroleum rises, the prices of coal and natural gas will tend to rise in sympathy, but there is little presumption that such changes will have a direct influence on the price of, say, copper or wheat.

Other commodity groupings can be constructed to bring out neater but important distinctions. For instance, the unit price provides a rough measure of the transportability of commodities. Products like coffee, wool or tin (average prices per ton in 1985−7, $3300, $5600, and $8100), can be transported around the world with ease, since even very long hauls involve costs that constitute minuscule proportions of price. In contrast, products like phosphate rock, iron ore and coal (average prices per ton in 1985−7, $33, $22 and $42), still command some local monopolies on account of the high proportion of the transport cost in total delivered price.

Commodities can also be classed into those which are easily stored and the ones which are not. Refrigeration and preservation have rendered all commodities storable to some extent. The hard-to-store commodities are predominantly found in the agricultural groups, but there are many agricultural materials (jute, rice) which are easily stored for long periods of time. Storability affects a commodity market in at least two ways. First, it commonly provides for an increase in the elasticity of supply. Depletion of stocks makes it possible to vary supply beyond the feasible variations of production. And secondly, it increases the scope for speculative activity (see chapter 5).

There are great variations among commodities in terms of the time it takes to add to production capacity. The production of some commodities, e.g. bananas, sugar or wheat, can be greatly expanded between two adjacent seasons, simply by extending the area on which the crop is grown. In other commodities, like coffee, palm oil and most minerals, several years are commonly required between the decision to increase capacity and the start-up of production from that capacity. Even though the long-run price elasticity of supply for the two groups may be of the same magnitude, the short-run price elasticity of supply for the latter will be much lower.[5] This distinction makes a great difference for established producers bent on monopolistic coordination of their market. Supply cuts will seldom be worthwhile to producers of the first group of commodities, because of the speed with which additional production can be established. The second group is much more amenable to monopolistic coordination, given that the producer benefits will ordinarily be far more durable (see chapter 6).

For some materials, primary supply is supplemented by supply from secondary sources. This is importantly true for precious metals, but also for base metals like iron/steel, copper and lead, and for some agricultural raw materials, e.g. rubber and wool. The secondary supply has determinants and a cost structure that typically differ from those that apply to primary supply. The control of secondary materials is usually out of reach of primary producers. The availability of secondary supply tends to increase the overall supply elasticity for the commodity. Where such supply is important it reduces the scope for monopolistic coordination by primary producers.

The level of the price elasticity of demand constitutes yet another important distinguishing mark between commodities. The ones with many close substitutes typically have high price elasticities of demand. If the price increases, demand is redirected in favor of the substitutes. This is true, for instance of bananas and lamb, the demand for which is easily shifted towards other fruits and meats. Commodities with important uses and without convenient substitutes will usually have very low price elasticities of demand. When the use of a commodity is in some way indispensable, demand will not be much affected by a change in price. Platinum and chromium are prime examples of indispensable materials with few substitutes in many uses and with very low price elasticities of demand. For a somewhat different reason, coffee, too, has a low price elasticity of demand. Though one can lead a comfortable life without it, a large part of humanity has become addicted to this beverage, and as a result, the demand for it is not very sensitive to price. Like the preceding distinction, the price elasticity of demand is important in singling out commodities suitable for successful monopolistic intervention by producers.

One should note that the price elasticity of demand for any commodity is usually much higher in the long than in the short run. With time, users frequently find alternatives to a raw material whose price they find excessive. History knows of many examples of commodity cartels which broke down because the participating producers failed to grasp the longer-term dynamics of demand determination.

A distinction is often made between exhaustible and renewable resource commodities, but this does not appear to be very relevant for the problems treated in the present book. For example, contrary to the claims of exhaustible resource theory, there is little empirical evidence of a difference in the determination of prices between the two commodity groups.

1.2 The importance of commodities in the international economy

Table 1.1 displays the global primary commodity export values subdivided by major commodity and country group. Figures are given for 3 years covering a 20-year period. Total exports of all categories of goods are also provided for comparison. Several important insights can be gained from a scrutiny of the data.

In 1985, primary commodities as defined here accounted for some 40 percent of overall exports of goods. The importance of commodities in total trade has been declining over time, and that of manufactures has been rising. The share of commodities was 48 percent in 1965 and 46 percent in 1975. Despite the decline, primary materials are still sufficiently important to have a substantial impact on the world macroeconomy. Changes in the prices of commodities are known to have strong repercussions, for instance on global inflation rates, or on the exchange rates and levels of economic activity of the raw material exporting countries.

The fuels group has emerged as a dominant component of overall commodity exports. Oil dominates the group. In the 1980s, nine-tenths of the value of fuel exports comprised oil. As a result of the petroleum price increases in the 1970s, the share of this group in primary commodity trade rose from 20 percent in 1965 to 42 percent in 1975 and 47 percent in 1985. In that year, the fuel commodities' share in global trade was almost 20 percent. With falling petroleum exports and energy prices from the mid-1980s, the share of fuels in total commodity exports and in global trade declined in subsequent years.

Primary commodities have always dominated the exports of developing

Geography of Production and Trade

Table 1.1 Exports by major country and commodity group (billion $)

Exports from	Food	Agric. raw mat.	Minerals and metals	Fuels	Total commod.	Total visible exports
1965						
I	19	8	15	5	47	128
D	12	5	4	11	32	35
S	3	2	4	2	11	22
W	34	15	23	18	90	186
1975						
I	73	21	63	29	186	577
D	33	9	12	125	179	210
S	9	4	10	15	38	85
W	115	34	85	169	403	872
1986						
I	124	40	100	100	364	1,275
D	62	15	25	199	301	441
S	15	10	15	61	101	208
W	201	65	140	360	766	1,924

I = Industrialized market economies (includes South Africa).
D = Developing countries.
S = Socialist countries (includes China, North Korea and Vietnam).
W = World.

Source: GATT, *International Trade*, 1986, 1987

countries, and they continue to do so. However, the dominance has been declining over time. In 1965, primary exports accounted for 91 percent of total exports from the developing countries. By 1985, this share had fallen to 68 percent. These figures give a picture that is heavily biased by the dominance of petroleum. In non-OPEC developing countries, the share of primary commodities (including oil) in total exports fell from 76 percent in 1970 to 53 percent in 1984. In the same years, commodities excluding petroleum accounted for 68 percent and 34 percent of overall exports in this country group.

To give a feel for the importance of individual commodities, using World Bank material table 1.2 presents the export values for the 17 most important commodities in international trade, between the early 1970s and the early 1980s. The ranking is by export value in 1981–3.[6] Though unsynchronized price cycles lead to some shifts in the relative values attained by individual commodities, the ranks do not undergo any drastic

Table 1.2 Average annual global export values for individual primary commodities (billion $)

	1970−2	*1975−7*	*1981−3*
Petroleum	27.9	135.8	267.4
Wheat	3.5	9.7	17.0
Timber	5.1	11.2	16.6
Coal	3.3	10.0	15.4
Sugar	2.9	8.6	12.3
Maize	2.0	7.0	10.3
Coffee	3.0	8.3	9.1
Beef	2.3	4.1	8.0
Copper	4.6	6.0	8.0
Iron ore	2.7	5.5	6.8
Cotton	2.8	5.1	6.7
Aluminum	1.2	2.6	6.0
Rice	1.2	2.8	4.5
Tobacco	1.4	2.8	4.4
Wool	1.4	2.5	3.7
Rubber	1.0	2.2	3.1
Tin	0.8	1.5	2.6
Zinc	0.8	2.0	2.4

Source: Coal from UN, *Yearbook of International Trade Statistics*, several issues; all other commodities from World Bank, *Commodity Trade and Price Trends*, annual, several issues

change over time. The most important products appear on top of the list throughout the period.

Even before its great price increases, petroleum was by far the most important commodity in international trade. The trade value of no less than eight of the most important commodities after petroleum had to be added up to match the revenue generated by oil exports. As is apparent from table 1.2, the prominence of petroleum among commodities became even more pronounced from the mid-1970s.

The great importance of oil was a major reason for the serious disturbances to the world economy, when its price was forced up in the early and late 1970s. Price rises of equal magnitude in any other commodity market would have had negligible effects in comparison.

The export values for individual commodities can be compared with those for some manufactured products. For instance, in 1982−3, the global average annual export value of road vehicles was $238 billion, office machines $31 billion, aircraft $26 billion, footwear $12 billion, furniture $10 billion, toys and sporting goods $9 billion, and alcoholic beverages $8 billion.[7]

The importance of primary commodity trade can alternatively be measured by weight, and when that is done, a distinctly different ranking emerges. Five commodities had 1984 export volumes of 100 million tons or more. These were petroleum (1090 million tons), iron ore (372 million), hard coal (305 million), wheat (116 million) and wood (187 million cubic meters). Other commodities with a large volume of exports in that year were maize (68 million), edible oils and their raw materials (65 million), phosphate rock (48 million), bauxite (35 million) and iron and steel in primary shapes (24 million).[8] The commodities enumerated comprise three-quarters or more of the volume of commodities in international trade. The developments in these commodity markets determine heavily the business conditions in bulk transport by sea. Many high-priced commodities with large export values, coffee and copper for example, are traded in quite small volumes in comparison with the products enumerated above (see table 1.3).

1.3   Where are traded commodities produced and consumed?

The emphasis of this book is on the international trade in commodities. Such trade will arise only when some countries have production in excess of their own consumption. Depending on the proportion that is domestically consumed, world trade will constitute varying shares of world production. In most cases, production is far greater than trade, and the international commodity market constitutes only a fraction of the overall market for that commodity. Table 1.3 provides the volume of production and trade in a recent year for a sample of important commodities. The comparison probably exaggerates the importance of trade, since large quantities of the commodities listed are re-exported, either in unchanged form, or after some limited degree of processing.

Painting a very broad picture, one can say that most commodity groups are produced in all the major country groups. The important exceptions are tropical agricultural products like rubber, jute, coffee, tea and cocoa, of which the tropical developing countries are the sole primary suppliers. Economic bauxite deposits predominantly occur in tropical and semi-tropical areas. Tin is unusual among minerals in that virtually all the rich ores happen to be located in the developing countries of South East Asia and in Brazil. A heavy concentration of ores also occurs in the case of niobium (Brazil) and platinum (South Africa and USSR). Trade commonly accounts for a high share of global output in products with geographically concentrated supply.

Table 1.3 World production and exports of selected commodities in 1984

	Production	Exports	
	000 tons	*000 tons*	*% of production*
Hard coal	2,942,000	305,000	10
Petroleum	2,700,000	1,090,000	40
Iron ore	881,000	372,000	42
Wheat	517,000	116,000	22
Rice	453,000	12,400	3
Sugar	100,600	28,300	28
Cotton	18,200	4,200	24
Aluminum	17,740	4,740	27
Copper	8,680	5,065	58
Coffee	5,180	4,060	78
Rubber	4,260	3,575	84
Tin	200	160	80

Source: Association of Iron Ore Exporting Countries, *Iron Ore Statistics*, 2, 1987; *Energy in Profile*, Shell Briefing Service, No. 4, 1985 and No. 4, 1987; FAO, *The State of Food and Agriculture 1985*, 1986; UN, *Monthly Bulletin of Statistics*, June 1987; World Bank, *Commodity Trade and Price Trends*, 1986 edition

Some commodities, for example, staple foods and products with low unit prices, enter international trade only in a very limited measure. As is revealed by table 1.3, this is clearly true of rice, most of which is consumed locally. Similarly, only a small proportion of hard coal enters international trade. This is primarily because the competitiveness of this cheap commodity is heavily diluted by transport distance.

Additional important features of world commodity trade are summarized in the matrices of table 1.4, and in figure 1.1. The matrices cover similar ground to the contents of table 1.1, but provide further detail on the direction of commodity trade in recent years. Though the level of aggregation is very high, a number of circumstances that characterized world trade in raw materials in the mid-1980s can be noted.[9]

The industrialized market economies dominate the world trade in commodities. At the same time they exhibit a surprising overall balance in their trade both with food, agricultural raw materials and minerals and metals. As will be revealed later in the chapter, this balance is importantly due to the export surpluses of Australia, Canada, South Africa and a few other smaller countries, which compensate for the large deficits of the European Community and Japan, and the smaller deficit recorded by the

Table 1.4 Matrices of world trade in commodities, 1983–5 averages, (billion $)

	Origin	Destination			
		I	*D*	*S*	*W*
Food	I	87	33	9	129
	D	35	16	10	61
	S	4	4	6	14
	W	126	53	25	204
Agric. raw materials	I	31	6	3	40
	D	8	5	2	15
	S	4	1	5	10
	W	43	12	10	65
Minerals and metals	I	69	19	10	98
	D	18	5	2	25
	S	4	2	9	15
	W	91	26	21	138
Fuels	I	88	7	1	96
	D	151	58	6	215
	S	32	6	24	62
	W	271	71	31	373

I = Industrialized market economies (includes South Africa).
D = Developing countries.
S = Socialist countries (includes China, North Korea and Vietnam).
W = World.

Source: GATT, *International Trade*, 1986, 1987

United States. Only in the case of fuels do the industrialized market economies in aggregate record a very large deficit, primarily *vis-à-vis* the developing countries (OPEC), but to a significant extent also in relation to the socialist countries.

The developing countries recorded an annual surplus of $8 billion in their food trade. The surplus in tropical products like beverages, tropical fruits and some edible oils was substantially larger. The tropical beverages alone provided a net export value in excess of $15 billion. At the same time, this country group had a sizable deficit in cereals. The large net import needs of wheat, rice and coarse grains are of relatively recent origin. In 1955 the tonnage of such imports was only 3 million tons, 1.3 percent of their cereal consumption. By 1985, the figure had grown to 72 million tons, more than 7 percent of consumption.[10] The developing

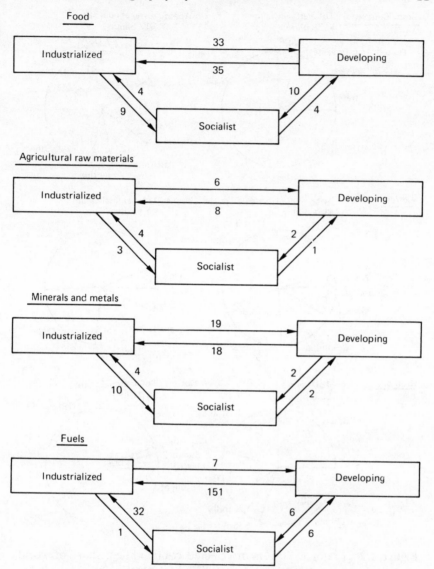

Figure 1.1 Inter-regional trade in commodities, 1983−5 averages (billion $)

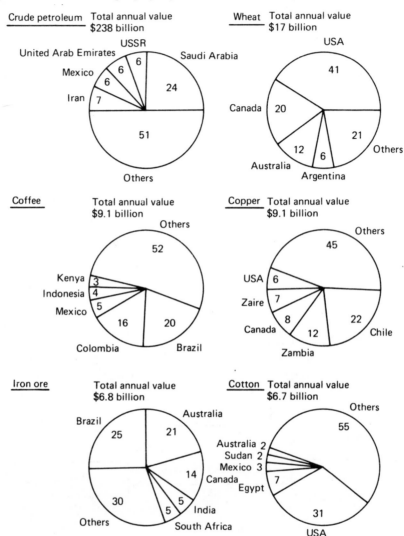

Figure 1.2   Major exporters of selected commodities: share of world
export value in 1981−3 (percent)

countries' export participation in agricultural raw materials and in minerals
and metals amounted to a little below 20 percent of the world total, but in
both product groups, imports were about as large as exports. These
findings do not tally with the common belief that the LDCs are very
important net suppliers of non-fuel commodities to the rest of the world.

The large exports of such products from many developing countries are increasingly being counterbalanced by sizable imports by other developing countries, such as Brazil, India and South Korea, to satisfy the large-scale needs of their processing and manufacturing industries. Only in the fuels group did the developing countries record a very sizable surplus, mainly due to the petroleum exports from the OPEC group.

Given the size of their economies, the socialist countries as a group (including China) play a relatively limited role in international commodity trade. The socialist countries' imports of food from the rest of the world in 1983–5 accounted for about 12 percent of global food trade. Their deficit in food equalled $11 million, 5 percent of global exports of food products. In agricultural raw materials, the overall trade of the country group was in balance, but this of course did not preclude significant trade flows for individual commodities or countries. In metals and minerals there was a $6 billion deficit. Only in the case of fuels did the socialist area exhibit a significant export surplus, amounting to $31 billion, more than 8 percent of world fuel trade. The exports of petroleum and natural gas from the USSR accounted for most of this surplus.

The trade balances for non-fuel commodities, quantified in table 1.4, deviate considerably from conventional wisdom perceptions. The view that the industrialized market economies in aggregate are heavily reliant on commodity imports from the developing countries is not borne out by the trade statistics. Both the industrialized countries and the developing countries have a reasonable balance in their trade with these commodity categories, recording surpluses of $7 billion and $10 billion respectively, corresponding to 1.7 percent and 2.5 percent of global trade in these products. The socialist countries emerge as the import dependent group for this category of goods. They absorbed the entire non-fuel commodities surplus generated by the industrialized and developing countries. Their imports of these commodities exceeded their exports by more than 40 percent.

One would have liked to compare these trade imbalances with overall commodity consumption, but consumption data for aggregate commodity groups are hard to obtain. However, given the small absolute size of the trade deficits and surpluses, and given also that for most commodities there is sizable domestic production which does not enter international trade, it follows that the trade balances recorded by each of the three geographical areas constitute minuscule proportions of total consumption. At the level of aggregation now considered, each area is by and large self-sufficient in non-fuel primary commodities.

In fuels, however, the conventional view is vindicated. The industrialized market economies depend heavily on imports, predominantly from the developing, but significantly also from the socialist countries.

Table 1.5   Industrialized market economies: GDP, total exports and trade in commodities. 1983−5 annual average (billion $)

	Japan	EEC	USA	Other	All
GDP	1,200	2,430	3,620	960	8,230
Total exports	164	280	203	239	886
NFC					
Exports	17.7	49.1	48.8	73.3	188.9
Imports	39.9	74.6	51.7	15.5	181.7
Balance	−22.2	−25.5	−2.9	57.8	7.2
F					
Exports	0.5	17.3	9.6	30.3	57.7
Imports	58.3	99.4	59.6	15.4	232.7
Balance	−57.8	−82.1	−50.0	14.9	−175.0
Percentage shares					
NFC imports/GDP	3.3	3.1	1.4	1.6	2.2
NFC balance/GDP	−1.8	−1.1	−0.1	6.0	0.1
F imports/GDP	4.8	4.1	1.6	1.6	2.8
F balance/GDP	−4.7	−3.4	−1.4	1.6	−2.1

NFC = non-fuel commodities.
 F = fuels.
International trade among EEC countries has been eliminated from the 'EEC' and 'All' figures.

Source: World Bank, *World Development Report*, 1985, 1986, 1987 editions; GATT, *International Trade*, 1986, 1987

Further disaggregations, both at the geographical and at the individual commodity level uncover more pronounced surpluses and deficits in commodity trade. In table 1.5, the commodity trade of Japan, the European Community and the United States is singled out from the industrialized market economies total, and an attempt is made to measure the relative import dependence of each. Since we are interested in the EEC area as a whole and not in the 12 individual countries of which it is composed, the figures in the table exclude the trade between these countries.

Looking first at the non-fuel commodities, the table reveals that the significant surplus generated by the industrialized countries in aggregate, is composed of very large deficits in Japan and the EEC, a small deficit in the United States, and a very sizable surplus in the remaining industrialized countries, notably Australia, Canada and South Africa. More than half of Japan's and the EEC's non-fuel commodity imports originate in other industrialized countries.

A somewhat similar pattern emerges when trade in fuels is considered. Although the aggregate for all industrialized countries is a huge deficit, the unspecified countries record a significant surplus, while big deficits occur not only in Japan and the EEC, but in the United States too.

Table 1.5 also assesses Japan's, the EEC's and the United States' relative dependence on foreign commodity supply. I have chosen to measure this dependence by relating total commodity imports and total deficits, respectively, to each area's GDP. Japan emerges as the most dependent and the United States as the least dependent under both measures, with the EEC figures closer to Japan's. This is true both for non-fuel commodities and for fuels. Since there may be significant re-exports of imported commodities to which little value has been added, the second measure seems more appropriate for assessing dependence. One could alternatively establish dependence by relating imports or deficits to total exports on the premise that the export proceeds must be used to finance commodity imports. Using that measure would increase US dependence, given its lower share of exports in relation to GDP.

With one exception − iron and steel − Japan did not accomplish any commodity exports of significance during the 1980s. Japan's foreign iron and steel sales in 1983−5 were valued at $14 billion, but all other non-fuel commodity exports amounted to no more than $5 billion. All commodity imports in these years, $98 billion per year, equalled 75 percent of overall Japanese imports, and accounted for almost 13 percent of global trade in primary commodities.

The European Community has a somewhat more balanced commodity trade position than Japan. Although deficits were recorded in every major category of commodities, there were nevertheless sizable exports in each. In 1983−5, the annual average sales to countries outside the area were more than $20 billion in the case of food, $3 billion in agricultural raw materials, $6 billion in non-ferrous metals and ores, and $14 billion in iron and steel. The EEC fuels exports amounted annually to more than $17 billion in these years. All commodity imports into the EEC, $174 billion, equalled 57 percent of total imports, and constituted 22 percent of global commodity trade.

The United States regularly achieves a sizable export surplus in food, and a smaller one in agricultural raw materials, but it usually has a deficit in non-ferrous metals and ores as well as in iron and steel. This was also true in 1983−5. All commodity imports into the United States in these years, $110 billion on average, corresponded to 35 percent of overall imports. (On account of the strong overvaluation of the US dollar in the early 1980s, the US trade balance recorded a large deficit. Average exports in 1983−5 were $203 billion, average imports amounted to $320 billion.)

Table 1.6 disaggregates the export flows both by country and by individual commodity. It demonstrates that a relatively small number of LDCs account for substantial proportions of the traded supply of major raw materials. Argentina, Brazil, Colombia, India, Kenya, Malaysia, the Philippines, Sri Lanka and Thailand generate a large share of the developing countries' total exports of agricultural products. Brazil, Chile, Mexico, and Peru in Latin America, Zaire and Zambia in Africa, along with India, Indonesia, Malaysia, the Philippines and Papua New Guinea (PNG) cover a major share of mineral and metal exports from the Third World. Australia, Canada, South Africa and the United States among the industrialized market economies account for a very substantial proportion of the global exports of a number of agricultural and mineral non-fuel commodities.

Not included in table 1.6 are the exports of petroleum. In 1982–3, Saudi Arabia generated 24 percent of world exports of crude oil. Iran, Indonesia, Mexico, Nigeria, the United Arab Republic and USSR each accounted for 5 percent or more of the global exports of this product.[11]

In summary, then, our broad survey of commodity production, consumption and trade patterns in recent years reveals the following major characteristics:

1   In value terms, the most important trade flow is that of fuels, from the OPEC countries, Mexico and the USSR to the industrialized market economies and to the oil importing developing countries.
2   Developing countries are, by and large, the sole producers of tropical food commodities. A very large proportion of the total output of these commodities is exported, predominantly to the industrialized market economies.
3   The United States, Canada, Australia and Argentina generate very sizable cereals surpluses which are exported to the USSR and to selected developing countries.
4   Japan and the European Community import large quantities of agricultural raw materials, ores and non-ferrous metals. More than half of these imports originate in a few industrialized market economies, primarily Australia, Canada and South Africa; to some extent also in the United States. The rest is bought from selected developing countries. Although Japan imports lesser commodity quantities than the European Community in absolute terms, it exhibits a greater net import dependence than the European country group.

1.4   The emergence and growth of Western Europe's and Japan's dependence on commodity imports

The large Western European and Japanese dependence on faraway supplies of raw materials is a phenomenon that has emerged, in the main, during

Table 1.6 Country share of world exports of selected commodities in 1981–3 (percent)

	Coffee	Sugar	Wheat	Cotton	Rubber	Wool	Copper	Iron ore	Tin
Kenya	2.7	0.1				0.1			
Zaire	1.3						7.3		
Zambia				0.1	0.6		12.2		0.5
India	2.1	1.1		1.6				5.2	
Indonesia	4.1				24.8		1.3		13.4
Malaysia	0.1	0.1			47.0		0.4		28.6
Philippines	0.5	3.5			0.2		4.2		
Sri Lanka	0.1				4.2				
Thailand	0.2	3.5			15.4				12.7
Argentina	20.0	1.4	5.7	0.5		5.6			0.2
Brazil		5.9		1.4		0.3		24.9	2.9
Chile	16.4					0.5	22.1	2.1	
Colombia		0.5		0.7					
Mexico	4.5			3.0			2.5		
Peru	1.2	0.1		0.9		0.1	4.8	1.2	1.1
PNG	1.2				0.1		3.6		
Australia		6.4	11.5	2.2		49.2	4.9	20.9	0.6
Canada			20.0				8.1	13.9	
S. Africa		2.1				9.1	5.5	4.8	
USA		2.3	40.9	30.6		1.4	5.9	2.8	
Total for above countries	54.4	27.0	78.1	41.0	92.3	66.3	82.8	75.8	60.0

Source: UN, *Yearbook of International Trade Statistics*, 1984; World Bank, *Commodity Trade and Price Trends*, 1986 edition

the present century. Two factors explain the very fast expansion of primary commodity imports into these areas. The first is the very impressive secular decline in transport costs. The second is the speedy pace of industrialization in the two regions, and the concomitant increase in their raw materials needs.

Prior to the mid-nineteenth century, freight rates on long hauls were prohibitively expensive except for goods with very high unit prices. In consequence, the international commodity trade at the time was small in volume and consisted in the main of highly valued luxuries like coffee, cocoa, spices and precious or semi-precious metals.[12] Since then, there has been a tremendous reduction in transport costs, both across oceans and on land. Representative transatlantic freight indices for bulk products in constant money fell from 100 in 1870 to 56 in 1900, 40 in 1950 and 25 in 1962,[13] and the fall has continued in more recent decades.[14] The construction of railways in the late nineteenth century increased the area of economic accessibility for low-cost products requiring overland transport. It was only in the final decades of last century that US cereals became competitive with those from Russia in the Western European markets. Even cheaper products, like bauxite, coal and iron ore from transoceanic sources, did not become competitive in the main industrialized country markets until the 1950s, after the introduction of revolutionary new systems for ocean transport and harbor handling of bulk products.[15]

While the progress of transport technology during the present century expanded the potential for international commodity trade, the economic developments in the industrial centers led to an explosive increase in their demand for raw materials. The Japanese economy's ascendancy to industrialized status and the ensuing expansion of its raw materials needs, have occurred entirely in the present century, and in the main during the period after 1945. Prior to that, this country's need to import primary commodities was relatively small. Western Europe's industrialization is much older, but this area's resource endowment is also richer, so that the raw material import needs remained limited through the beginning of the present century.

Japan's and Western Europe's dependence on imported primary commodities would have been much more pronounced, if these areas had not adopted highly protective agricultural policies (see chapter 2). With existing policies, Western Europe regularly generates sizable export surpluses of major agricultural products like wheat, sugar, butter and milk powder. In an internationally competitive environment, the production of food in Japan and Western Europe would shrink substantially from present levels.

In comparison with Japan and Western Europe, dependence on imported raw materials in the United States is still limited. The country's sparse population and vast resource base made it into a large net exporter

Table 1.7 Commercial energy at the primary
stage: ratio of production to consumption

	1925	1967	1987
USA	1.07	0.95	0.86
Western Europe	1.03	0.46	0.61
Japan	1.08	0.24	0.20
USSR	1.07	1.14	1.21

Source: J. Darmstadter et al., *Energy in the World Economy*, Resources for the Future, 1971; BP, *Statistical Review of World Energy*, June 1988

of commodities in aggregate over long periods of time. In the past few decades, however, marginal deficits in US non-fuel commodity trade have become more common. With increasing industrial needs and a gradual depletion of domestic resources, the net import needs are likely to increase over time. In the case of fuels, the deficit has already grown to a considerable value.

The case of energy provides a striking illustration of the long-run increase in the industrialized areas' import dependence. Table 1.7 depicts the declining self-sufficiency in fuel commodities in the United States, as well as in Western Europe and Japan. The recent increase in Western Europe's self-sufficiency is due to the opening up of oil and gas production in the North Sea. It probably represents an aberration in the very long-run trend. The figures in the table demonstrate both how recent are the net import needs in the industrialized market economies, and how extreme is the import dependence of Japan. They also show that the largely untapped resource wealth of the USSR has permitted that country to expand fuels production up until the present at a rate faster than domestic use.

NOTES

1 See for instance World Bank, *World Tables 1976*, 1976.
2 K. Morton and P. Tulloch, *Trade and Developing Countries*, Croom Helm, London, 1977.
3 UNCTAD, *Handbook of International Trade and Development Statistics*, 1986.
4 GATT, *International Trade*, 1986.
5 Price elasticities are defined as the (absolute) percentage changes in quantities supplied or demanded, resulting from a 1 percent change in price.
6 The iron and steel group had an average export value in 1981–3 of about $70 billion (GATT, *International Trade*, annual, several issues), making it the most important item after oil. It is not included in the list because iron and

steel exports cannot really be regarded as a single commodity. They comprise a great variety of products, some in crude form, others at a high degree of processing.

7   UNCTAD, *Handbook of International Trade and Development Statistics*, 1986.

8   Association of Iron Ore Exporting Countries, *Iron Ore Statistics*, 2, 1987; *Energy in Profile*, Shell Briefing Service no. 4, 1985 and no. 4, London, 1987; FAO, *The State of Food and Agriculture*, 1985; UN, *Monthly Bulletin of Statistics*, June 1987; UNCTAD, *Yearbook of International Commodity Statistics 1986*, 1987; World Bank, *Commodity Trade and Price Trends*, 1986 edition.

9   GATT, *International Trade*, 1986, 1987.

10 World Bank, *Price Prospects for Major Primary Commodities*, Report no. 814, 1975 and 1986.

11 UNCTAD, *Handbook of International Trade and Development Statistics*, 1986.

12 D. S. Landes, "The Great Drain and Industrialisation: Commodity Flows from Periphery to Centre in Historical Perspective," in R. C. O. Matthews (ed.), *Economic Growth and Resources*, vol. 2, *Trends and Factors*, Macmillan, London, 1980.

13 P. Bairoch, "La baisse des couts des transports et le développement économique," *Révue de l'Institut de Sociologie*, Brussels, 1965.

14 M. Radetzki, "Regional Development Benefits of Mineral Projects," *Resources Policy*, September 1982.

15 G. Manners, *The Changing World Market for Iron Ore 1950–1980*, Resources for the Future, Washington, DC, 1971.

2

Comparative Advantage, Trade Policy and the Dislocation of Commodity Production

In a world where commodities could be traded without policy restrictions, we would expect production to be located so as to minimize global costs, including the cost of transporting the product to the final user. Comparative advantage based on climate, natural resource endowment or low cost of labor and other input needs would reign in this world, and the countries possessing such advantage would supply their output to the others.[1] The real world deviates considerably from this ideal. A great number of countries have established various barriers to trade. Where such barriers prevent a free commodity inflow, they provide protection for local production that can thrive by being assured of the national market even when the cost of local output is higher than that of imports. The ultimate consequence of national policies that restrict trade is to obstruct the establishment of an optimal location pattern in commodity industries.

This chapter looks first at the national policies that affect commodity production and trade, and explores the reasons for their establishment. I shall then provide some quantitative measures of the extent of trade restricting policies affecting commodities. There follows an analysis of the distortions to the location of production and to the trade flows in different commodity groups, caused by the restrictions to trade. A final section focuses on commodity processing and explores how the location of this activity has been distorted, not only by trade restraining policies in a strict sense, but also by a broad array of colonial legacies.

2.1   What policies, by whom and for what reasons?

Protection comes in a great many forms. Not all of it is clearly visible. Its rationale is often hard to establish. We begin by considering the menu of measures adopted by the commodity importing countries.

Traditional analyses of trade policy distinguish between tariff barriers to trade which restrict imports by raising the import price, and non-tariff barriers, comprising all other protection measures. It is useful to make a further distinction by subdividing non-tariff barriers into the ones that restrict imports directly and those that do it indirectly, by promoting domestic production. The tools to be enumerated are not exclusive to commodity trade. Most of them are equally employed to restrain manufactures trade too.

Import tariffs, which raise the imported price, and so reduce the volume of imports, constitute the classical measure for protecting domestic production from more efficient foreign competition. Tariffs can come in different forms and under different names. A very important form of tariffs in recent times has been the so called **variable import levy**, employed, amongst others, by the European Community to protect agriculture. The purpose of the levy is to keep domestic production and imports stable over the price cycle in the international commodity markets. It involves the maintenance of a domestic price which is high enough to assure simultaneously an adequate *and* stable profitability to domestic production, and the imposition of a levy on imports which varies inversely with the international price, so as to always equate the total import price with the domestic price.

A very straightforward measure to restrict imports is to establish **import quotas**. Imports are then permitted only up to the level of the quota. Any remaining demand has to be satisfied from domestic output. The allocation of quotas among importers regularly raises controversies, when quotas are effective in reducing imports. Even when no specific limit on the imported quantity has been set, the institution of **import licenses** often involves a bureaucratic hazzle that in effect leads to a restriction of the import flow. **Voluntary export restraints** are a special type of quotas. The concept is a misnomer: the restraints are typically not voluntary at all, but adopted by the exporting country under threat from the importing government of even more severe suppression of trade. Restrictions of the import volume are often implemented with the help of **national standards**. In primary commodities, this tool would be most common for agricultural products. On health grounds, the importing country can impose a general prohibition on imports of food from areas claimed to be infested by a disease, or where a particular insecticide has been used. Alternatively, the importing government can require elaborate and costly veterinary inspections as a precondition for import.

Instead of reducing the competitiveness or availability of imports, the protective measures can aim at inducing expanded domestic output, by improving its competitiveness, or by directing demand specifically towards that output. Overt **subsidies** involving direct payments, loan finance at low interest, or the write-off of loans, will reduce the domestic production costs. **Tax concessions** can have a similar effect. **Public procurement** exclusively from domestic sources will add to the demand for domestic output, to the detriment of imported supply.

Commodity exporting nations, too, can use policy to affect the competitiveness and/or volume of their export supply. By and large the same arsenal as has been listed above comes into use. But while the importing countries' measures invariably have the aim of restricting imports, the exporting nations differ in their policy objectives. Some provide incentives to expand exports — through subsidies, tax concessions and favorable treatment of foreign exchange earnings. Others adopt policies to discourage sales abroad — by establishing elaborate export license procedures, or by imposing taxes and quotas on export sales.

Exchange rate policy can be a very powerful tool for determining the competitiveness of a country's export production. However, since this tool is not product-specific, it is not considered part of the arsenal of protection. It will be discussed in greater detail in chapter 8, where the macroeconomic problems of commodity exporting countries are analyzed.

Several rationales are put forth in justification of the importing countries' restrictive policies related to commodity imports. The most important is probably a concern about the labor and capital employed in existing domestic production. Underlying this concern may be a variety of economic or political considerations.

In many cases, uncontrolled imports could swiftly annihilate an uncompetitive domestic commodity industry. This would usually involve uneconomic destruction of capital and skills. Hence, it is argued, imports should be expanded only gradually, in line with the depreciation of these assets, to avoid this undesirable outcome. In practice, the application of such a policy frequently results in semi-permanent protection. In numerous industrialized countries, agricultural producers have a vocal lobby whose political support for government policies in general is conditioned on continued agricultural protection. Strategic concerns constitute another common justification for protection. Some degree of self-sufficiency in crucial commodities like basic foods or indispensable minerals is considered essential, so protection is used to maintain domestic production even if its costs exceed the import price (this point is treated in detail in chapter 5).

Alternatively, import restrictions are seen as a way to ease a strained balance of payments situation. Also, especially in developing countries, taxes on foreign trade often make up an important source of public revenue.

Policies to promote foreign sales in commodity exporting countries are regularly justified by a perennial scarcity of foreign exchange. This scarcity is typically the result of an overvalued exchange rate. The export promotion measures can then be seen as a way to overcome the distorting impact of currency overvaluation.

There are at least three rationales for policies that restrict foreign commodity sales from exporting countries. One is a desire to safeguard supplies for domestic use. Another is to raise international prices, usually through coordinated international producer action. A third is to assure public revenues through export taxes. The third rationale becomes especially important in countries whose economies are heavily dependent on a single commodity.

2.2   Measuring the extent of trade restrictions in international commodity trade

Assessing the degree of protection against imports of primary commodities in a country raises a number of methodological and practical difficulties. The level of tariff protection is relatively easy to establish, even though it will fluctuate over time where variable import levies are applied. Tariffs have been lowered substantially over the past decades. In more recent times, as non-tariff barriers have grown in importance, tariffs have probably made up only a minor share of the total protective barrier.

Since non-tariff barriers come in so many different forms, the measurement of their protective impact is quite tricky. At the simplest level, the relative importance of non-tariff barriers among commodity groups and over time has been demonstrated by the frequency with which they occur for each group or at each time. At a more sophisticated level, the aggregate protective impact of tariff and non-tariff barriers is measured by the **Nominal Protection Coefficient** (NPC), defined as the ratio between the price received by the domestic producers of a commodity and the international price. A coefficient of less than one denotes negative protection, i.e. that taxes and other policy measures discriminate against domestic producers in favor of imports.

To the extent that purchased inputs constitute a significant proportion of the commodity price, the NPC measure may give a distorted picture of the protection afforded to the domestic producers of the commodity. Rather than comparing prices, it would be more appropriate to measure the extent of protection as the ratio between the value added by the commodity producers at domestic prices, and the value added at international prices. This would provide the **Effective Protection Rate** (EPR), but given the practical problems in estimating this measure, there have

Table 2.1   Average tariff barriers in major
industrialized countries in 1984 (percent)

	EEC	Japan	USA
Manufactures	7.0	6.7	6.7
Food	13.8	19.5	7.1
Agric. raw materials	3.3	2.3	1.7
Fuels	3.4	3.0	1.0
Ores and metals	4.0	3.9	3.8

Source: R. Erzan and G. Karsenty, "Products Facing
High Tariffs in Major Developed Market Economy
Countries: An area of priority for developing
countries in the Uruguay Round?", Seminar Paper
No. 401, Institute for International Economic Studies,
University of Stockholm, December 1987

been few attempts to establish it (the EPR should not be confused with
the Effective Tariff, which will be discussed in the last section of the
present chapter).

Most data on the extent of protection are for the industrialized market
economies. The evidence from developing countries is uneven and scattered. Measuring protection in socialist countries is not very meaningful,
given their foreign trade monopolies, and the tenuous relationship between
prices and costs in these economies.

Some of the relevant and available data on protection against commodity
imports are displayed in tables 2.1 through 2.3.

Table 2.1 exhibits the tariffs imposed by major industrialized countries
since the Tokyo Round of tariff negotiations. At that negotiation, tariffs
for all major categories of goods were substantially reduced. For most
primary commodities, tariffs in industrialized countries are lower than for
manufactures. With the exception of food imported by the EEC and
Japan, the tariff levels on primary commodities are insignificant, and
cannot by themselves constitute any serious impediment to trade. The
average tariffs imposed on commodities by developing countries are probably much more severe, but there is no general information to illuminate
this point. For eight countries in South and South-East Asia, the un-
weighted average tariffs on food products, applicable in the mid-1980s,
amounted to 51 percent, with the highest tariff level, 119 percent, imposed
by India. In the case of agricultural raw materials, the corresponding
figure was 34 percent, with the Indian figure, again the highest, at 92
percent.[2] The import duty on refined copper in Brazil in the mid-1980s

Table 2.2 Share of imports into major industrialized countries, subject to non-tariff barriers in 1984 (percent)

	1981	1984	1986
Manufactures	18.6	19.9	20.5
Food and beverages	40.8	43.3	42.5
Meat and live animals		52.2	
Dairy products		54.6	
Sugar and confectionery		70.0	
Cereals		29.0	
Tea, coffee, cocoa		6.6	
Agric. raw materials	2.8	3.5	8.4
Fuels	42.4	15.5	15.5
Iron and steel	29.0	50.6	64.2
Non-ferrous metals	3.8	6.3	6.4

Source: UNCTAD, *Revitalizing Development, Growth and International Trade*, 1987, p. A36; World Bank, *World Development Report*, 1986 edition, p. 117

was 15 percent on material from Latin America, and 20 percent on imports from elsewhere. In India in the same period, the duty was in excess of 100 percent.[3]

Table 2.2 assesses the extent to which non-tariff barriers are employed by major industrialized countries to restrict commodity imports. The table does not permit a judgment about the importance of such barriers. A variety of measures are involved. Some of them can have a heavily restrictive impact on trade, while others may be quite lax.

For the period covered, table 2.2 reveals that while there has been some expansion of the non-tariff barriers affecting agricultural raw materials and non-ferrous metals, virtually all imports of these goods continue to be unimpeded by such barriers. The low incidence of non-tariff barriers also applies to the beverages group. In contrast, a very large share of foods other than beverages have long been subject to widespread non-tariff protection. Non-tariff barriers have recently become a dominant feature in iron and steel trade, but their importance has receded in fuels.

No systematic investigations have been published on the application of non-tariff barriers by developing countries. In the mid 1980s, prohibitions or restrictive licensing affected more than 40 percent of imported food products in Bangladesh, India, Indonesia, Pakistan, the Philippines and Thailand, but not by Sri Lanka, Malaysia, Hong Kong, South Korea and Singapore. In the case of agricultural raw materials, this frequency was exceeded within the country group only by Bangladesh, India, Pakistan

Table 2.3 Nominal protection coefficients for major food products in the early 1980s

	Wheat	Rice	Beef/lamb	Sugar	Dairy prod.
Australia	1.0	1.2	1.0	1.0	1.3
Canada	1.2	1.0	1.0	1.3	1.2
EEC	1.3	1.4	1.9	1.5	1.7
Other Europe	1.7	1.0	2.1	1.8	2.4
Japan	3.8	3.3	4.0	3.0	2.9
USA	1.1	1.3	1.0	1.4	2.0
Argentina	0.6	1.1	0.7		
Brazil		1.0	0.7		
India	0.7			0.6	
Pakistan	0.9	0.7		0.7	
Philippines		0.8			

Source: World Bank, *World Development Report*, 1986 edition

and Indonesia.[4] All non-ferrous metals imports to Brazil and India are subject to such barriers.[5]

Table 2.3, displays the NPCs for key food products in major industrialized countries and a few developing countries in the early 1980s. As discussed above, the figures indicate the ratio of domestic producer prices in each country, to the international market prices. The overall impact of tariff and non-tariff measures conveyed by the NPCs indicates a very high level of protection in Japan. Japanese food producers received prices at least three times as high as the international prices for corresponding products. Agricultural protection was quite high also in Europe. Agricultural protection was moderate, or none at all in Australia, Canada and the United States. The figures show that developing countries, in contrast, often impose negative protection on their farmers.

In India in the mid-1980s, the NPCs for copper, lead, nickel and zinc were all above 2. For aluminum, the figure was 1.8. This implies a very high level of protection for India's non-ferrous metals industries.[6] In Brazil and South Korea in the same year, the NPCs for refined copper were 1.6 and 1.2.[7] National policy measures have certainly affected the competitiveness of commodity exports from many developing countries. For instance, it is likely that Brazilian iron ore exports have benefited from subsidized capital contributions to the state owned producers. Obversely, it is probable that Zambia's copper producers have been exposed to negative protection during the copper price trough in the early part of the 1980s. In the absence of alternative sources for public revenue, the government has extracted very heavy dues from the copper industry over these years. The substantial losses incurred by the copper corporation have led to a significant shrinkage of the country's copper production.

2.3   An assessment of the locational and economic impact of trade distortions

Although the available evidence is severely incomplete, it nevertheless permits us to formulate some conjectures about the causes motivating the protective arrangements in international commodity trade, and to provide some clues about the impact of these arrangements.

The protective policies applying to **food** excepting beverages (world exports in 1986 $205 billion) in industrialized and developing countries, constitute, without comparison, the most important distortion to international trade in primary commodities. In official policy statements, the heavy agricultural protection in Japan and Europe is motivated, in the first place, by strategic considerations. If opened to international competition, a large part of European and Japanese food production would have to wind up. The maintenance of a relatively high degree of self-sufficiency is regarded as an important insurance against blockades during war, and other supply disruptions. In practice, a more important reason for the heavy agricultural protection is that the farmers' lobby has a strong political clout in many countries, with parliamentary representations substantially above the share of agriculture in total employment. Protective measures that maintain agricultural employment, along with rising agricultural productivity have resulted in substantial exportable surpluses of important food products in many European countries.

The negative protection of agricultural output in the Third World is an additional factor that influences world food trade flows. The fiscal burden imposed on agriculture, predominantly through price controls on farm output and publicly owned marketing channels, has arisen from the dominance of the sector, and the desire to industrialize. Extraction of the agricultural surplus has been seen as a key to providing the savings surplus needed for industrial investments. The result has been a disappointing stagnation in food production, and increasing import needs to feed the population. In the late 1980s the disappointments are leading to a gradual shift of fiscal policy in favor of agriculture in many developing countries. The impact of this shift is not yet evident.

In a world without these distorting policies, the distribution of world food production and trade would be quite different from the present pattern. Western Europe and Japan would produce considerably less and would import far more than under current arrangements. The developing countries would produce and export much more, as a result of the greater demand from Europe and Japan, and of the easing of existing fiscal restraints. The exports of Australia, Canada and the United States would increase as a result of dismantled European and Japanese protection, on the one hand, but there would be a shrinkage of exports to developing countries, and more competition from Third World producers, on the other. On balance, however, the first impact would probably be stronger, leading to a net rise of production and exports by Australia, Canada and the United States.

Agricultural protection encourages high cost production, and suppresses many low-cost producers. As a result, it involves a heavy social cost to the world economy. Protection also reduces the import demand for food products, and so it makes the international market more marginal. This leads to lower international price levels on average, and more unstable price trends in the international market, all in comparison with a world without protection.

Some attempts have been made to measure the impact of the protective policies pursued by the industrialized countries. A recent study[8] has estimated that the dismantling of agricultural protection in the industrialized market economies would have increased the net economic welfare of these countries in the early 1980s by more than $20 billion, corresponding to $28 per capita. In the EFTA countries and Japan, where protection is particularly severe, the per capita gains would have been about twice as high.

The net economic welfare is composed of a loss in the agricultural producer benefit of $58 billion, and a gain in consumer benefit of almost $80 billion. These figures can be compared with overall 1984 food exports and imports by the industrialized countries of $133 billion and $129 billion, respectively. In a global perspective, the removal of OECD agricultural protection would lead to substantial increases in the agricultural producer benefit in the developing nations and socialist countries, but net economic welfare would change only marginally (negatively) in these two country groups.

There would be very substantial price effects from a removal of the industrialized countries' barriers to agricultural trade. The availability of low cost international supply would greatly reduce internal prices, especially in the heavily protected Japanese and European markets. The expanded import demand would lead to some increase of the international prices which are being kept depressed by protection. Table 2.4 summarises some of the results.

Finally, the study concludes that by widening the international markets for foods, the removal of OECD agricultural protection would reduce price instability in these markets by about one-third.

Table 2.4   The impact on real prices in the early 1980s from a removal of OECD agricultural protection (percent)

	Wheat	*Rice*	*Beef/lamb*	*Dairy prod.*	*Sugar*
Internal prices					
EEC	−22	−21	−35	−8	−26
EFTA	−34	11	−45	−34	−28
Japan	−72	−67	−55	−44	−63
USA	−5	−11	16	−19	−20
International price	10	11	27	61	11

Source: R. Tyers and K. Anderson, "Liberalising OECD Agricultural Policies in the Uruguay Round: Effects on Trade and Welfare," *Journal of Agricultural Economics*, May 1988

It could be that Tyers and Anderson underestimate the benefits of a removal of agricultural trade barriers. This is because their study uses a partial equilibrium approach and so misses the effects of liberalization on the non-agricultural parts of the economy. For instance, a concurrent study that adopted a general equilibrium approach concluded, in contrast to the findings of Tyers and Anderson, that the net economic welfare of developing countries would rise substantially in consequence of removed agricultural protection in the industrialized world.[9]

Steel (world exports in 1986 $73 billion) is another important commodity whose trade is heavily distorted by restrictive measures. But in distinction from agriculture and food, where protection has long prevailed, the barriers to steel trade are relatively new (for some evidence, see table 2.2).

The depressive developments of steel demand in the industrialized countries since the mid-1970s provide a major explanation for the establishment of the barriers. Prior to 1975, Western Europe and Japan were the major steel exporting regions. The United States was, by and large, self-sufficient. The steel industries of these countries have been in a constant state of depression since the late 1970s, with repeated restructurings and cut-downs of production capacity. The capacity of these industries proved highly excessive, as domestic steel consumption declined, and as the continued fast demand growth in developing countries became increasingly satisfied by local production.

Protection, mainly in the form of non-tariff barriers, was greatly expanded in the 1980s, primarily in reaction to the increasing export potential from newly industrializing countries (NICs) like Brazil and South Korea.

The United States, the EEC and Canada have established a complex system of often overlapping and ad hoc government intervention to manage and restrict the imports of steel.

The modern plants of the NICs have lower costs on average than the more ancient installations of the older industrial centers. In an international steel market unhampered by protection, a substantially greater proportion of global supply would originate in the NICs. Protection has been employed as a tool to slow down this process, and so to permit a less painful adjustment to the emergent competitive situation. In effect the trade barriers are becoming an increasingly entrenched and perennial phenomenon.

In comparison to food and steel, the remaining major commodity groups experience relatively limited impediments to international trade. Protection in the industrialized nations, the major importing group, is less restrictive, on average, for these products than for manufactures. The anecdotal evidence of the barriers maintained by developing countries suggests that though they are higher than in industrial nations, their impact is less than for food and steel.

There is no strong reason to protect against the imports of **cocoa, coffee and tea** (world exports in 1986 $22 billion) in the industrialized countries, since the three beverages are not produced in this country group. The climatic requirements of these products provide a very strong comparative advantage to the present producers. Some importing nations impose special sales taxes on the beverages, and when there is no local production, a sales tax will of course be tantamount to a tariff. However, the prime rationale of the taxes is to raise fiscal revenue and not to restrict imports. Though the existing policies may restrict global demand and trade flows, it is unlikely that they have any important impact on the location of production for this product group.

For **agricultural raw materials** (world exports in 1986 $72 billion), with major products like timber, cotton, wool and rubber, both tariff and non-tariff protection in the industrialized countries is quite limited.[10] The contrast with the high protection of food is a bit surprising, given that many importing nations produce identical materials (timber, wool) or close substitutes (synthetic fibers and rubber). Of course, the analogy with agriculture may not be appropriate in the case of synthetics which are produced by large, capital-intensive industrial firms. Also, the natural fibers and rubber may be more of complements than substitutes to the synthetic products.

Deregulation of the **petroleum and natural gas markets** in the United States in the 1980s involved a substantial reduction of the share of international fuels trade (world exports in 1986 $272 billion) subject to non-tariff barriers (table 2.2), but it is by no means clear that these non-tariff barriers had been effective in constraining imports to the United States.

A major share of the coal production in the United Kingdom and West Germany could not compete with substantially cheaper imports from transoceanic sources like South Africa, Australia and Canada. Its survival is assured by the procurement policies imposed on the United Kingdom and German electrical utilities, requiring them to rely heavily on the domestic supply.[11] Employment arguments and a desire to maintain a high degree of self-sufficiency in energy are used to justify these coal policies.

Severe trade intervention in **non-ferrous minerals and metals** (world exports in 1986 $73 billion) is by and large limited to selected developing countries which have ambitions to provide local supply for their growing industrial needs. This is the case, for example, in India, Argentina, Brazil and Mexico, where many local production units with costs exceeding the international price level have been set up.[12] The survival of such activities is assured through a combination of high tariffs, and non-tariff measures like the issuance of import licenses only after the domestic supply has been fully absorbed. The countries that pursue such policies, account for quite limited shares of world demand. The major industrial nations permit a reasonably free trade flow in these product groups. Hence, on the whole, the existing trade restrictions do not lead to any serious distortions of production and trade worldwide.

2.4   Location of commodity processing activities: colonial legacies and distorting trade policies

The raw materials extracted from the ground or picked from plants typically undergo one or several processing stages before they are used for consumption or as inputs in the production of manufactured goods. In many cases, very substantial value is added to the product througʰ the processing activity. Bauxite typically comprises 10 percent or less of the aluminum ingot value. Natural rubber roughly doubles in value when it is converted to sheets, plates and tubes. In others, the processing value added is more limited. Conversion of copper concentrates to refined metal adds no more than about 30 percent to the concentrate price. Cocoa butter and powder cost only some 20 percent more than cocoa beans.

Available trade data point to a distinct and persistent tendency for the commodity exports of developing countries to be biased towards unprocessed products. In the case of commodities produced both by industrialized and developing countries, the extent of processing before exports in the former tends to be much greater than in the latter. In the case of tropical materials produced almost exclusively by developing countries, like coffee,

Table 2.5 Selected primary commodities by processing stage: share of developing countries in the imports of industrialized countries (percent)

	Average 1970−2	*Average 1978−80*
Cocoa beans	98.2	97.5
Cocoa powder	22.5	26.0
Cocoa butter and paste	51.0	53.1
Natural rubber	96.4	97.9
Rubber products	1.0	4.3
Hides and skins	24.3	15.6
Leather	32.7	38.4
Timber in the rough	52.8	52.7
Timber, shaped and plywood	15.4	18.1
Bauxite	73.3	71.8
Alumina	32.5	24.6
Aluminum metal	9.7	13.0
Lead concentrates	40.4	44.4
Lead metal	18.0	13.5
Manganese concentrates	56.6	46.7
Ferromanganese	6.4	7.1

Source: UNCTAD, "The Processing and Marketing of Primary Commodities," TD/B/C.1/PSC/23, 24 November 1981

cocoa and rubber, a significant proportion of the processed exports are generated by industrialized countries which imported the raw material in the first place. In 1978−80, the developing countries accounted for one-third out of the total imports of 25 important primary commodities by industrial countries. When these imports are sub-divided according to processing stage, it emerges that the developing countries' share of the total was 49 percent of the unprocessed products, but only 22 percent of the processed ones.[13] Further details for some individual commodities are provided in table 2.5.

There are basically three alternatives for the location of commodity processing facilities: (a) in the proximity of the raw material production; (b) close to the market for the processed product; and (c) at a distance from both. The existing locational pattern is the result, in part, of important economic considerations. But the pattern is far from economically optimal, because additional, non-economic factors have also been at play.

In the rest of this section I shall look first at the economic considerations that influence the location of commodity processing and then scrutinize the causes and impact of two important policy-induced distortions to a globally optimal location pattern.

The **cost of processing** is a first important economic consideration for the location of processing activities. The cost, in turn, will depend on the relative prices of the factors needed for the specific activity. A poor country with abundant unskilled labor resources will tend to be more competitive in relatively labor-intensive processing (preservation of fruit or preparation of fish and meat), than in activities that are intensive users of capital, complex technology and managerial talent (copper smelting, steel production or chocolate making). However, in an age of increasing mobility for capital, technology and management, trans-border movements of these factors do not add greatly to their costs. Where large amounts of energy are needed in processing (smelting of aluminum or nickel), there will be a distinct competitive edge for locations where cheap energy is available. Energy constitutes a much greater proportion of the cost of aluminum metal than does bauxite. This makes it economical to locate aluminum smelting in the proximity of low cost power (for example, Bahrein, which has a surplus of natural gas), even if both the bauxite input and the aluminum output have to be transported over long distances. In some cases, the cost balance is tilted in favor of locations that provide superior infrastructural facilities that benefit the processing activity in an indirect way.

Economies of scale provide a further important cost consideration. There is a minimum economic unit in many processing activities. If the raw material output of a country is less than that minimum, processing abroad may be a more economical option.

Transport costs constitute a very important economic consideration in the location of some commodity processing. Costs will decline very substantially with the preservation of perishables or the concentration of lean mineral ores. The cost of transporting tinned mango by ship is only a fraction of the cost of the air freight for the fresh fruit. Non-ferrous metal ores normally contain 5 percent or less metal, so transporting the unprocessed ores involves volumes at least 20 times greater than the metal content. Virtually all such ores are concentrated at the mine, to increase the metal content to 25−30 percent, and thus to reduce the weight of the material by 80 percent per unit of metal. The content of gold is typically 5 grams or less per ton of ore (0.0005 percent), and concentration of such ores is a must, to make transporting over any distance economically feasible. In contrast, local concentration of minerals like bauxite and iron ore, though economical in many cases, is less essential, given that the ores contain some 25 percent aluminum and 50 percent iron, on average.

The weight loss in processing is limited for most agricultural commodities. The usable content of cereals, sugar, coffee, rubber and wool, constitutes a very high proportion of the unprocessed raw material, so the transport gain from local processing will be negligible.

Reduced weight unambiguously results in lower transport costs only so long as the processed commodity remains homogenous and amenable to bulk handling. At later stages in the commodity transformation, the product may require more careful handling and more space per unit of weight (copper tubes), become fragile (aluminum foil), and require packaging (roasted coffee). All of these characteristics will tend to add to the transport costs. Thus, for a number of commodities, the cost of transport per unit of the "pure" commodity may have a U-shaped form, with the lowest cost somewhere in the middle of the processing chain.[14] Studies of liner conferences' pricing practices show a tendency for transport profit margins to be higher for high value (processed) items, the rationale being a belief that such items are less sensitive to transport costs.[15] Such practices result in higher transport charges for processed products than warranted by the cost of transport. They consequently discourage processing in the country where the commodity is produced.

It has been suggested that **proximity to the final market** may be an important economic factor for products that are highly differentiated. While such proximity cannot matter for homogenous products, it may be valuable and convenient for the producers of, for example, chocolate or ferronickel to be located close to the final users. Such proximity, it is claimed, will facilitate monitoring changes in tastes or technological requirements of the users. This could be true, but one may argue about the economic importance of the factor in an age of fast transports and cheap instantaneous communications. After all, the garments industry is thriving in faraway South and East Asian locations, despite the exceedingly speedy change in European and North American fashions.

The location of commodity processing activities would be globally optimal if it were entirely determined by economic factors like those discussed above. The economics of locating the processing activity in the country of exports, or of imports, or in a third country, would vary, depending on the circumstances in each case. In practice, location is also strongly influenced by two further factors which clearly create a bias in favor of processing in the importing countries.

I refer to the first factor as the **colonial legacies**, *de facto*, if not always *de jure*. Traditionally, commodity exports from developing countries emerged in response to the increasing demand in Europe, North America, and later, Japan. The export oriented production was predominantly handled by multinational firms domiciled in the United States and in the major colonial powers of Europe. The developing countries were typically supplying the raw material only; most processing took place in the corporations' homes. Despite the numerous nationalizations of foreign ownership positions, and the emergence of a large state-owned enterprise universe in the decades since the Third World gained its political independence, the multinational firms in base resource industries continue to maintain a very important role as owners and managers of commodity production and exports. There are several reasons why these firms are reluctant to establish commodity processing in the developing countries where the commodities are produced.

Even where pure cost considerations favor the location of processing in the exporting country, the existence of processing installations at home will deter the multinationals from building up new capacity in the developing countries, at least in the short run. The common corporate accounting habit of depreciation in excess of physical and technological decay creates a bias in favor of existing installations. The short run tends to be quite durable, however. The life of processing plants is often extended over very long periods by reinvestments, partial replacements and expansions. In this way, the company's short-run reluctance to relocate the processing activity develops into semi-permanence.

The multinational company's feeling of exposure to "political risk" is probably a major factor inhibiting decisions to locate commodity processing in developing countries. Whether warranted or not, the fear that the host country might increase taxation, nationalize without compensation, or otherwise fail to honor the agreement it has signed with the corporation, creates a desire to minimize the resources at stake. The additional cost of producing the raw material elsewhere may be prohibitive. In processing the material, on the other hand, the cost differences of alternative locations are seldom as large, so the company's desire to minimize the political risk exposure may be instrumental for decisions to process at home.

A related but more general factor is the multinational's unfamiliarity with the social and economic environment in developing countries. The difficulty of obtaining, and the barrier to absorbing, the relevant information is a deterrent to processing in the developing country, even when a longer-run and more impartial attitude would have warranted the opposite choice.

The second distorting factor has to do with the **trade policies** of the industrialized, commodity importing countries. By a tendency to escalate tariffs with increasing degrees of processing, and by subjecting a greater share of processed products to non-tariff barriers, these policies are distinctly biased against processing in the developing countries.

Table 2.6 provides the incidence of tariff escalation and non-tariff barriers for some agricultural commodities. Tariff escalation is equally common for minerals. For example, the EEC and Japan have no tariffs on lead and zinc concentrates, but impose duties of 6—7 percent on lead and zinc metal. The EEC, Japan and the United States import bauxite

Table 2.6 Tariff and non-tariff barriers in industrialized countries on imports of selected agricultural commodities at different stages of processing

	Average tariff rates (%)	Percent of imports subject to non-tariff barriers
Vegetables		
Fresh or dried	8.9	39
Prepared	12.4	48
Fruit		
Fresh	4.8	20
Prepared	14.4	54
Coffee		
Green, roasted	6.8	11
Processed	9.4	17
Edible oils		
Seeds	2.7	33
Oils	8.1	56
Rubber		
Natural	2.3	0
Processed	2.9	6

Source: World Bank, *World Development Report*, 1986 edition

and iron ore duty-free, but impose duties of between 4 and 10 percent on aluminum and steel.[16] The actual average tariff rates imposed on imports of both crude and processed materials from the Third World are probably lower than the figures given in table 2.6. This is because specified quantities of certain products from developing countries are imported duty-free under the General System of Preferences, GSP.[17] Hence, the main constraints to trade may be in the non-tariff barriers.

Nevertheless, even though the nominal tariffs on processed commodities may be low, and escalation moderate, one must establish the "effective tariff" levels, to get a full impression of the impact on trade. The "effective tariff" level is obtained by relating tariff escalation to the value added in processing. Suppose processing increases the value of the commodity by 20 percent or from $100 to $120. If there is no tariff on the unprocessed commodity, but a 10 percent tariff on the processed one, the effective tariff imposed on the processing activity will be obtained by comparing the tariff, $12, with the processing value added, $20. The nominal tariff of 10 percent corresponds to an effective tariff of 60 percent in this case. For several of the agricultural processing chains contained in table 2.6, and also for iron ore/steel, the effective tariffs are of such orders of magnitude. The World Bank quotes some extreme cases relating to Sweden in the 1970s, where moderate nominal tariff protection resulted in effective tariff rates above 1,000 percent for edible oils, and above 100 percent for cereal flours.[18]

The industrialized nations' motivations for creating a bias against commodity processing in the countries producing the raw materials has varied grounds. These probably include some post-colonial desire to maintain the economic dependence of the exporting country by obstructing its economic diversification. Another ground could be a wish to protect the processing installations at home, along with the employment they create. In both objectives there is likely to be a communality of interest between the importing country and the extractive multinationals which have it as their home.

Trade in processed primary commodities has been hampered by tariff escalation in the developing importing countries too, and a recent investigation suggests that such escalation is generally far greater than in the industrialized countries.[19]

The result of the colonial legacies and trade policies described here is that significantly less commodity processing is taking place in the developing countries that produce and export primary commodities than would be the case in an undistorted, economically optimal situation.

The importance of the existing distortions is hard to quantify, especially since some of the exporting developing countries have introduced countermeasures which distort in the opposite direction, to rectify the initial imbalance. For instance, some commodity producing countries have introduced export tax structures that provide incentives to local processing, by taxing the raw materials exports particularly heavily. In other cases, quantitative restrictions have been imposed on the unprocessed materials exports. Furthermore, the involvement of foreign direct investors is often looked upon much more favorably by the host governments, if the investments include not only the extraction of the raw material, but also its processing.

Leather is a case where such counter-measures have had a strong impact. As appears from table 2.5, the developing countries' share of the finished leather market in industrialized nations is much larger than their share of raw hides and skins. For some time now, the industrialized nations have in fact been net exporters of raw hides to developing countries, and have imported the processed product in return.[20]

Even though the impact of the distorting policies is difficult to establish unambiguously, it is clear that significant global economic gains could be achieved from a move towards economic optimality in the location of commodity processing.

NOTES

1   J. Tilton, "Comparative Advantage in Mining," IIASA Working Paper WP−83−91, September 1983, Laxenburg, Austria.
2   D. DeRosa, "Agricultural Trade and Protection in Asia," IMF Working Paper/88/63, July 1988. The countries were: Bangladesh, India, Indonesia, Malaysia, Pakistan, Philippines, Sri Lanka and Thailand.
3   M. Radetzki and K. Takeuchi, "Growth Patterns in Copper Consumption in Industrializing Countries," *World Bank Staff Commodity Working Paper* no. 21, 1989, Washington, DC.
4   DeRosa, "Agricultural Trade and Protection in Asia."
5   M. Radetzki, "Developing Countries: The New Growth Markets," in J.E. Tilton (ed.), *World Metal Demand: Past Trends and Future Prospects*, Resources for the Future, Washington, DC, (forthcoming).
6   Ibid.
7   Radetzki and Takeuchi, "Growth Patterns in Copper Consumption."
8   R. Tyers and K. Anderson, "Liberalising OECD Agricultural Policies in the Uruguay Round: Effects on Trade and Welfare," *Journal of Agricultural Economics*, May 1988.
9   T. Loo and E. Tower, "Agricultural Protectionism and the Less Developed Countries," Center for International Economics, Canberra, 1988, as reported in *The Economist*, June 4, 1988.
10 UNCTAD, *Revitalizing Development, Growth and International Trade*, 1987, p. 135.
11 R. L. Gordon, *World Coal, Economics, Policies and Prospects*, Cambridge University Press, Cambridge, 1987.
12 M. Radetzki, "Developing Countries. The New Growth Markets."
13 UNCTAD, "The Processing and Marketing of Primary Commodities," TD/B/C.1/PSC/23, 24 November 1981.
14 For some empirical evidence see A. J. Yeats, "Do International Transport Costs Increase with Fabrication? Some Empirical Evidence," *Oxford Economic Papers*, November 1977.
15 UNCTAD, "Processing and Marketing of Primary Commodities."
16 A. I. MacBean and D. T. Nguyen, *Commodity Policies, Problems and Prospects*, Croom Helm, London, 1987.
17 R. J. Langhammer and A. Sapir, *Economic Impact of Generalized Tariff Preferences*, Trade Policy Research Centre, London, 1987; UNCTAD, *Revitalizing Development*, p. 132.
18 World Bank, *World Development Report*, 1986 edition.
19 S. Laird and A. J. Yeats, "Empirical Evidence Concerning the Magnitude and Effects of Developing Country Tariff Escalation," UNCTAD Discussion Paper, 1986.
20 World Bank, "Export Oriented Processing of Primary Commodities in Developing Countries," Commodity Note No. 14, September 1979.

3

Price Formation and Price Trends in Commodities

3.1 Factors determining price levels in the short and long run

Just like in all other markets, the basic forces determining price in an international commodity market are supply and demand. Despite the national tariffs and taxes which in some cases result in sizable differences between the internal prices and international price quotations (see chapter 2), the latter are usually very important also for the determination of domestic price levels.

In what follows, we briefly sketch the main factors that shape the demand, supply and price of commodities. Maximization of utility or profit among all agents is assumed. Though it may appear a bit tedious, the account is important, and will be repeatedly drawn upon in the present and later chapters. Those acquainted with basic microeconomics can proceed to the following section. The reader interested in further detail is referred to any standard text on microeconomics.

In the short run, the price of a commodity in the international market will tend to settle at a level like P_1 in figure 3.1, determined by the intersection of D_1 and S_1, the demand and supply schedules. The demand schedule for commodities is ordinarily steeply downward sloping. It depicts the quantity demanded for consumption and inventory holding at different prices. The supply schedule represents the horizontal addition of the marginal cost curves of individual producers. It typically slopes gently upwards until the level of full capacity utilization, where it becomes vertical.

The price will rise to a level like P_2 in consequence of a rightward shift in the demand schedule from D_1 to D_2. Such a shift can be caused, for

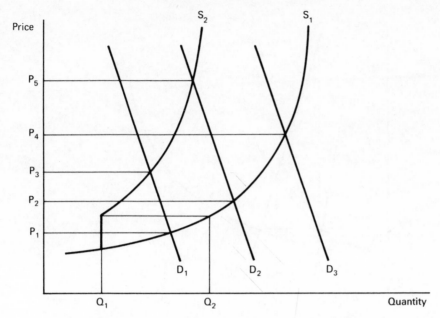

Figure 3.1 Competitive demand and supply

instance, by the secular economic growth from one year to the next, by an upturn in business conditions, which increases the demand for current consumption as well as for user inventories, or by the expectations, rational or irrational, of an impending price increase, which result in a surge in inventory demand for speculative purposes.

The price will rise to a level like P_3 in consequence of a disruption immobilizing the producers in the Q_1Q_2 segment of the original supply schedule. Such disruption may be the result of a crop failure due to disease or weather, a strike, or a political upheaval that arrests exports. The relevant supply schedule will now be like S_2, with a vertical portion at a supply volume of Q_1.

Notice that the higher is the initial capacity utilization, the greater will be the price impact of given shifts in the demand or supply schedules. If the demand schedule shifts once more by the same volume, or from D_2 to D_3, then price will rise from P_2 to P_4, a much stronger move than that from P_1 to P_2, caused by the initial shift in the demand schedule. Similarly, the leftward shift in the supply schedule from S_1 to S_2 will cause price to rise from P_2 to P_5, with the demand schedule at D_2, which is much more than with the demand schedule at D_1.

Everything else being equal, the steeper the demand curve, the lesser

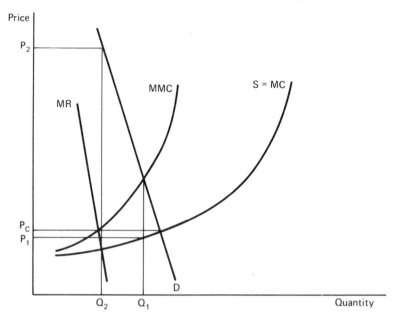

Figure 3.2 Monopolistic demand and supply

the price elasticity of demand. We have drawn the demand curves in figure 3.1 quite steep to reflect the relatively low short-run price elasticities of demand for a majority of commodities. Some of the reasons why these elasticities are low will be explored in section 3.3.

The short-run supply schedule, S_1, subsumes a given production capacity (or a given area of land under a specific crop cultivation). As noted, the schedule has been obtained by the horizontal addition of the marginal cost curves of individual producers, ranked according to their cost levels from left to right. Natural advantage, managerial efficiency, a high proportion of fixed costs and public subsidies will yield low variable and marginal cost levels. Taxes related to export revenue or export volume will push the schedule upward. At low levels of capacity utilization, the price elasticity of supply, defined as the percentage change in supply in response to a 1 percent change in price, will be high. As full capacity utilization is being reached, the supply schedule will tend to become increasingly steep, and the price elasticity of supply will decline. Very large price increases will be needed to generate additional output.

International commodity markets sometimes contain monopolistic features which result in prices different from those expected to prevail under competitive conditions. Figure 3.2, with initial demand and supply schedules identical to those of figure 3.1, illuminates the range within which prices are postulated to settle if the markets are not competitive. When the sellers have full monopoly control over the market, they will reduce supply to Q_2, where their marginal cost equals their marginal revenue from additional sales. This is given by the intersection of the MC (=S) and MR schedules. Price will rise to P_2 in consequence. If the monopoly control is less than complete, price will settle somewhere between P_2 and P_c, the competitive price. When the buyers have full monopsony control over the market, they will reduce demand to Q_1, given by the intersection between D and MMC. The latter is marginal to the S=MC schedule, and represents the buyers' marginal cost from additional purchases. The emergent monopsony price will be at P_1. If the monopsony control is less than complete, price will settle somewhere between P_1 and P_c. When there are monopolistic elements among both buyers and sellers, price will settle somewhere between P_1 and P_2, and the level will depend on their bargaining strength. Microeconomic theory leaves a very substantial void when it comes to price determination in non-competitive markets.

More complex price determination processes are involved when production results in the output of more than one commodity.[1] This is frequently the case in the exploitation of polymetallic ore bodies (copper and nickel; lead and zinc; gold and copper), but also hides along with beef; or wool along with mutton. Where one commodity dominates the revenue, the joint commodity will tend to be supplied irrespective of price. The plans to exploit deep-sea nodules for their nickel and cobalt content provide an extreme case of the influence of byproduct supply on price. The economics of nodule exploitation are dominated by the revenue from nickel sales. However, the metal composition of the nodules is very different from the composition of world demand for the two metals. If nodule exploitation provided a small fraction of world nickel supply, the simultaneous supply of cobalt would swamp the world market, resulting in a collapse of cobalt prices.

So far, we have considered price determination in the short run, when capacity, and hence the MC (=S) schedule, is given. The capital cost that was needed to create that capacity is a sunk cost and will not affect short-run price formation. In the long run, in contrast, price will tend to settle at a level that will cover the cost of capital, including profits, in those new production facilities that will be needed to replace worn-out installations, or to expand capacity in line with the trend growth of demand.

Because it will have to cover capital costs too, the long-run price will often correspond to a marginal cost relatively far to the right on the existing supply curve, e.g. like P_4 in figure 3.1. Subsidies to or taxes on new projects will affect the long-run price that is needed to assure market equilibrium. The long-run price will tend to rise over time if the total

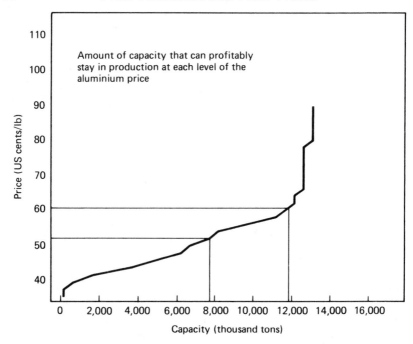

Figure 3.3 Aluminum supply curve, 1986. (Reproduced with permission from Anthony Bird Associates, *Aluminium Analysis* (Kingston upon Thames, UK), No. 29, April 1986)

costs of new projects increase, for instance because of depletion or the need to use less productive agricultural land. These tendencies can be neutralized or even reversed by cost-reducing technical progress. See section 3.7 for an empirical verification of long-run commodity price trends.

3.2 Exit barriers and the impact of price on cost

The neat relationships depicted in figures 3.1 and 3.2. are hard to vindicate in empirical analysis. In the real world, these relationships will be quite blurred. This present section will discuss one important reason why the supply curve may be hard to identify. It will also show that the causality does not run uniformly from cost to price. It is in fact common that costs adjust in response to persistently high or low price levels.

Figure 3.3 contains a supply schedule for the non-socialist world aluminum industry in 1986. It is conceptually identical to the supply curves in figures 3.1 and 3.2, and was constructed early in the year on the basis of detailed cost considerations for each individual aluminum smelter.[2] In the competitive circumstances characterizing the international aluminum market of the mid-1980s, profit maximizing producers should have kept their plants operating only if price exceeded their operating costs, as given by the schedule.

A scrutiny of actual events in 1986 indicates[3] that a large segment of capacity with variable costs in excess of price was kept in operation. Price in that year (London Metal Exchange, spot) was very stable, recording an average of 52 cents/lb. The supply curve suggests an output of less than 8 million tons in response to that price. Actual output was 11.95 million tons. One-third of the operating capacity could not cover its operating costs, and would have been better off by closing down. Why didn't it?

There are many answers, and not all of them are completely clear. First, there are several problems concerning the cost figures. The cost reporting could have been faulty. Some producers may have reduced their dollar costs in the course of 1986, for instance through improved efficiency of operations, or because their currencies were devalued. Some costs, for example, the cost of labor, typically assumed to vary with the level of operation, may in fact not do so, if the firm is prevented from sacking its workers. The supply curve will then in fact be lower than shown for the firms whose labor cost is unavoidable. The distinction between fixed costs, which should not be included in the supply schedule, and variable costs, which should be, also depends on the time horizon that is adopted. Servicing of installations is normally an obvious part of the operating costs. In the very short run, however, the service costs can be neglected without impediment to operations, with an ensuing downward shift in the very short-run cost of supply.

In this vein, one possible interpretation of the high-cost producer insistence on continued operations may run as follows: the price during 1986 was very low, both in relation to the industry's costs, and in a constant money comparison with earlier periods. The prevalent opinion was that prices would improve in a not too distant future. The combination of (a) the high technical and marketing cost of closing and reopening the production facilities, (b) the unavoidability of some cost items (e.g. wages) even when production closed down, and (c) the possibility of deferring some cost items (e.g. servicing of installations) into the future suggested that it was economically rational to continue operations during the temporary price trough, even though prices appeared to be below that portion of the supply schedule.

Other interpretations of continued operations are possible. The public authorities could have coerced or induced a certain behavior, through legislation and taxes, or through subsidies. There could also have been social or political pressure on the firm to continue operations even when it was not strictly economical to do so.

Deviations from the profit maximization goal provide a further possible explanation for loss-making operations. In many firms, return on capital is only one of several criteria that guide operations. This is true of many state owned corporations, or cooperatives that process the raw material supplied by their members. Goals other than profit maximization could then motivate continued operations even when price does not fully cover operating costs. Even in firms that profess the profit maximization goal, such deviations could nevertheless result from the managers' short-run urge to secure their own jobs.

The present discussion has brought out a number of "exit barriers" which prevent or at least delay the closure of production units which should have discontinued operations if the microeconomic rules for profit maximization had been applied without reservations. We started out from the example of aluminum smelting in 1986, but the argument has applicability to all commodities, both mineral and agricultural. The important revelation brought out by the above discussion is that many suppliers do not pursue profit maximization as their sole goal, that all categorizations of costs are fuzzy, that the traditional supply schedule is ambiguous within wide ranges, and that consequently one has to be cautious when using it as a tool for supply determination.

The preceding section which summarized the microeconomic insights into price determination, indicated that the supply schedule is based on the cost of supply; and that, with given demand, price is determined by the level and shape of this schedule. The suggested causality would go from costs to prices. This view must now be qualified, for there are many reasons to believe that prices also have an influence on costs. This adds another ambiguity to the supply schedule.

The findings and predictions of the behavioral theory of the firm,[4] that high price and profit levels push up costs and increase the organizational slack, and that obversely, low prices and profits lead to cost reductions and squeeze the slack, have clear applications to the industries producing raw materials.

Using copper as an example, we find a remarkable increase in the average level of the industry's average variable costs of production between 1950 and 1972 (see table 3.1). In the 1970s, the major explanation for this increase was widely believed to be resource exhaustion, but as I have argued elsewhere, increasing organizational slack, permitted by the high price levels, was probably a far more important factor.[5] In the 1980s, the costs have experienced a very impressive fall. This was partly because the highest cost production units were closed down due to the slack demand conditions. More importantly, however, producers whose survival was

Table 3.1 Average operating costs in
the copper industry outside the
socialist countries, and copper prices
(LME spot) (constant 1986 $/lb)

	Operating costs	Price
1950	65	113
1960	84	122
1972	110	138
1982	85	78
1986	56	62

Source: Costs 1950 through 1972
from M. Radetzki, "The Rising Costs
of Base Materials – the Case of
Copper", *Mining Magazine*, April
1979; costs 1982 through 1986 from
Metals Analysis and Outlook, *Five
Year Outlook 1987–1991*, August
1987; prices and deflator from World
Bank, *Commodity Trade and Price
Trends*, annual, several issues

threatened by the price depression undertook draconian measures to cut
existing slack out of their systems. During the 1980s, the entire supply
schedule for copper in the non-socialist world declined by an order of
magnitude of 0.25–0.30 constant 1986 dollars per lb.[6] The efforts of the
US and Canadian producers yielded particularly impressive results.
Admittedly, some of this cost decline was not sustainable in the longer
run, and involved a mere deferral of costs, to permit survival during the
low-price period. But a substantial part of the cost decreases were based
on pushes for technical advance and improved managerial efficiency, and
thus of a permanent nature.

Copper, our example, is not exceptional. Similar stories could be told
for many other commodities. During the 1980s, when virtually all commodity prices experienced substantial price declines in real terms, the
producers of most commodities succeeded in substantially cutting the cost
of output, measured in dollars. Apart from the permanent closure of
redundant high cost installations, improved technology and a greater
managerial pressure for cost minimization, the cost reductions were brought
about through the acceptance of lower returns by labor and by the
providers of production inputs. With the depressed prices and demand
levels plaguing many commodities, the sellers of inputs like machinery or

power accepted lower prices in many cases, rather than risking that their clients would close down. On similar grounds, labor was agreeable to wage cuts in many industries and countries.

The efforts to reduce the cost of supply were facilitated in many countries by aggressive reductions in the real exchange rates which lowered the dollar cost of inputs and factors without the need to reduce the nominal amounts paid in local currency.[7] Such exchange rate policies have been particularly common in developing countries whose exports are dominated by the commodities whose prices declined.

A common arrangement in the 1980s to induce factors of production and input suppliers to accept lower prices and remunerations, has been to relate the wage or the input price to the price of the commodity output. Labor contracts in many industries and countries have been structured to permit labor a share in any increase in the price of the output. Similar provisions have been written into the input supply agreements, for instance for power or alumina in the case of aluminum smelters.

The aggressive devaluations undertaken by many commodity exporting countries, and the establishment of a causal link from prices to costs, have further blurred the supply schedule. These practices have probably also added to the instability of commodity prices, for, by lowering the supply schedule in consequence of a price weakness, they must have induced prices to fall even more.

3.3   Price instability: causes and consequences

This section considers the instability of commodity prices in the relatively short run. The long-run trends will be discussed later in the chapter.

Pointing out drastic movements in commodity prices is easy.[8] The annual average sugar price fluctuated between 1.9 cents per lb in 1968, 29.7 cents in 1974, 7.8 cents in 1978, 28.7 cents in 1980 and 4.1 cents in 1985. The price of petroleum rose threefold between 1973 and 1974. The price of rice fell from 630 dollars per ton in April 1974 to 240 dollars in April 1976. The price of copper was 137 cents per lb in April 1974, but had fallen to only 58 cents in December of the same year. In one week during December 1987, the price of nickel rose by 26 percent, but early in January 1988, it fell by 20 percent in a single day.

Designing a systematic and meaningful measure of price instability in commodity markets is less straightforward. I will point to some of the difficulties by reference to the price graphs for rubber, in nominal and real terms, depicted in figure 3.4. Consider first the lower curve of nominal prices. The simplest procedure to measure instability is to fit a trend line to the price curve, and then to measure instability as the

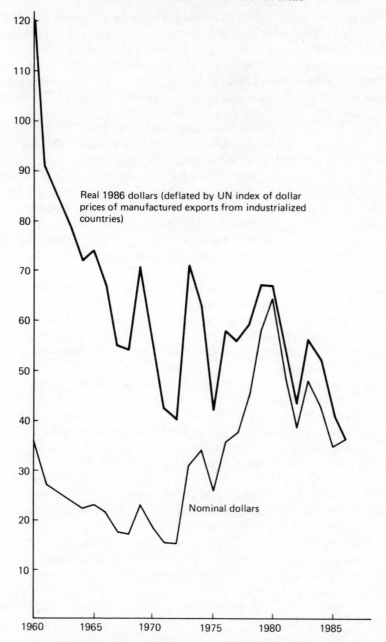

Figure 3.4 Price of rubber (Singapore No. 1 RSS, f.o.b.), US cents/lb. (*Source*: UNCTAD, *Monthly Commodity Price Bulletin*, several issues)

average percentage deviation of actual prices from the trend line. Notice that the curve consists of annual average quotations which smoothen out the very short price fluctuations. Instability will be greater if instead it is measured on the basis of monthly or daily variations around the trend. Instability will be smaller, and the fit will improve when convenient sub-periods with steadier price movements, e.g. 1960–72, or 1972–80, are chosen instead of the entire period shown.

Part of the instability in nominal prices is clearly caused by the inflation of the 1970s, and it may be more relevant to determine the instability measure from deflated, real dollar prices, as given by the upper curve in figure 3.4. The shape of this curve points to the appropriateness of yet another approach to determining instability. The curve depicts a continuous but decelerating decline over time, when measured in absolute terms. This suggests that a straight line trend does not catch the essence of the longer-run price movements. An exponential trend line, declining by a given percentage per year, is likely to provide a better fit, with a lesser extent of instability in this case.

Aggregation across several commodities will tend to reduce price instability. An index of prices of industrial raw materials is bound to be smoother than the prices of the individual commodities included, because the price movements will not be fully synchronized. Analogously, an aggregate price index for all commodities will exhibit an even greater degree of stability.

Fitting quarterly price observations to an exponential trend for the 1957–82 period, Chu and Morrison[9] concluded that the average percentage price deviations for an aggregate index of non-oil commodities amounted to 17, with higher values recorded for the food, beverages and agricultural raw materials groups, but lower ones for the metals group. The instability turns out lower for all these commodity categories when two separate periods, 1958–71, and 1972–82, are considered, but it is higher in the second sub-period than in the first. Manufactures exhibit a lower price instability than the aggregate commodity price index, for the whole period, as well as for each of the two sub-periods.

A. I. MacBean and D. T. Nguyen[10] measure instability for a number of individual commodities by percentage deviations of annual averages from an exponential trend in the 1951–80 period. In their results, sugar, sisal, coffee and cocoa, all with deviations above 40, emerge as the most unstable commodities. In contrast, jute, tea, bananas and tobacco, with deviations below 20, exhibit the least instability. The instability ranking among commodities undergoes considerable change over time, when sub-periods are considered. The authors also compare the price instability in 1971–80 of manufactures exports from major industrialized countries, disaggregated into 26 groups, on the one hand, with the instability of individual major commodities over the same period, on the other. Like Chu and Morrison, they conclude that the instability in manufactures is less than in commodities. This finding confirms a very common belief, but one should realize that it may be due to the higher level of manufactures aggregation in the comparison.

It is clear that the prices of many commodities can vary a lot, even within relatively short spans of time. But as should by now be apparent, there are many ways to measure price instability, and the results can differ considerably depending on the approach that is chosen.

The price variations that occur in competitive commodity markets can be seen as efforts to restore equilibrium between the quantities that are supplied and demanded. Starting out from an equilibrium price like P_1, given by the intersection between S_1 and D_1 in figure 3.1, the price will rise if there is a rightward shift in the demand schedule, or a leftward one in the supply schedule. The price will decline if the opposite shifts occur. The relative magnitude of the price change will depend on the size of the shift as well as on the price elasticities of supply and demand. Other things being equal, the lower the (absolute) elasticities, the sharper will be the price swing.

The price reaction pattern becomes much more complicated if there is a lag in the adjustment of supply or demand to a changed price. For instance, if the supply adjustment is lagged, and the price elasticity of supply exceeds the (absolute) price elasticity of demand, price will start oscillating in an explosive way, without automatically finding an equilibrium level. The literature refers to this as the "hog cycle."[11]

Even when we do not consider the complication of lagged reaction patterns, it is necessary to examine both the price elasticities and the possible shifts in supply and demand to explain prevailing price instability. The following discussion relates to the short-run price elasticities of supply and demand. All price elasticity values are hard to determine and elusive. The numbers contained in table 3.2 should therefore be taken with a pinch of salt.

Supply elasticities vary with the commodity. For one-year crops, the elasticity is low in the very short run, but may be quite high over two crop seasons. Where output is dependent on capital investments with extended gestation periods, the supply elasticity will depend on the extent of slack in the utilization of existing capital. The elasticity will be high so long as such slack remains, but will decline as full capacity is approached. In distinction from the elasticity of output, the elasticity of supply will normally be higher where inventories exist and can be drawn upon. Since exports ordinarily account for only a part of output, the elasticity of export supply will usually be greater than the elasticity of output.

Price elasticities of demand (absolute values) will be high for com-

Table 3.2 Estimated short-run price
elasticities

	Demand	Supply
Coffee[a]	−0.17	0.06
Tea[a]	−0.2	0.15
Rice[a]	−0.25	0.5
Bananas[a]	−0.37	High
Rubber[a]	−0.2	0.15
Copper[b]	−0.3	0.06
Tin[b]	−0.5	0.19
Chromium[c]	−0.05	0.2

[a] World Bank Commodity Handbooks:
Coffee, June 1985; Tea, February
1982; Rice, February 1981; Bananas,
June 1985; Rubber, February 1981.
[b] W. Labys, *Market Structure,
Bargaining Power and Resource Price
Formation*, Lexington Books,
Lexington, Mass., 1980.
[c] M. Radetzki, Strategic Metal
Markets, *Resources Policy*, December
1984.

modities with close substitutes, especially luxuries which are easily dispensable. The demand elasticity will be higher if the price of a commodity
rises alone rather than in conjunction with its substitutes. The price
elasticities of demand will be low for basic necessities and "indispensable"
materials without close substitutes, base food products like cereals, for
example, or strategic metals like manganese and chrome. Where processing and manufacturing costs are high, the price of and hence the demand
for the final products may be only marginally dependent on the price of
the raw material (steel and tyres made from iron ore and rubber respectively). Demand elasticity will be low in such cases.

A variety of events can cause supply and demand to change. The shifts
will tend to be stronger where there is a heavy geographical concentration
in the production or consumption of a raw material. Agricultural commodities experience harvest variations. Strikes can sharply affect the
supply of minerals. Political disturbances may cut the supplies of all types

of commodities. Business cycles are known to cause variations in demand, especially for goods with high income elasticities. The demand for some commodities is strongly affected by inventory fluctuations. Inventory cycles may in turn be caused by speculative, commercial or political triggers. Technological shifts, too, can sometimes change the demand for a commodity.

International markets for agricultural commodities often experience an especially high degree of volatility. This is because the major industrialized countries often isolate their domestic markets through agricultural protection. The export supply of these countries, sometimes constituting a large share of the total international market, will be determined by national policies that determine national production and consumption, and will not be influenced by the international market price. Sugar provides an illustrative example. Suppose the crop in industrialized countries is above average. With existing agricultural policies, the price in the domestic markets will not be permitted to fall. Domestic consumption will therefore not increase, and the surplus thrown into the international market will be larger than in the absence of domestic price stabilization.

The low short-term price elasticities and the considerable variability in demand and supply for many commodities provide an entirely plausible reason for the observation that commodities experience a greater degree of price instability than do manufactured goods. The sharp price fluctuations, in turn, create a variety of problems.

General commodity price booms such as the ones culminating in 1951 and 1974, with the quarterly price indices for all non-fuel commodities rising by more than 50 percent within a 12-month time span,[12] have been claimed to cause a rise in global inflation through the so-called "ratchet effect,"[13] whereby the prices of manufactures and services rise in response to the higher commodity prices, but do not fall when commodity prices decline. Similar effects probably ensued from the oil price shocks in 1973 and 1979, given the importance of this commodity in international trade.

Sharp variations in commodity prices cause serious macroeconomic destabilization in countries like Jamaica, Chile, Liberia, Niger, Uganda, Mauritius and Iceland, where one single commodity accounts for more than 50 percent of total exports.[14] The issue of high national dependence on the exports of one or a few commodities is treated in detail in chapter 8.

Price swings of individual commodities destabilize the earnings of commodity producing firms. Furthermore, by their unpredictability the price variations tend to disrupt the process of investments in new capacity.

Finally, the instability of commodity prices complicates the commodity users' purchasing operations. Where the raw material weighs importantly in total cost, the organization and timing of purchases become crucial both for profitability and for relative competitiveness. In stainless steel production in industrial countries, for example, the nickel- and chromium-containing raw materials typically account for no less than 45 percent and 15 percent respectively of overall costs. Labor and capital costs, in contrast, amount to no more than 20 percent and 10 percent of the total. Any change in nickel and chromium prices will have a very strong impact on the total costs of the stainless steel producer. The raw materials user can sometimes price his output in parallel with the fluctuations of his raw material costs, and so shift the burden of swinging raw materials downstream. Such practice is hardly feasible to those who, because of bad luck or imprudent purchase policies, have to pay more than their competitors to satisfy their raw materials needs.

3.4 Alternative trading arrangements and their implications for price formation

A myriad of arrangements is being practiced in cross-border commodity trade, and the discussion in the present section cannot be exhaustive. My ambition is to classify the trading arrangements into a few major forms, to indicate some of the markets in which they are practiced, and to point to the major implications of each form. The logical order of my classification is from the most public and transparent arrangement to the most private and opaque one. Commodity exchanges, auctions, producer dictated prices, user dictated prices, bilateral contracts and transfer prices are discussed in turn.

Commodity exchanges

Chapter 4 is devoted entirely to commodity exchanges, so they can be treated quite briefly in the present context. Commodity exchanges are markets where many buyers and sellers meet simultaneously, and enter into numerous transactions regarding the commodities traded on that exchange. Depending on the institutional arrangements, the exchange can provide the opportunity for spot transactions, as well as forward or futures trade. The prices are monitored and published. The commodities traded on exchanges are characterized by a sizable number of sellers and buyers, and by relatively few quality grades. The most important internationally oriented commodity exchanges are found in London, New York, Chicago and Kuala Lumpur. They maintain markets for a great number of commodities, of agricultural as well as mineral origin.

Perhaps the most crucial function of the exchanges is to determine a uniform and representative price level. The prices set by the exchanges are often used to determine price levels in deals outside the exchange. The uniformity of the price facilitates transactions. The need for price haggling is virtually eliminated. Transaction costs on the exchanges are usually quite low. The prices at the exchanges are instantaneously influenced by events in the outside world. Hence, there tends to be a much greater short-run price instability on the exchanges than under most other trading arrangements, though some claim that the order of causality is the reverse, i.e. that a high inherent price instability of a commodity makes it a favored candidate for exchange trade.[15]

Auctions

Auctions commonly also accommodate many sellers and buyers, but unlike exchanges which operate continuously, business is transacted only at irregular intervals. In distinction from exchanges, where the double auction principle is applied, i.e. buyers and sellers are equally active in trade, the auction markets apply the principle of single auction, with a more passive role assigned to the sellers (ordinary auction) or to the buyers (Dutch auction). In ordinary auctions, the practice is to deal with the sellers consecutively, and to offer the supply of each at a time. Normally, the buyers make successively higher bids, with the transaction priced at the highest bid. In Dutch auctions, the procedure is reversed; the seller makes successively lower offers, with the transaction priced at the first accepted offer. As in the case of exchanges, auction prices are public and transparent, but they may lack continuity if auctions are irregularly held.

Tea and wool are the two main commodities for which auctions constitute the major trading arrangement. London is the most important venue, but auctions are also held in the major producing countries, e.g. India and Kenya for tea, and Australia and New Zealand for wool. The purported reason for trade at auctions rather than at fully fledged exchanges is the great variety of grades across producers and over time, in which these commodities are sold.[16]

Bilateral contracts

This is probably the predominant arrangement in international commodity trade. It involves a pair of agents who independently agree on the terms that will apply to the trade between them. The crucial terms on which all contracts have to be explicit concern the commodity specification, the quantity, the time and place of delivery and the price. Other than that, bilateral contracts come in many different forms. Thus, some contracts can relate to a single immediate transaction, while others concern repeated deliveries stretching over periods from a few months to a decade or more.

Bilateral contracts often use the price levels set by commodity exchanges. The price determination becomes more tricky for commodities that are not traded on exchanges. In principle, each bilateral pair has to negotiate and agree on the price that will apply in each contract. This will be arduous and time consuming. Since prices of contractual agreements are not regularly published, the negotiations may result in a wide range of price levels at a particular point in time.

In practice, there are often conventions which simplify the procedure and help avoiding blatant deviations from the average price level. In manganese, for instance, where most trade is transacted through annual bilateral contracts, a commercial practice has developed where a major supplier enters into preliminary discussions with a major customer, while the rest of the industry defers its contract negotiations. As soon as this pair reaches an agreement, all other suppliers and users adopt the agreed price as a guideline for their own negotiations.[17] Very similar practices apply to the annual contracts under which a large proportion of international iron ore trade is transacted. Until about 1970, the annual contractual arrangements between the Swedish iron ore exporter and the steel mills of Germany set the pace for other contract negotiations. From then on, the Brazilian company CVRD has taken over the Swedish role.[18] In more recent years, the lead roles have oscillated between the Brazilians, Australians and Canadians on the supply side, and the Germans and Japanese on the demand side.[19]

In other cases the price transparency in bilateral contract markets is quite limited. This is true, for instance, of the international markets for sisal and jute or of phosphates, chromite and uranium, though in all these cases there are trade associations or specialized journals which publish prices or price ranges purported to reflect the levels of actual transactions. In the case of uranium, the published series relates to spot sales, while the evidence of prices applied in the long-term contracts that dominate uranium trade is scattered and less systematic.[20]

In some cases, the true price may not even be clearly apparent from the content of the contract. This would be the case when the contracted price is preferential, to take account of the provision of long-term investment finance, or equity participation, by the buyer. Similarly, barter deals make it very hard to determine the true commodity price contained in the contract.

Especially in cases with lacking transparency, there is a likelihood that small parties with lesser access to information and with weaker bargaining skills will get a worse deal in bilateral contracts than they would in the more transparent and impartial arrangements characterizing exchanges and auctions.

Producer dictated prices

Producer dictated prices occur in commodity markets where the number of producers is relatively small, and where each sells to relatively many customers. Producer pricing implies some degree of monopoly power; it also affords the producer a certain degree of convenience.[21] The commodity is sold on a take-it or leave-it basis, and, at least in theory, the need to bargain with each customer is obviated.

Markets where producer pricing prevails are mainly found among minor minerals. World output of cobalt is dominated by the state owned mining firms in Zaire and Zambia, and the two set the prices at which they are prepared to supply. A very large share of world molybdenum is produced by Amax Inc. in the United States, and the company has long been announcing producer prices for this material. A few South African mining companies account for a large share of world platinum production, and also set the price for their production. Quite often one of the producers in such markets ·becomes the price leader, with the others stepping in line.

Producer price quotations can coexist with prices set by commodity exchanges or the prices monitored by trade journals from bilateral contracts, but such coexistence tends to dilute the pricing power of the producers. Producer prices typically react with a lag to market developments, and alter less frequently and less violently than prices on commodity exchanges. Producers have to introduce rationing when their price is below the exchange price, and are forced to offer hidden rebates when the commodity price falls below their quotations. A time series of producer prices therefore tends to give a distorted picture of transaction prices.

In earlier times, prices set by producers could remain for extended periods of time. The proliferation of commodity exchanges has forced the price setting producers to alter their prices more frequently and to adjust more fully to the exchange quotations. The introduction of petroleum, aluminum and nickel on commodity exchanges along with a substantial decline in producer concentration during the past decade has greatly reduced the relevance of the producer price systems which traditionally dominated in these three markets.

User dictated prices

One could think of identical arrangements, but with the roles reversed, with the buyers being few and able to dictate prices to prolific producers. Such arrangements are certainly not common. An example is the military procurement of uranium by the US and UK authorities, whose complete dominance of demand until the early 1960s permitted them to set the terms of their purchases.[22]

Transfer prices

Transfer pricing in international commodity trade occurs when the producer/exporter and the user/importer are part of the same vertically integrated corporation. The prices in such trade are internal to the firm, and can be set at any level. They appear only in the accounts of the firm, and are ordinarily not published. In principle, they do not affect the corporate profit before tax.

The profit maximizing firm will have an interest in setting the transfer prices so as to minimize the sum total of profits tax, export tax and import duty. Import duties on raw materials are usually low, so ordinarily the major corporate concern is with profits and export taxes. If the transfer price is set low, profits will be shifted to the importing country. This will reduce the tax burden, if the profits tax in the importing country is lower. Governments of exporting countries desirous to maintain their tax income have instituted "posted prices" in many cases, to be applied for the purpose of tax assessment in the exporting unit of the integrated firm. These prices have sometimes been derived from production costs; in other cases they have been based on perceptions of prevailing price levels in trade between independent parties. The institution of posted prices has reduced the corporate benefit from transfer price manipulation.

Where transfer prices dominate a market, the price transparency will usually be quite low. Even if the prices were known, it is unclear whether they would at all reflect the costs of production or the price levels that would emerge in arm's length transactions.

In the 1980s, bauxite trade probably offers the best example of a commodity market based predominantly on transfer prices. The extent of vertical integration from bauxite to alumina and aluminum is still quite high, and a major share of the bauxite that enters international trade is in internal corporate deals. There are no proper price quotations for bauxite. The World Bank publishes two "price" series.[23] One of these is based on the estimated Jamaican cost of production, freight and export tax. The other is the US import price. Presumably, this is based on the customs declarations of importers into the United States. This series would then represent a mix of transfer prices and prices of arm's length transactions.

Transfer price arrangements account for minor shares of all international transactions in, for example, iron ore, tea, rubber, and some edible oils, where the processors in industrialized countries still own some of their sources of primary supply. Transfer prices were far more common in the 1950s and 1960s, for example in petroleum, iron ore, copper and many food products. Since then, there has been a wholesale vertical disintegration of the industries producing and processing these materials. The disintegration resulted from the widespread nationalizations of the raw material producing industries in developing countries. In consequence, the significance of transfer pricing has been greatly reduced.

3.5 The actual price quotations

Commodity price data may appear confusing and mystifying to the uninitiated. The purpose of this section is to clarify some of the concepts used and point to the sources where current quotations and long time series are found.

Commodity price quotations come in many different formats, and one has to be clear about the precise information they convey, in order to evaluate them or compare alternatives. At the most basic level, one must be careful to note the **currency** in which the quotation is made. The **unit of measurement** is equally important, but can be more tricky to clarify. Tons come in at least three varieties, and ounces, bushels and gallons differ depending on country and product, so it may be useful to refer to a handbook of weights and measures. For unprocessed metal minerals, e.g. iron ore, conventions differ between quotations per unit of gross weight on the one hand, and per unit of metal content on the other. In the case of some mineral concentrates, e.g. chromite, the quotation could be (a) per unit of gross weight, (b) per unit of metal oxide (Cr_2O_3), or (c) per unit of metal content.

The **stage of processing** at which the material is sold is also important for the price. Sugar is alternatively traded as raw or refined; uranium comes either as uranium oxide (U_3O_8) or uranium hexafluoride (UF_6), and the additional processing costs explain existing price differences. The **quality** of the product will obviously make a difference to price, and one must clarify the specific quality to which the price quotation refers. Coffees are divided into robustas and arabicas, with the latter commanding a price premium over the former. In cotton, long fibers usually command a higher price. And the price of chrome ore is strongly influenced by its carbon and iron content.

The **time of delivery** is very important for the price level. When supplies for immediate delivery are ample, the prices for future delivery, quoted on commodity exchanges, will be higher than prices for spot transactions, the difference (contango in the United Kingdom; premium in the United States) providing for the cost of carrying inventories. When the supplies for immediate delivery are scarce, spot transactions may be priced higher than deals with later delivery times, and the difference (backwardation in the United Kingdom; discount in the United States) can be quite large.[24] In November 1987 copper for immediate delivery was hard to obtain, and price on the LME was 1,420 pounds sterling per ton, up from £1,100 in September. Supply early in 1988 was expected to be more ample, so the price in November for delivery in February was only £1,217, the backwardation amounting to more than 14 percent of the spot price.[25] Forward and future contracts usually cover delivery times between 3 and 18 months into the future. The 1980s have seen the development of commodity bonds permitting the pricing and payment today for commodities to be delivered several years into the future. Bonds involving repayment in gold, silver and petroluem have been issued.[26] The provision of finance for investment in commodity production has been the major rationale for the issuance of commodity bonds, with the pricing of future commodity supply playing a subsidiary role.

The **delivery place** is equally important. From one extreme to the other, the places of delivery can be ex garden, ex mine or ex refinery for agricultural products, minerals and metals respectively; free on rail (f.o.r.); free alongside ship (f.a.s.); free on board (f.o.b.); and cost insurance freight (c.i.f.). The price differences are most important for commodities with low values per unit of weight and long transport distances. The price of iron ore f.o.r. in Brazil or manganese ore f.o.r. in South Africa is much less than one half of the c.i.f. price in the user country. Depending on the point of delivery, the price may or may not include export taxes and import duties. These range from insignificant for many commodities to very high for instance for highly protected agricultural products in industrialized countries. The point of delivery for transactions on commodity exchanges is usually from the exchange warehouses. Most of these are located in the major industrialized countries.

Daily quotations from the most important commodity exchanges are regularly published by business oriented newspapers in major business centers. *The Financial Times* and the *Wall Street Journal* give a wide coverage of prices from the exchanges. The two newspapers also provide regular quotations for numerous important commodities which are not traded on the exchanges. These include, for instance, minor metals, jute or coconut oil. To track the non-exchange commodities in greater detail, one has to go to specialized journals, newsletters or government publications which provide, for example, producer and trader quotations, or price ranges from bilateral deals for specific commodities. Thus, *Metal Bulletin* in the United Kingdom and *Metals Week* in the United States contain a wealth of price information on ferrous and non-ferrous metals and minerals. *Preise und Preisindices fuer Aussenhandelgueter* published by Statistisches Bundesamt, Wiesbaden, West Germany, provides often quoted price series for products like iron ore, maize or bananas. *Oil World*, published from Hamburg, contains detailed price data for edible oil seeds and oils. *Public Ledger*, published from Watford in the United

Kingdom, has, among others, price series for maize, pepper, jute and sisal. Cereals price developments are regularly found in *Grain and Feed Market News*, issued by the US Department of Agriculture.

More extended time series for prices of a wide range of commodities in international trade, as well as price indices for major commodity groups, are contained in *International Financial Statistics*, issued monthly by the International Monetary Fund, in UNCTAD's *Monthly Commodity Price Bulletin*, and in *Commodity Trade and Price Trends*, published by the World Bank once a year. The World Bank publication provides annual price series expressed in current dollars, stretching back to 1950 in most cases. The high levels of inflation over the past decades reduce the relevance of these series when such long periods of time are considered. The nominal price data have to be converted into real ones, expressed in constant dollars. A number of approaches can be employed to make such conversions, and the World Bank document presents no less than four alternative price deflators. These are in turn, (a) the implicit deflator of GDPs for the OECD area as a whole, expressed in US dollars; (b) the implicit GDP deflator for the United States; (c) the US producer price index; and (d) the index of dollar prices of manufactures exports (c.i.f.) from major industrialized countries.

Each of the deflators can be used to convert the nominal commodity price series into real or constant dollar series, but one must be careful in the selection of the index used, since each can yield very different results over specific time periods. For example, between 1980 and 1984, inflation in the United States amounted to 27 percent by index (b) and 15 percent by index (c). Over the period, the US dollar appreciated strongly. As a result, inflation was −1 percent when measured by index (a), and −5 percent when measured by index (d). The international value of the US dollar increased because the appreciation of the US currency more than offset the decline of its value due to price increases in the United States. International price deflators like (a) and (d) are more appropriate when the real commodity price series are to be used in an international context. Commodity price series expressed in real terms should be treated with caution until it is clarified what kind of deflator has been used to obtain them.

Given its primary interest in the developing countries' real earnings from commodity exports, the World Bank uses index (d) to convert the nominal price series for individual commodities into real ones. This is also the deflator that will be employed later in the chapter when we consider commodity price trends over even more extended periods. First, however, we have to attend to a more technical question, i.e. how exchange rate changes for a currency affect the price of a commodity, quoted in that currency.

3.6   Exchange rates and commodity prices

A majority of the commodity price quotations in international trade are expressed in US dollars. When other currencies are used, such as pounds sterling or Malaysian dollars, their equivalents in US dollars at current exchange rates are often quoted alongside. An issue which has often been raised is whether suppliers to an international market reap an advantage by quoting their prices in an appreciating currency, or a disadvantage by having quotations in a currency which tends to depreciate against others. The issue may be highly relevant in a non-competitive market where producers set the price after arduous negotiations. The case of OPEC between 1974 and 1983 is an illustrative example. Because it is difficult to change the price, the producers will tend to gain from having set their quotations in an appreciating Swiss franc than in a depreciating pound sterling. The purchasing power of a price set in the former currency will increase over time in relation to that of a price set in the latter.

In a competitive market, in contrast, where price can change flexibly, the forces of demand and supply will determine the level, with automatic adjustments for any exchange rate change of the currency in which the price is quoted, so it should not matter which currency is used. The mechanics of the price adjustments to exchange rate changes have been subject to considerable confusion, especially during the 1980s, when the dollar first rose against most other currencies, and then fell again. The purpose of the present section is to clarify the adjustment process by showing what must happen to the dollar price of a commodity traded in a competitive market, as the dollar appreciates or depreciates.[27] To isolate the problem under scrutiny, we will assume that everything else remains constant while the dollar's exchange rate shifts. At least in the short run, this is not a serious distortion of reality. For simplicity we will initially assume that there are only two currencies, and that the Deutschmark is used throughout the world outside the United States.

I shall begin by putting forth the following general proposition: the greater the economic weight of the dollar, the less dollar prices of commodities in international trade will be affected by exchange rate changes. This is easily demonstrated by considering two extreme cases. In both the value of the dollar is assumed to increase by 100 percent against the DMark. In the first extreme, 99 percent of world economic activity takes place in the United States. Given the unimportance of the rest of the world (ROW) and the DMark, the dollar appreciation will have an insignificant effect on global supply and demand. Hence, the dollar price of commodities will remain virtually unchanged. In the second extreme, only 1 percent of world economic activity takes place in the United States. A doubling of the value of the dollar will make commodities much

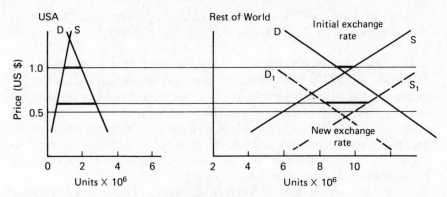

Figure 3.5 Effects of dollar appreciation on dollar prices in international commodity markets.

Assumptions: Rest of world (ROW) currency is DMark, initial exchange rate is 1 DMark = 1 dollar. At initial exchange rate equilibrium price is $1, US demand = 22 percent of world demand, while US supply = 11 percent of world supply. The US import surplus amounts to 1 million units. The initial demand and supply schedules have been drawn so that a 50 percent decline in price results in a 50 percent change in the quantity demanded and supplied. After dollar appreciation the exchange rate is 2 DMark = $1. The ROW demand and supply schedules shift to D_1 and S_1. The new equilibrium price is $0.6 and the US import surplus is 2.2 million units.

dearer in terms of DMarks. Since virtually all production and consumption takes place in the ROW, the old DMark price has to be restored for the initial demand and supply of commodities to be maintained. Hence, the dollar price of commodities must be halved.

The extremes just described also apply to specific commodities, though in the individual cases, the relative dominance of the United States as producer and consumer of the commodity under scrutiny has to be substituted for the relative dominance of the dollar in the world economy.

Less extreme and more realistic cases for a number of commodity markets can be disentangled with the help of figure 3.5.[28] The figure shows an initial equilibrium between demand and supply at the price of $1.0 per unit. The full S and D lines depict the initial demand and supply schedules in the United States and ROW respectively, with the US accounting for 22 percent of world demand and 11 percent of world supply, and importing 1 million units.

What happens when the value of the dollar doubles from 1 to 2 DMarks? Abstracting from international trade in factors and inputs used in the production of the commodity under scrutiny, the US supply and demand schedules will remain unchanged, while those in the ROW will shift downwards to the positions indicated by the dotted lines in figure 3.5.

The new schedules indicate that at a price of $1.0 (now equal to 2 DMarks), the ROW will generate a huge export surplus. Since the US import surplus at this price remains at 1 million units, the price must fall to bring about market equilibrium. The new schedules also show that at a price of $0.5 (1 DMark), the ROW will continue to generate the same export surplus of 1 million units as before the exchange rate change. This surplus is insufficient to satisfy the expanded import demand from the United States, so the price must settle higher.

It is apparent from figure 3.5 that equilibrium will be attained at a price of $0.6 (equal to 1.2 DMarks), when the export surplus from the ROW (2.2 million units) equals the US import requirements. With the assumptions underlying the figure, therefore, a doubling of the exchange rate of the dollar results, *ceteris paribus*, in a 40 percent decline of the dollar price. The figure can of course also be used in reverse, to analyze the effects of a dollar depreciation: if the exchange rate of the dollar falls back to 1 DMark, the effect will be to push the price up from $0.6 to $1.0 per unit.

Additional insights can be gained from various adaptations in the figure. For instance, as already discussed, the sensitivity of the dollar price to exchange rate changes will be reduced as the US share in world supply or world demand increases. Similarly, this sensitivity will be reduced with increases in the price elasticity of supply or demand in the United States, and with decreases in the corresponding price elasticities in the ROW. Along with data on shares and elasticities for a given commodity, the figure can be used to assess how the dollar price of that commodity will fare as the dollar exchange rate moves up or down.

Admittedly, the analysis is based on a number of simplifying assumptions which reflect real events somewhat artificially. The two-currency world may be a reasonable representation of what went on between 1980 and 1985, when the dollar appreciated in splendid solitude against all other currencies. The picture was more complex in subsequent years, because then the dollar depreciated in parallel with the currencies of a number of other important countries, including the major commodity producers. The dollar's importance, in terms of this analysis, was much greater during its decline, which should have reduced the impact of that decline on the dollar price quotations for commodities. It must also be underlined that by focusing exclusively on exchange rate movements, and abstracting from other simultaneous changes affecting commodity markets, the present analysis becomes highly partial. This may be all right when the exchange rate change studied is instantaneous, but could mislead when the period considered extends over years during which many other factors are also at work. These caveats notwithstanding, figure 3.5 and its underlying arguments are instructive for understanding how exchange rate changes affect commodity prices.

3.7 The long-run commodity price trends

Attempts to track the very long-run price trends for commodities in international trade have a long and confusing tradition. To be at all meaningful, the commodity prices have to be expressed in real or relative terms. It has been common to use an index of dollar prices of manufactured goods in international trade as deflator to obtain real dollar commodity price series. There have been many such attempts, and they have yielded very varied results.[29] Depending on the end points of the series, the countries whose trade is covered, and the commodities and manufactures included, these investigations have yielded a variety of results ranging between stagnant and substantially declining long-run trends for real commodity prices.

Figure 3.6 presents the gist of a recent painstaking effort to clarify the long-run trend of real commodity prices.[30] The real prices are measured as an index of the dollar prices of 24 major commodities in international trade, accounting for 54 percent of total non-fuel commodity trade in 1977–9, divided by an index of manufacturing unit values, expressed in dollars, exported from major industrialized countries. The index contained in the figure depicts a statistically significant trend rate of decline of 0.59 percent per year for the real prices of non-fuel commodities over the first 86 years of the present century. This amounts to a cumulative trend fall of some 40 percent. Elaborate tests in which the weights of the commodity basket are varied, and the impact of the end points of the period studied explored, confirm the stability of the negative trend and the size of the decline.

Additional insights are obtained when the material is disaggregated into major commodity groups. The annual trend decline is 0.84 percent for metals, 0.82 percent for agricultural non-foods, and 0.54 percent for foods excluding beverages. Beverages is the only group exhibiting a positive trend. The real prices of coffee, tea and cocoa have been rising by an average of 0.63 percent per year over the present century.

With one exception, no significant reversals in the above trends have taken place over the period studied. Only in the case of metals can one identify a clear break, occurring in the early 1940s. From 1900 to about 1941, the real metals price index shows a negative trend of 1.7 percent

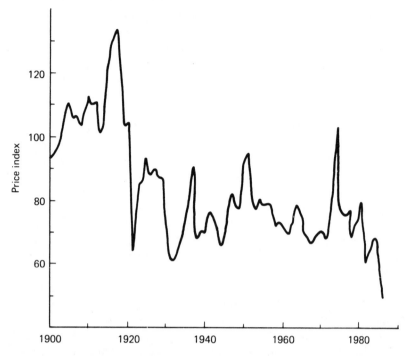

Note: The index of relative commodity prices has been obtained by deflating
      an index of dollar prices of 24 internationally traded non-fuel commodities
      by an index of dollar export prices of manufactured goods from major
      industrialized countries.

Figure 3.6   Index of relative prices of non-fuel primary commodities,
1900–86 (1913 = 100) (*Source*: E.R. Grilli and Maw Cheng Yang, *World
Bank Economic Review*, January 1988)

per year, but during the remainder of the period, the trend price rises by
some 0.5 percent per year.

How can one explain the long-run price performance of commodities
versus manufactures? It is first worth noting that the evidence of falling
relative commodity price trends revealed by Grilli and Yang's and many
others' investigations[31] is contrary to the theories and expectations of a
row of classical economists. These economists postulated rising relative
price trends for raw materials in consequence of the productivity loss
caused by the need to employ increasingly more meager land and mineral
deposits in commodity production. Elaborating on the works of Adam
Smith and David Ricardo, John Stuart Mill synthesized the classical
argument for rising real commodity prices:

The tendency, then, being to a perpetual increase of the productive power of labour in manufactures, while in agriculture and mining there is a conflict between two tendencies, the one towards an increase of productive power, the other towards a diminution of it, the cost of production being lessened by every improvement in the process, and augmented by every addition to population: it follows that the exchange value of manufactured articles, compared with the products of agriculture and of mines, have, as population and industry advance, a certain and decided tendency to fall.[32]

The notions about rising raw materials prices due to increasing pressures on land and mineral depletion remained out of vogue for a long period of time. From the early 1970s, however, they attracted intensive concern, as a result of the strong and widespread commodity boom, the dramatic price increases implemented by the oil producers, and the publication of the Club of Rome's reports. In the case of exhaustible resource commodities, the Hotelling rule[33] was rediscovered and attracted widespread attention both in economic research and among the public at large. Under a set of restrictive assumptions, this rule stipulates that the price of an undeveloped resource in the ground will rise over time at the rate of interest. Intellectually impressive research efforts were carried out in the 1970s and 1980s to elaborate and refine this rule, but the theoretical constructs have tended to lead their own separate life, without any convincing empirical vindication. A vulgar version of the Hotelling rule enjoying wide popularity claimed that the price of extracted resources would rise at the rate of interest. Based on this notion, virtually all long-term analyses of the petroleum market in the late 1970s and early 1980s forecast that real oil prices would rise continuously at 2−3 percent per year. Both versions of the Hotelling rule abstract from the continuous resource discoveries and the cost reducing technical progress which play instrumental roles for long-term price trends in exhaustible resource commodities.

The first attempts to explain the falling real commodity price trend were mounted by Prebish and Singer,[34] who argued that there is an asymmetry in the response of prices to productivity gains between commodities and manufactures. The markets for the former are highly competitive, so any productivity improvement leads to a price decline. The monopolistic organization of the labor and capital employed in manufactures production, in contrast, enables the factors of production to reap the benefit of productivity gains in the form of higher income. The Prebish and Singer explanation of falling commodity price trends aroused an extended debate. The critics argued that it contained a logical flaw: falling commodity prices would boost commodity demand until the original commodity/manufactures price ratio had been restored.

There are several other, less controversial, reasons that could explain the long-run decline of real commodity prices. First, the income elasticity of demand for most commodities (defined as the percentage change in demand due to a 1 percent change in income), is lower than for manufactures, and so, with expanding income, the lower growth of commodity demand is likely to result in a weaker commodity price development. The second reason is that transport costs ordinarily constitute a higher proportion of the delivered price of commodities than of manufactures. The secular fall in transport costs discussed in the preceding chapter should therefore have resulted in a stronger decline in commodity price quotations. Third, and probably most important, the manufactures prices index is tricky to construct and interpret because of the continuous shifts in its product composition, and of the quality changes over time of individual products. The increasing size and efficiency of, say, harvesters or mine loaders during the past 40 years has involved a much greater improvement than any quality change of the cereals or ores in whose production these machines are employed. It is quite possible that the relative shifts in quality are enough to explain why manufactures prices have risen in relation to commodity prices.

Finally, it seems that the classical economists exaggerated the detrimental impact on productivity from the need to employ inferior lands and mineral deposits in commodity production. Improvements in agricultural productivity have assured global supply without the need to employ increasingly unfertile lands. On the contrary, there have been tendencies, especially in North America, to stop using the least productive land so as to avoid burdensome surpluses. Advanced methods of exploration for minerals have not only expanded the quantity of reserves, but also ameliorated the quality of the exploited resource base over time.

The debate over declining real commodity prices in the past several decades has arisen mainly out of concerns about the developing countries which are heavily dependent on commodity exports. In the final chapter of this book we will revert to the issues with which such countries are confronted. At the present time it suffices to note that these countries would obviously be better off if real commodity prices were rising instead of falling. But one would have to go far behind the evidence of figure 3.6, and explore productivity trends as well as quality changes in commodities and manufactures before one could conclude that the benefits reaped by these countries from their foreign trade have deteriorated over time.

NOTES

1   For a formal treatment see, for instance, P. R. G. Layard and A. A. Walters, *Microeconomic Theory*, McGraw-Hill, New York, 1978.
2   Anthony Bird Associates, *Aluminum Analysis*, No. 29, April 1986.

3 Ibid., No. 33, April 1987.
4 See for instance R. M. Cyert and J. G. March, *A Behavioral Theory of the Firm*, Prentice-Hall, Englewood Cliffs, NJ, 1963.
5 M. Radetzki, "The Rising Costs of Base Materials – the Case of Copper," *Mining Magazine*, April 1979.
6 P. Crowson, "The Global Distribution and Availability of Mineral Resources," paper presented to a symposium on mining and petroleum at the Delft University of Technology, 3–4 November 1987.
7 The issue of real devaluation will be treated in greater detail in chapter 8.
8 Two standard references to commodity prices, from which the following examples have been taken, are World Bank, *Commodity Trade and Price Trends*, annual; and UNCTAD, *Monthly Commodity Price Bulletin*.
9 Ke-Young Chu and T. K. Morrison, "The 1981–82 Recession and Non-Oil Primary Commodity Prices," *IMF Staff Papers*, March 1984.
10 A. I. MacBean and D. T. Nguyen, *Commodity Policies: Problems and Prospects*, Croom Helm, London, 1987.
11 Layard and Walters, *Microeconomic Theory*.
12 M. Radetzki, "Commodity Prices during Two Booms, 1950 and 1973," *Skandinaviska Enskilda Banken Quarterly Review*, No. 4, 1974.
13 B. P. Bosworth and R. Z. Lawrence, *Commodity Prices and the New Inflation*, chapter 1, Brookings Institution, Washington DC, 1982.
14 UNCTAD, *Handbook of International Trade and Development Statistics*, 1986.
15 L. G. Telser, "Why There Are Organized Futures Markets," *Journal of Law and Economics*, April 1981.
16 UNCTAD, "Marketing and Processing of Tea: Areas for International Co-operation," TD/B/C.1/PSC/28/Rev.1, 1984.
17 UNCTAD, "The Processing and Marketing of Manganese: Areas for International Cooperation," TD/B/C.1/PSC/20, August 1981.
18 World Bank, *Price Prospects for Major Primary Commodities*, Report No. 814/86, October 1986.
19 UNCTAD, "Review of the Current Market Situation and Outlook for Iron Ore," TD/B/IPC/IRON ORE/AC.1/8, September 1987; private communication with RTZ Ltd, October 1988.
20 M. Radetzki, *Uranium, A Strategic Source of Energy*, Croom Helm, London, 1981.
21 T. Scitovsky, *Welfare and Competition*, Unwin, London, 1952.
22 Radetzki, *Uranium*.
23 World Bank, *Price Prospects for Major Primary Commodities*, Report No. 814/86, October 1986.
24 Futures and forward trading on the commodity exchanges are considered in greater detail in the following chapter.
25 Drexel, Burnham, Lambert, *Futures and Options Monthly Report* (New York), January 15, 1988.
26 T. Priovolos, "Commodity Bonds, A Risk Management Instrument for Developing Countries," World Bank Commodity Markets Division, Working Paper No. 1987–12, Washington, DC, 1987.
27 A broader analysis of what happens to the prices, traded volumes and trade revenues of commodity exporting countries in consequence of exchange rate variations is found in D. Ridler and C. A. Yandle, "A Simplified Method for Analyzing the Effects of Exchange Rate Changes on Exports of Primary

Commodities," *IMF Staff Papers*, November 1972.

28 An algebraic analysis with similar conclusions can be found in H. Fliessing and S. Van Wijnbergen, "Primary Commodity Prices, the Business Cycle, and the Real Exchange Rate of the Dollar," World Bank Background Paper WDR–1985, Washington DC, 1985.

29 MacBean and Nguyen, *Commodity Policies*, chapter 3.

30 E. R. Grilli and Maw Cheng Yang, "Primary Commodity Prices, Manufactured Goods Prices and the Terms of Trade of Developing Countries: What the Long Run Shows," *World Bank Economic Review*, January 1988.

31 C. Kindleberger, *The Terms of Trade, A European Case Study*. John Wiley, New York, 1956; W. A. Lewis, "World Production, Prices and Trade 1870– 1960," *Manchester School of Social and Economic Studies*, May 1952; R. Prebish, "The Economic Development of Latin America and Its Principal Problems," *Economic Bulletin for Latin America*, 1962, pp. 1–22; D. Sapsford, "The Statistical Debate on the Net Barter Terms of Trade between Primary Commodities and Manufactures: A Comment and Some Additional Evidence," *Economic Journal*, 1985, pp. 781–8.

32 J. S. Mill, *Principles of Political Economy*, John W. Parker, London, 1848, vol. II, p. 254.

33 H. Hotelling, "The Economics of Exhaustible Resources," *Journal of Political Economy*, April 1931.

34 R. Prebish, "The Economic Development of Latin America and Its Principal Problems," *Economic Bulletin for Latin America*, 1962, pp. 1–22; H. Singer, "The Distribution of Gains between Investing and Borrowing Countries," *American Economic Review*, 1950, pp. 473–85.

4

The Commodity Exchanges

4.1 The commodity exchanges and the commodities traded there

Throughout this book, the concept "international commodity markets" is being used in a very loose sense, to describe the buyers and sellers and the transactions they enter into. Commodity markets can be much more strictly defined as places where buyers and sellers of commodities meet to conduct their trade. In all countries there are many such markets of various sizes and levels of sophistication. Local rural markets provide a place for the exchange of food and other agricultural commodities. Nationwide and international markets for specific products or groups of products are also common. Spot transactions with immediate physical delivery usually dominate the trade activities of commodity markets, but there may also be forward deals, involving delivery some time in the future.

The commodity exchanges which are the subject of the present chapter form a small subset of commodity markets. This subset is distinguished by having developed particular features in response to a variety of specific needs. Commodity exchanges exhibit several distinct characteristics:

1 Trade is exclusive to a limited membership, but the members of the exchange can conclude deals both on their own behalf and on behalf of their clients. The latter are usually far more important.
2 Trade has the form of open outcry, now increasingly recorded on computers. The double auction principle is applied. The price of bids to buy is gradually raised, that of offers to sell reduced, until a commonly agreed price is reached.
3 There is a strict standardization of trade practices, with regard to, for

example, volumes, qualities, delivery times, margins and payment terms. Some exchanges stipulate a maximum permitted price change from the previous day.
4 Futures transactions with a high degree of transferability usually dominate trade (the distinction between forward and futures trade is discussed below). Physical trade has a subordinate position, as a majority of the futures contracts are cancelled by the issue of opposite contracts before delivery falls due.
5 As a rule there is a clearing house, established and financially guaranteed by the members of the exchange. All futures contracts issued by the members have the clearing house as the opposite party. The net position of the clearing house for a particular commodity and delivery date must always be zero.[1]

The most important commodity exchanges, located in London, New York and Chicago, are listed in table 4.1, along with details about commodities traded, instruments used, contract specifications and volume of trade. Some of these exchanges (e.g. the LME or the CBT) have operated for over a century, while others (e.g. COMEX and NYMEX) are of a more recent vintage. The specialization in terms of commodity coverage, usually the result of historical accident, varies considerably among the exchanges. Commodity exchanges of significance also operate in many other places, including Kuala Lumpur (tin, rubber, palm oil), Sydney (wool), Paris (sugar), Kansas City and Minneapolis (cereals). National transactions dominate trade on some of the exchanges, while others are truly international in character.

Not all commodities are suited for trade on exchanges. A number of conditions must be satisfied for futures markets in a commodity to function reasonably:[2]

1 There must be many buyers and sellers.
2 There must be a preparedness among those who trade the physical commodity to use the market for hedging, i.e. for fixing the price of known future sales or purchase needs.
3 The inherent price variability in the commodity must be considerable, i.e. its supply and demand schedules should experience a significant instability and have a low price elasticity.
4 The commodity must be storable so that a comprehensible relationship between cash and futures prices can exist. With the development of preservation and refrigeration, virtually all commodities have been storable in recent times.
5 The commodity must be easy to grade, or else it will be difficult to specify the quality covered by futures contracts.

Table 4.1 The major commodity exchanges in London, New York and Chicago

Exchange	Commodities traded	Instruments	Contract unit	Number of contracts traded in 1987 Futures	Options
London Metal Exchange (LME)	Aluminum, High grade	F O	25 tonnes	49,847	105[a]
	Aluminum, Primary	F O	25 tonnes	1,057,024	43,986[a,b]
	Nickel	F O	6 tonnes	163,329	457[a]
	Copper, Grade A	F O	25 tonnes	1,375,703	50,831[a]
	Copper, Standard grade	F	25 tonnes	3,237[a,c]	
	Lead	F O	25 tonnes	291,680	244[a,d]
	Zinc, Special high grade	F	25 tonnes		
	Zinc, Standard grade	F O	25 tonnes	238,910	1,035[a]
	Silver	F	2,000 ounces	27[a,c]	
	Silver	F O	10,000 ounces	7,694	0[a,c]
London FOX, the Futures and Options Exchange	Cocoa	F O	10 tonnes	926,335	281
	White sugar	F	50 tonnes	200,340	
	Raw sugar (FOBS)	F O	50 tonnes	762,053	3,457
	Coffee	F O	5 tonnes	906,930	5,505
International Petroleum Exchange (IPE), London	Gas oil	F O	100 tonnes	1,102,148	7,518
	Premium leaded gasoline	F	100 tonnes	1,584	
	Heavy fuel oil	F	100 tonnes	3,019	
	Crude Oil	F	1,000 barrels	171	

Table 4.1 *(con't)*

Exchange	Commodities traded	Instruments		Contract unit	Number of contracts traded in 1987	
					Futures	Options
Baltic Exchange, London	Soybeans	F		20 tonnes	52,310	
	Barley	F		100 tonnes	25,914[e]	
	Wheat	F	O	100 tonnes	61,249[e,f]	
	Pigmeat	F		50 pigs at 65 kg	2,474	
	Live cattle	F		5,000 kg	275	
	Potatoes	F	O	40 tonnes	206,196[f]	
New York Mercantile Exchange (NYMEX)	Platinum	F		50 troy ounces	1,361,546	
	Palladium	F		100 troy ounces	160,284	
	WTI crude oil	F	O	1,000 barrels	14,581,614	3,117,037
	Unleaded regular gasoline	F		1,000 barrels	2,056,238	
	Heating oil No. 2	F	O	1,000 barrels	4,293,395	143,605
	Propane	F		1,000 barrels	15,312[g]	
Commodity Exchange (COMEX), New York	Copper	F	O	25,000 lb	2,569,178	612,850
	Silver	F	O	5,000 oz	5,055,652	918,064
	Gold	F	O	100 oz	10,239,805	2,080,067
	Aluminium	F		40,000 lb	8,500	
New York Cotton Exchange (CTN)	Cotton	F	O	50,000 lb	1,395,980	73,480
	Frozen conc. orange juice	F	O	15,000 lb	266,641	685
New York Coffee, Sugar and Cocoa	Coffee	F	O	37,500 lb	964,586	25,639
	Raw sugar	F	O	50 long ton	3,853,499	432,927

Exchange	Commodity	F	O	Unit		
(CSCE)	White sugar	F		50 metric ton	903	
	Cocoa	F	O	10 metric ton	895,465	13,910
Chicago Board of Trade (CBT)	Gold	F		1 kg	159,627	
	Silver	F	O	1,000 oz	509,965	10,009
	Soybeans	F	O	5,000 bushel	7,378,760	1,242,072
	Soybean meal	F	O	100 tons	3,912,417	81,213
	Soybean oil	F	O	60,000 lb	3,797,970	85,735
	Corn	F	O	5,000 bushel	7,253,212	661,519
	Oats	F		5,000 bushel	291,108	
	Wheat	F	O	5,000 bushel	1,929,306	124,598
Chicago Mercantile Exchange (CME)	Gold	F		100 oz	261,639	
	Lumber	F	O	130,000 board ft.	437,089	6,483
	Live cattle	F	O	40,000 heads	5,229,294	1,222,397
	Live hogs	F	O	30,000 heads	2,040,478	147,859
	Pork bellies	F	O	38,000 lb	1,097,010	15,112
	Feeder cattle	F	O	42,000 lb	645,877	134,830

F = Futures contract, O = Traded option.

[a] Trading statistics for 29/5–31/12 1987.
[b] The trading ceased in 1988.
[c] The trading ceased in 1989.
[d] The trading started in 1988.
[e] Trading statistics for 10/1987–10/88.
[f] The trading of options started in 1988.
[g] The trading started 21/8 1987.

Source: Based on publications collected from the exchanges and clearing houses in 1988 by U. Améen, R. Gyllenram and Å. Holmström (The Royal Institute of Technology, Stockholm).

For successful introduction on an exchange, it is important that the contract specification in terms of quality, volume, expiration date and place of delivery suits the needs of those who buy and sell the physical commodity. At the same time, the contract should be attractive to the small individual investors whose business provides continuity and liquidity to the market. For example, the size of the contract, and hence the margin payments, should not exceed the financial capacity of such investors. Attempts are continuously being made to widen the group of commodities that are traded on the exchanges, and in some cases the successes and failures of the efforts are hard to explain. For example, some years back, the Chicago Mercantile Exchange created markets for ham and bacon. The first was a failure, but the second an enormous success.[3]

In some cases, commodities are not traded on exchanges because an important producer or government plays a successful role as stabilizer of prices. This was true for nickel in the 1960s, when INCO dominated world output. It is also the case for groundnuts and tobacco, where the US government maintains large stockpiles and price support schemes. Incidentally, the same applied to currencies in which there was no futures trading until the exchange rates started to fluctuate after the breakdown of the Bretton Woods system in 1971.[4]

Producer unwillingness to relegate the pricing function to an independent institution, combined maybe with historical accidents probably explains why paper pulp as well as iron, manganese and chrome ores are not traded on exchanges.

Recent additions of commodities traded on exchanges include aluminum, nickel and petroleum. Until at least the early 1970s, the markets for the three products were characterized by implicit collaboration among small groups of producers who dominated their respective markets, and assured stable prices over months, or even years. The limited number of sellers and the price stability made the commodities unsuitable for trade on the exchanges. These conditions changed in the course of the 1970s. As the number of producers proliferated, collaboration and market control became harder to maintain. Traders assumed a greater role in marketing. In the more unstable economic environment of the 1970s, the producers were forced to adjust their quotations much more frequently and fully to the independent market quotations. This prepared the ground for the introduction of aluminum and nickel on the LME, aluminum on COMEX, and petroleum on NYMEX and London's International Petroleum Exchange.

4.2   Functions and instruments

Broadly, the commodity exchanges have the following function:

1 They constitute authoritative mechanisms for price determination.
2 They provide an opportunity for hedging through which producers and users of a commodity can obtain a kind of price insurance.
3 They greatly facilitate both very safe and highly speculative investments in commodity inventories and commodity-related trade instruments.
4 They establish a physical trade outlet through spot transactions and through futures contracts at their termination.

Before discussing what the exchanges do, however, it is necessary to describe the instruments with the help of which they perform their roles. There are basically two instruments, namely futures contracts covering a continuum in time, and options on such contracts. Both are highly standardized.

Futures contracts

A **futures contract** is an agreement to buy or to sell a specified quantity of a commodity for the agreed price at a particular future time. The quantities covered by a contract, and the periods when futures contracts fall due, are determined by the trade practices of the exchange. For instance, the copper contract on the LME involves 25 tons, and falls due either immediately or in three months' time.[5] In distinction, the copper contract on COMEX covers 25,000 pounds (11.3 tons), and can be made to fall due immediately or in January, March, May, July, September or December within the next 18 months. A coffee future on the London FOX covers 5 tons, but on the Coffee, Sugar and Cocoa Exchange in New York, the quantity is 37,500 pounds (17 tons). Contract months on both exchanges include March, May, July and September, but January and November only in London, and December only in New York.[6]

The standard features of futures contracts makes them easily transferable and highly liquid. The owner of a contract can sell it at any time at the going price for that commodity and delivery month. **Forward contracts** are a wider concept that comprises futures contracts. Any contract that stipulates delivery in the future is a forward contract. Forward contracts need not have standardized provisions regarding quantities, grades and dates when they fall due. Since each forward contract is unique, it is much less easy to trade. A transfer of a forward contract is dependent on finding a party interested in its particular specifications. The distinction between the tradeability of the two contract forms is akin to the distinction between trade with the help with money, and barter trade.

A member of the exchange entering into a futures contract to buy, does not need to pay for his purchase at the time he signs a contract, but he is required to provide a **margin** representing about 10 percent of the purchase value, as a commitment to the deal. This margin is held by the clearing house of the exchange, which is formally the opposite party to the contract. If the price declines after the buyer has signed the contract, a need arises to top up his payments, so that the margin always represents 10−20 percent of the current value of the contract. Suppose that in March a buyer has signed a December futures contract on COMEX to buy copper at $1 per pound, for a total of $25,000, and paid a margin of $2,500. By May, however, the December futures price has fallen to $0.90, reducing the value of a December contract to $22,500. The price fall has depleted the entire margin, and the buyer no longer has any financial reason to fulfill his contractual obligation. Before the price has fallen that far, the buyer will be asked to make additional margin payments. Failing that, the contract will be forcibly liquidated. This will take the form of issuing a December futures sales contract at the going, lower price, to the buyer. The two contracts will cancel out each other, and the loss, amounting to the difference between their values, will be recovered from the original margin payment. If on the other hand, the price rises, payments will be made to the futures buyer, since he is not required to hold margins above the 10−20 percent level.

Analogous conditions apply when members of the exchange enter into futures contracts to sell. In any normal circumstances, the margins will provide a complete financial guarantee for the commitments entered into by the clearing house. In principle, therefore, commodity futures trade involves no risk that the opposite party defaults. This adds considerably to the fungibility of futures contracts.

The tin debacle on the LME, which at the time did not have any clearing house, is one of the few examples of futures contract issuers defaulting on their obligations. The debacle led to a fundamental reorganization of the LME, and a clearing house has since then been established. In practice, the existence of a clearing house does not offer an iron-clad guarantee against default. When price movements are very fast, the call for additional margin payments may not be speedy enough to assure that margins are positive on all contracts at all times. The possibility of default will be there as soon as margins reach a zero level.

The majority of futures contracts are entered into for the purpose of hedging or investments, with no intention to provide or take physical delivery at the contract's expiry. Physical transactions, therefore, ordinarily represent only a minor part of the values traded on commodity exchanges. A major proportion of the futures contracts are voluntarily liquidated through the procedure described above, before delivery falls due. The liquidated futures purchase transaction will yield a loss if the price falls between the issuance of the original contract and liquidation. The transaction will yield a profit if the price rises. The reverse will be true for futures sales transactions.

The price for future delivery quoted today is usually not the same as today's spot price. Depending on current market conditions and expectations about the future, there will ordinarily be a difference between the two. The term **contango** (premium in the United States) refers to a situation where the futures price exceeds the spot price, while **backwardation** (discount in the United States) involves a futures price below the spot level.

A contango market results from an abundance of immediate supply relative to the expected future supply. The current abundance will depress the price for immediate delivery, as compared to delivery in the future. Notice, however, that the possibility of arbitrage limits the size of the contango to the cost of storing the commodity between now and the time of future delivery. The 12 month futures price cannot exceed the spot price by much more than 15 percent when the cost of physical storage, including deterioration, is 3 percent per year, and the rate of interest is 12 percent. A higher contango will make it profitable to invest in commodity stocks by buying spot, taking physical delivery, incurring the cost of storage and immediately making a 12-months futures sale. Such action would increase spot demand and raise spot prices until the contango declined to just above the 15 percent level. The contango provides a neat mechanism for financing excess inventories without risk. (Such financing of physical commodity stocks is discussed later in the present section.)

A backwardation market indicates a shortage of immediate supply and a perception of more ample supplies in the future. In contrast to the contango, there is no maximum in the difference between spot and futures prices when the market is in backwardation, since arbitraging is not possible. A shortage today can cause spot prices to explode, irrespective of what is expected of the future. The futures price could remain at only a small fraction of the inflated spot price, if it is known with reasonable certainty that the current shortage will soon be overcome, for instance because new production facilities are being opened up.

Options

The **traded options** dealt with on commodity exchanges are directly related to the futures contracts. One must distinguish between the **issuers** and **holders** of options, since their involvements are highly asymmetrical. There are **call** and **put** options. A call option gives the holder the right (but not the obligation) to buy a futures contract at a predetermined price, the **strike price**, at any time until the option's expiry. Analogously, a put option gives the holder the right (but no obligation) to sell a futures contract at a predetermined price. The issuer is obliged to comply with the option holder's rights.

Options are freely transferable. The price of the option is called the **premium**. This is what the issuer charges when he first issues the option and what the holder is paid when he transfers the option to another holder.

Options have a limited life and lapse on their **expiry**. The life ordinarily extends from anywhere between one and 12 months. The premium will fluctuate through the life of the option in a pattern determined by two factors, i.e. the "time value," which depends on the remaining time until expiry (the shorter the remaining time, the lesser the value), and the "intrinsic value," which depends on the relationship between the strike price and the underlying futures contract price. The intrinsic value will fluctuate in parallel with the futures contract price development. At the time of expiry, the time value will be zero, and the intrinsic value will represent the entire premium.

The option holders' only obligation is to pay the premium. To them, options are distinctly different from futures contracts, in that they do not carry any responsibility for taking or making deliveries. From the issuers' point of view, the option carries a strong resemblance to a futures contract in that their obligation is precisely to issue such a contract whenever the option holder chooses to exercise his right.

The holder will reap a profit if the option premium rises from the time he acquired it and until he exercises his right. He will lose if there is a decline in the premium. The holder's loss cannot exceed the premium he paid, for he can always choose to do nothing and to let the option lapse. The issuer's gains and losses are opposite to those of the holder. The gains are limited to the initial premium received, but the potential losses are infinite.

As in the case of futures contracts, the issue of options is guaranteed by the clearing house of the commodity exchange. Also, in a majority of cases, the option rights to acquire futures contracts are not exercised. Instead, the options are sold at the going premium when it is positive, or not exercised at all when the premium is zero.

Some exchanges still transact in **dealer options** (non-traded options in the United States). These options are not traded during their life, and the option holder's right can be exercised only by the time of the option's expiry.

After having described the instruments employed by the commodity exchanges, I shall now discuss the major functions that the exchanges perform. The functions are treated in the same order as they were listed at the beginning of the present section. Let us look first at the price setting function.

Price formation

Whenever an international commodity exchange succeeds in establishing a broad-based and continuous trade in a commodity, the price quotation in that trade usually comes to be regarded as the representative price level for the commodity. The broad base and continuity are essential for an efficient price setting process. When the market is thin, a few transactions may unduly influence the price developments in an ad hoc manner. With a thin market, there is also the likelihood that gaps will occur in the time series of futures prices, because there are no contracts expiring in some of the months covered by the trading period. The aluminum market on COMEX has been plagued by these problems in the 1980s.

Different prices may be quoted when a commodity is traded on several exchanges. Ordinarily, the prices will run in parallel. Also, the possibilities for arbitraging will prevent the price difference from widening beyond what is warranted by differences in the specified quality that is traded, and to reflect the different levels of transport costs.

The price quotations on commodity exchanges are sometimes accused of reflecting distortions caused by intentional manipulation or unorganized speculation. However, since the alternatives for authoritative price setting are usually inferior, the influence of commodity exchange quotations is not surprising. The most common alternatives are (a) quotations by trade journals or trade associations based on their collection of public and private information, and (b) the sales prices announced by leading producers. The representativeness of the former is often hard to judge; the latter frequently hides discounts and premiums which at times can be substantial.

A great attraction of the prices set by the exchanges is that they are immediately available and widely published. This contributes significantly to the influence they carry in trade and industry. Where trade in a commodity has been successfully established on an exchange, its prices tend to replace other price quotations, and dilute the price setting power of producers. Since the late 1950s, *Metal Bulletin* regularly quoted a price for aluminum in Europe, entitled "Certain Other Transactions," which at times differed substantially from the dominant Alcan quotation. After the introduction of aluminum on the LME in 1979, the *Metal Bulletin* quotation became superfluous and was discontinued. In the course of the 1980s, the Alcan price, too, became increasingly irrelevant, and this leading aluminum company has accepted the quotation on LME as the authoritative reference price. The developments have been similar in the case of nickel. The ability of the oil producing countries to set prices has been severely undermined by the lively petroleum trade on the New York and London exchanges.

Producers find it hard to exceed the widely quoted exchange price levels for long and by more than the narrow margins that buyers are prepared to pay for the increased convenience and security offered by a long-standing trade relationship. This is most clearly evident in the case of copper, where a major share of trade is transacted under contracts that employ the LME quotation, though usually with a small premium to cover superior quality specifications and the cost of delivering at the customer's gate. Where producers quote their own prices, these quotations tend to change much more frequently and more tightly in line with the market, once an exchange starts to provide a pricing rod.

The exchange prices are influenced instantaneously by events in the outside world. Their daily variations can therefore be quite large. Prices in transactions outside the exchange tend to be more stable, either because producers maintain their own quotations for much longer than a day, or because they employ, for example, monthly averages of exchange prices when they sell to their customers.

Speculation and other forces that determine developments on an exchange can sometimes yield price levels that have little relationship with the costs of production. This has been true of nickel in the late 1980s. The average LME price for this metal in January–June 1987 was $1.80 per lb, substantially below the average variable costs of the production that remained in operation,[7] and the industry suffered severely. Many firms continued producing even though prices did not cover their variable costs because of the exit barriers (see chapter 3) and the hope for an impending price recovery. In January–June of 1988, the average price, at $6.27, was 3.5 times as high, and even the highest cost producers could reap record profits,[8] while users had a difficult time. A change in consumption levels amplified by shifting inventory behavior among users along with a reduced availability of scrap explain the development of nickel prices. With this experience in mind, major nickel producers and consumers have been discussing contractual arrangements in which prices would normally be determined by the LME, but with fixed maxima and minima, if the LME quotation went outside a broad band related to the production costs for the metal.[9]

Hedging

The actors on commodity exchanges are either looking for or trying to avoid risk. The present treatment of the investment (risk taking) and hedging (risk avoiding) techniques provides only a brief introduction, aimed to bring out the bare bones of what is involved. Both activities can be performed at high levels of complexity and sophistication. The more advanced techniques are described in a voluminous specialist literature.[10]

The existence of futures markets and options provides producers and users of commodities with a convenient facility for hedging, to protect themselves against unexpected variations in price. Hedgers are characterized by their high dependence on a commodity; hence the need to insure against moving prices. The general principle of hedging is to open a futures position opposite to that anticipated in the spot market position. It can also involve the acquisition of an option assuring the hedger the right to dispose of commodities he knows he will possess, or to acquire commodities he knows he will need but which he does not yet own.

The hedger is interested in safeguarding against one of two fundamental risks:

1 The first risk is that the value of unsold products will decline if the commodity price falls.

An owner of commodity stocks (wholesaler, processor) who is not interested in price speculation, can assure himself against this risk by making a **short hedge** at the time he acquires his inventory, i.e. by futures sales involving quantities and due dates that correspond to the planned disposal of his physical inventory. In this way he assures himself of the current commodity price for these future disposals. Each time he makes a physical disposal, the owner will buy a corresponding amount spot on the exchange. The initial futures and later spot transactions on the exchange cancel out each other. If the price has fallen in the period between physical acquisition and disposal, there will be a loss from the physical transactions, but a compensating gain from the futures purchase and spot sale on the exchange. If the price has risen, the exchange transactions loss will be compensated by the gain in the physical trade. The cost of this hedge will be the interest on the margin payment, the brokerage fee plus any contango, or minus any backwardation that prevails in the market at the time the futures contract is signed.

The wholesaler can alternatively acquire a put option with a strike price close to his physical purchase price, and expiry about the time of his planned physical sale. If the price falls, the wholesaler will compensate his physical loss by the gain on the option premium. If the price rises, there will be a gain from the physical trade, but the premium of the option may fall to zero. The cost of these transactions will be the premium paid for the option and the brokerage fee for its purchase and sale.

The specific circumstances of each case will determine which of the two hedges provides the best and cheapest price insurance. The futures hedge will involve an expanded financial cost of additional margin payments, and an ensuing temporary need for more cash, if a loss is incurred in the exchange transaction. The options hedge can yield a speculative gain if rising prices result in a profit from physical transactions that is larger than the premium paid for the option.

Commodity producers often make short hedges when they consider the current price attractive. The commodity exchanges provide them with a means to lock in that price for their future output. In 1980, when precious metals prices exploded, many producers sold most of their anticipated output for the next 2–3 years through the futures markets.

2   The second risk is that the cost of future commodity purchases will increase if the commodity price rises.

When a commodity user believes that the current price is attractive, or when he tenders for manufactured deliveries with a high content of the commodity several years into the future, he might find it advantageous and prudent to lock in the current price for his future purchase needs. He can do this through a **long hedge**. This involves futures purchases timed to coincide with his future physical commodity needs. The futures contracts can be cancelled by spot sales on the exchange at the time of the physical purchases. Alternatively, a call option can be acquired to make a long hedge. The assurance against price risk, as well as the cost and the relative merits of the futures versus options instruments are analogous to those in the short hedge.

The possibility of hedging a specific commodity is not entirely contingent on it having a developed futures market. An incomplete, but often satisfactory hedge can be attained with the help of a closely related commodity whose price is likely to move in parallel with the one on which the hedger is dependent. An edible oil not traded on any exchange can be reasonably hedged with the help of another closely related edible oil. Arabica coffee futures can in most cases provide a satisfactory hedge for robustas, while crude oil is a reasonably close hedging substitute for bunker oil.

Commodity investments

Investments in commodities through the instruments with which trade is transacted on the exchanges play an instrumental role for the smooth functioning of these exchanges. Although anybody can be a commodity investor, the investment activity is dominated by agents with no interest in the physical commodity as such. Their involvements are motivated purely by the gains from their financial operations.

The high level of standardization and the ensuing liquidity of the futures contracts and options makes it very easy to move funds in and out of commodity markets. This characteristic is a precondition for the widespread interest of financiers to invest in commodities. Two distinctly different types of investment objectives are common, and the instruments employed on commodity exchanges can be used to provide the satisfaction of either.

The first, briefly touched upon earlier in the chapter, seeks a safe short-run placement for financial resources at anything fractionally above the going rate of return in financial markets. A contango that assures an adequate level of return, provides the scope for a profitable holding of physical commodity stocks. By buying spot and immediately selling futures, investors can reap this "risk-free" return. Banks like to do this, aiming for what they call a "full financing contango." Although strictly speaking, these investor actions represent a long hedge, the different nature of the agents and of the basic purpose for their action warrants their classification under a separate category.

By continuing financing of inventories for which there is no immediate need, the safety-seeking investors perform a very useful function for the commodity markets. Producers know that they can always dispose of their output on the exchange at the spot price, provided the specifications are right, if they cannot find other takers. Without the exchanges with their strict trading rules and standards, this financing function would be costlier and more difficult to perform.

The objective pursued by the second group of investors is to reap very high profits in return for taking very high risks. This group is commonly referred to as "speculators," who, according to the *Shorter Oxford English Dictionary*, buy and sell "in order to profit by the rise or fall in the market value, as distinct from regular trading or investment." The difference between hedgers' and speculators' behavior can be explained either by a difference in risk aversion, or by the greater ability of speculators to diversify their positions. The role of speculation can therefore be seen as a means for the transfer of risk among agents with different preferences.

The commodity exchanges provide the speculators with attractive opportunities for highly geared investments. The limited margin payments on futures contracts stretch the speculators' money at least by a factor of five, as compared with speculation in physical commodities. The potential return – and loss – for a given investment, is multiplied in equal measure. The issue of options involves speculators in a risk of unlimited losses. But although there is an upper limit on the gains from options, these gains are massive in relation to the small capital that needs to be committed.

Combinations of futures contracts and options permit the speculator to set the degree of risk in accordance to his desire. For example, he can enter a futures contract to sell, if he expects prices to decline. If, instead, prices rise, he will lose, and there is no limit to the size of his loss. Such a limit can be established at, say, 50 percent of the value of the contract, by acquiring a call option at a strike price 50 percent above the futures sales price.

Since the clearing house of a commodity exchange must maintain a balanced position in any commodity for any future date, the minimum role that the speculators must play is to establish futures contracts that fill the imbalance between short and long hedges.[11] Because, by definition, they do not hold any offsetting positions on these minimum investments, the speculators carry the entire risk of loss or potential for gain from price movements.

Speculators are always there to respond to hedgers' needs regarding volume and timing of futures and options, at a price. Ordinarily, however, their actions go far beyond the satisfactions of hedgers' requirements. A large part of the positions they assume constitute bets against other speculators. In these ways, speculation improves the continuity and increases the liquidity in commodity exchange trade.

A physical trade outlet

A dominant proportion of commodity trade on the exchanges is in "pure paper" with no physical products changing hands. Although the exchanges do provide a facility for physical trade, most such trade is in fact transacted elsewhere. Nevertheless, the exchanges do offer a convenient facility for the buyer or seller without standing trading connections. They always stand ready, in principle, to absorb and release the commodity on a spot basis, at the going price. The importance of this function should not be underrated. For instance, while the physical delivery of gasoline through NYMEX in 1987 was only 0.67 percent of the traded futures volume, it simultaneously represented no less than 8 percent of total US consumption of that product. Figures of similar magnitude have been recorded for other commodities on US exchanges, for example, live hogs on the Chicago Mercantile Exchange.[12]

Socialist countries are particularly important users of the exchanges for their physical trade. Much of the somewhat irregular supply of USSR aluminum and nickel has been disposed through the LME. Similarly, Chinese requirements for metal imports are importantly satisfied through purchases on the LME. Producers who have been unable to place their entire output directly with clients, often dispose of their marginal supplies on the exchanges. The exchange stocks provide a convenient supply of last resort when other supply sources dry up.

4.3 Impact on price formation and other influences

The basic presumption is that under normal circumstances the operations of a commodity exchange will even out price variations. The speculators' actions are essential in this regard. Theoretical analysis demonstrates unequivocally that speculator behavior will normally have a stabilizing effect on prices.[13] After harvest, when the price is low, they will bid up futures prices until the contango is sufficient to make investments in stocks worthwhile. The demand for inventories will strengthen the spot price level. At the height of an industrial boom, they will bid down futures prices, and so make stockholding unprofitable. The liquidation of stocks will reduce the inflated spot price. In this way, speculator foresight stretching across seasons or phases of a business cycle, generates profits, and at the same time evens out the inherent commodity price instability.

This theoretical analysis may seem to be contradicted by the observation that commodities traded on the exchanges tend to have less stable prices than commodities which are not. As already noted, the causality could be the other way round. Commodity exchanges perform especially valuable functions for commodities with inherently volatile prices, and their services are simply not needed for materials whose prices are stable.[14] In this view, commodities which are traded on exchanges constitute a kind of "adverse selection" insofar as price instability is concerned.

The speculators' activities would destabilize commodity markets only if their forecasts proved persistently wrong. Say that the industrial boom and the high commodity prices were not followed by a recession and low prices, but by a strike and even higher prices. Then, the depletion of existing inventories caused by the wrong speculator expectations would amplify the ensuing price rise, and the speculators would lose wholesale from their investments.

Whether speculators gain or lose on average is an empirical question, to which there are no unambiguous answers.[15] If in fact they lose, and so destabilize prices, there may nevertheless be a positive consequence of their activity in that the losses would correspond to a lowering of the average price paid by users and/or an increase in the average price received by producers.[16] The net social effect of such destabilizing speculation would depend on whether this benefit is greater or smaller than the discomfort of greater price instability. It may be that producers would feel the need to insure themselves against the higher price volatility, and that the cost of the measures would absorb their price gain.[17]

Even if commodity speculation normally yields a gain, and so stabilizes prices on average, this does not preclude the existence of speculative bubbles which on occasion will drive prices to extreme highs or lows. Bubbles have to do with the fact that speculators are often more interested in what others believe and do, than in the fundamentals of the commodity market. This is readily apparent from the importance that investors attach to so-called "technical analysis," which uses the historical experience of price movements as reflected in price charts, to determine buying and selling recommendations.[18] Even if there are no fundamental factors behind these recommendations, their impact on actual prices can be large, if there is a sufficient following.

Keynes distinguished between large, professional and well-informed speculators, on the one hand, and small amateur speculators, on the other.[19] It could be that the former profit from speculation, while the latter lose. Speculators who are successful become large, and those who are not leave the market and are replaced by other small speculators. This distinction provides an interesting possibility for the emergence of speculative bubbles.

Commodity markets are occasionally invaded by amateur speculators. The invasion could result from disappointments in other markets, or the expectation of a commodity boom. The speculators' entry often results in a strong price boost, even when the fundamentals for higher prices are not there. The professionals will then tend to follow the amateurs and amplify the price increase in the confident belief that they can profit both from the price rise and from the subsequent decline. Once the amateur money inflow has been exhausted and the price ceases to rise, the professionals sell out, and the bubble bursts. In these circumstances, profitable speculation by the professionals will have a destabilizing impact on prices.[20]

An episode of intensive commodity speculation coincident with extreme price volatility occurred in the early 1970s.[21] In 1973–4, the confluence of high inflation, unstable currency markets and low real interest rates on the one hand, and a high demand for primary commodities on the other, resulted in a huge inflow of speculative funds into a number of commodity exchanges. This speculation contributed significantly to the exceptionally strong commodity boom of that period, as well as to the ensuing bust, when the speculative funds left for other more profitable objects.

Other impacts of commodity exchanges on commodity markets and commodity producing industries have been suggested,[22] although firm empirical evidence remains to be provided. For instance, it is plausible that producers will tend to adjust the quality of their output towards the standards adopted by the exchanges for the purpose of futures trading, even when the commodity is sold through other channels. This is because a correspondence with the exchange quality will normally make the commodity more widely marketable than otherwise. In this way, the exchanges would tend to promote standardization and uniformity of quality.

Also, by providing an assured outlet for physical trade, the existence of exchanges would reduce the incentive for vertical upstream integration by commodity users. Such integration has been a common response to potential threats to raw materials supply, for instance because of producers' monopoly power.[23] This line of reasoning suggests a lesser extent of vertical integration in industries that use commodities which are traded on exchanges. One can of course argue the direction of causality in this logic: commodities will not be traded on the exchanges until there is a reasonable degree of competition among producers.

NOTES

1 F. R. Edwards, "The Clearing Association in Futures Markets: Guarantor and Regulator," in R. W. Anderson (ed.), *The Industrial Organization of Futures Markets*, Lexington Books, Lexington, Mass., 1984.

2 C. W. J. Granger, "The Purpose and Workings of Commodity Markets," in C. W. J. Granger (ed.), *Trading in Commodities*, Woodhead Faulkner, Cambridge, 1974; L. G. Telser, "Why There Are Organized Futures Markets," *Journal of Law and Economics*, April 1981; D. Black, *Success and Failure of Futures Contracts: Theory and Empirical Evidence*, Monograph Series in Finance and Economics, New York University, 1986.

3 Granger, ibid.

4 Telser, "Organized Futures Markets."

5 During 1988, the range of delivery times on the LME has been widened and extended to 12 months into the future.

6 Shearson Lehman Brothers, *Futures Facts*, undated, circa 1985.

7 IMF, "Commodity Price Statistics," *Metals Analysis and Outlook* (quarterly), several issues.

8 Ibid.

9 Metallgesellschaft, "Pressmeldungen über die Metallmärkte", 30 June 1988.

10 For example, M. E. Streit (ed.), *Futures Markets, Modelling, Managing and Monitoring Futures Trading*, Basil Blackwell, Oxford, 1983; or the series of pamphlets issued by Drexel, Burnham, Lambert: *Managing Basis Risk Using Futures and Options, Framework for Analysis and Simulation; Options Hedging and Trading Techniques in the Metals Industries; Understanding the Delta or Hedge Ratio in Options Trading and Hedging;* and *Fine Tuning the Options Instrument — Synthetic Options for Metals Hedgers and Traders*, all published in New York, 1986.

11 S. Ghosh, C. L. Gilbert and A. J. Hughes Hallet, *Stabilizing Speculative Commodity Markets*, Clarendon Press, Oxford, 1987.

12 Information collected from the exchanges by U. Améen, R. Gyllenram and A. Holmström in 1988.

13 Telser, "Organized Futures Markets."

14 Ibid.

15 A study of a sample of grain futures speculators in the United States between 1924 and 1932 concluded that a majority incurred losses on average, and that total losses considerably exceeded total gains. See B. Stewart, "An Analysis of Speculative Trading in Grain Futures," *US Department of Agriculture Technical Bulletin 1001*, 1949.

16 M. Friedman, "In Defence of Destabilizing Speculation," in *The Optimum*

Quantity of Money and Other Essays, Macmillan, London, 1969.

17 This point was brought out in private communication with John Tilton, Colorado School of Mines.

18 Drexel, Burnham, Lambert, *An Introduction to Technical Analysis of the Futures Markets*, New York, 1987.

19 J. M. Keynes, *The General Theory of Employment, Interest and Money*, Harcourt, New York, 1936.

20 J. L. Stein, "Destabilizing Speculative Activity Can Be Profitable," *Review of Economics and Statistics*, vol. 43, 1981.

21 B. P. Bosworth and R. Z. Lawrence, *Commodity Prices and the New Inflation*, Brookings Institution, Washington DC, 1982; W. C. Labys and H. C. Thomas, "Speculation, Hedging and Commodity Price Behavior: An International Comparison," *Applied Economics*, No. 7, 1975.

22 U. Améen, R. Gyllenram and A. Holmström, draft working papers, Royal Institute of Technology, Stockholm, 1988.

23 F. M. Scherer, *Industrial Market Structure and Economic Performance*, Rand McNally, Chicago, 1980.

5

The Issue of Supply Security

The discussions of chapter 1 showed how, in the course of the present century, Japan, the United States and Western Europe, the world's industrial centers, have become increasingly dependent on imported commodity supply. Expanded needs due to industrialization and income growth, a gradual depletion of the domestic resource base, and the secular decline in transport costs, explain why it has become increasingly economical for the advanced nations to replace the domestic production of a multitude of raw materials by imported supply. Primarily on account of differences in resource endowments, the dependence on imported primary commodities is most pronounced in Japan and least in the United States, with Western Europe in between.

The apparent indispensability of many commodities, and the threat of international supply disruptions through wars and other disorders, have for long caused concern to the importing nations. Writing as early as 1933, J. M. Keynes expressed the view that the reliance on far-away raw materials supply in the leading economies of the time had become excessive, and that a greater self-sufficiency might be warranted both on political and economic grounds, even when local production cost more than the imported supply.[1] In more recent times, the major industrialized countries have launched a variety of proposals and actions to overcome the perceived problems of commodity imports insecurity. I say perceived because the greater risks of relying on imported supply, as distinct from domestic supply, are not clearly borne out by historical evidence. In fact, one can claim that the wider potential diversity of import sources may well make imports more secure than domestic supply. The breakdown of domestic coal availability in the United Kingdom during the extended coal strike in 1984 provides a salient illustration of this point.

The purpose of the present chapter is to explore the ramifications of the issue of imported supply security, and to scrutinize the alternative measures that have been used for overcoming the difficulties that an unreliable supply of raw materials from far-away sources could cause. Domestic supply is subsumed through the analysis to remain secure and stable.

Even though the analyses should be of relevance to any country heavily dependent on commodity imports, the subject will be treated mainly with reference to the major industrialized nations. The focus is on supply disruptions which are unanticipated, occur suddenly, and prevail only in the short-to-medium term. No attention is given to the gradual and long-run supply changes that stretch over time periods long enough to permit full economic and technical adjustments.

The supply disruptions to be considered involve cuts in the quantity supplied, caused by events like monopolistic producer coordination, embargoes, wars, strikes, and natural disasters. The cuts in supply will result in rising prices, and physical shortages if the price is prevented from rising freely.

My emphasis is on alleviating actions initiated or supported by the governments of the importing countries, although actions can of course also be taken by the commodity using industries. Quite often the government actions are implemented in conjunction with the major importing firms.

In section 5.1 I shall look at the factors which make supply disruptions especially serious. Section 5.2 explores the difficulties likely to emerge in consequence of disrupted supply. The menu of policies to overcome the problems is discussed in section 5.3. Finally, section 5.4 considers the conditions under which the policies make economic sense.

5.1 When will supply disruptions be serious to the importing economy?

The severity of a commodity supply crisis for an importing economy will depend on a number of factors. Some of these will be due to conditions in the importing country, while others will have to do with circumstances in the producing/exporting areas. We will review these factors, starting out with the ones that originate in the importing country.

Import dependence. Everything else being equal, the severity of the supply crisis in a given commodity will vary with the share of imports in total use in the importing country. An interruption of imported supply is unlikely to be serious if imports constitute a limited share of consumption, since in such a case the impact on total availability will be small, and only the less important, marginal uses of the commodity will be affected.

Value of the commodity import in relation to the size of the importing country's economy. Between two equally indispensable materials, a reduction in supply, or an increase in price will be more painful if it involves the one representing the greater import value.

Substitutability of the commodity in its major uses. An import supply crisis will have the most severe consequences for materials which have no readily available substitutes. Apart from the ease with which the functions of one material can be performed by another, substitutability has an economical and a time dimension. Easy substitution implies that the substitute material is available at a cost not much higher than the material in crisis. In this sense, palm oil is a good substitute for groundnut oil, since both have comparable costs and prices. In contrast, silver is not a good substitute for copper, for although silver has most of copper's technical attributes, its cost per unit of weight is about 100 times that of copper. If there is a supply crisis in copper, copper prices can rise a lot, before it becomes economical to substitute it for silver on a large scale. The time it takes before a raw material can be substituted for another depends importantly on the technology of its usage. If there is capital equipment that is specific to the use of the original material, substitution will be delayed by the need to rebuild that equipment.

Indispensability of the final product in which the commodity is used. A supply crisis will have the most severe repercussions if the commodity is employed to make products vital to the functioning of key industries in the importing nation. With all else equal, an import disturbance in nickel, employed in the manufacture of stainless steel, will be more severe than a disruption in the imports of cocoa, since stainless steel is harder to forgo than chocolate.

The severity of a supply disruption will also be related to the circumstances characterizing the export sources.

Concentration of export supply. The greater the geographic proximity among major supply sources, the easier will it be to bring about coordinated supply restrictions. Also, with geographically concentrated supply, the impact of natural or man-made disruptions, for example, droughts, earthquakes, strikes, and political upheavals will tend to increase. The same argument applies to national and corporate concentration of exports.

Affinity of values and established collaboration among major suppliers. The greater this affinity in political or economic terms, the greater is the risk that the major suppliers will act collectively to restrict supply to their own benefit.

Difficulty in substituting new sources of international supply for current ones. Disruption of supply from traditional import sources will be most severe when capacity utilization is high world wide, with little prospect for switching to alternative sources. The severity of the disruption will also vary with the length of time it takes to develop new capacity, and the differential between the cost levels of this new capacity and those of traditional suppliers.

Circumstances on the supply side also permit some judgment about the risk that a supply disruption will occur. Indications of political instability are taken as a sign of an increased likelihood for a supply disruption. The history of earthquakes, climatic fluctuations or strikes in major supply regions can also help in assessing the risk.

This list of factors is helpful in singling out the commodities which may warrant special action to assure stable import flows. The degree of risk aversion among policy-makers will determine how many commodities will be included in this group and how much will be done about them. This risk aversion appears to be greater in the United States than in Western Europe and Japan. Despite its much lower import dependence for most commodities, the United States has been by far the most energetic among the three, in launching efforts to assure its imported commodity supply.

A group of "strategic" metals probably come highest on the list of candidates for action to secure import supply.[2] Products like chromium, cobalt, manganese, niobium (columbium in the United States), platinum and its sister metals, tungsten and vanadium, satisfy almost all the above characteristics of products likely to cause severe disturbances in the importing economy when there is an import failure. There is very little production of these materials either in Japan, the United States or Western Europe, so the import dependence is almost complete. They are all hard to substitute and satisfy vital needs in the production of indispensable alloys and catalysts. Their supply is heavily concentrated. For example, more than 80 percent of the world output of niobium comes from Brazil, while Zaire and Zambia together account for two-thirds of global cobalt production. World supply of chromium, manganese, platinum and vanadium is completely dominated by South Africa and the USSR, countries which for different political reasons are regarded as unreliable suppliers.

After the market interventions of the OPEC cartel and OAPEC's embargo actions in the early 1970s, petroleum too has entered the list of products that warrant action to assure supply. In distinction from the strategic metals whose trade values are quite small, petroleum trade weighs very heavily in the importing countries' economies.

Other important metals, for example, copper, nickel, tin and uranium have sometimes prompted action aimed at averting the risks of uncertain foreign availability. Iron ore and lead, in contrast, have attracted less attention in this respect, importantly because of a greater diversification of their sources of supply.

Among agricultural raw materials, natural rubber has been seen as a risk, on account of its importance for transport and other key industries, and the concentration of its supply to South East Asia. However, the availability of synthetic rubber, a good substitute for many purposes, has reduced the fear of supply cuts. Wool and cotton, on the other hand, have prompted far fewer worries.

Base foods like cereals, pulses, and meats have not been prominent among the materials causing worries about supply security, despite their nature as essential goods. The reason is probably a low degree of import dependence. In Europe and Japan this has been the result of subsidies and protection (see chapter 2), motivated primarily by concerns about agricultural employment. But since a high degree of self-sufficiency has been a subsidiary motivation for the support of domestic output, one can argue that the essential foods have not caused worries in recent times precisely because the protective measures have rendered the desired results.

Import dependence and supply concentration are very high in the case of tropical beverages, but supply disruptions have not been seen as a serious threat, probably because these products are regarded as dispensable.

5.2 The nature of problems caused by disrupted commodity supply

The first consequence of the reduced availability of a commodity following a disruption in supply is a rise of its price. Given the low price elasticity of demand for indispensable raw materials, the price reaction can be quite strong. For the strategic metals, this elasticity is probably below $(-)0.1$, so price will more than double in consequence of a 10 percent supply shortfall.

The price rise will have some direct macroeconomic effects. Where the price elasticity is low, there will be a deterioration in the importing country's current account. The rate of inflation will tend to accelerate. For these effects to be perceptible, however, the imports and consumption of the commodity must represent a large value in relation to the importing nation's economy. This may be true of oil and copper, but hardly for any one of the strategic metals.

The reduced supply will ordinarily limit usage. Rationing of what is available can be done by price or by regulation. Whichever method is employed, some former users will have to do without the commodity.

Both the price rise and the physical unavailability will cause microeconomic dislocation, which will eventually also affect macroeconomic performance. The commodity users who can afford the higher price in the short run, may find it economical to initiate long-term adjustments, to substitute in favor of other raw materials, or to invest in capital that is more appropriate to the higher commodity price. These adjustments will impact negatively on productivity and slow down economic growth. The reduced availability of the commodity may force some users to close down their installations. This will tend to raise unemployment and reduce GDP. Closures will also have a dislocating effect further down the production chain. The latter can be quite severe if the output of the commodity using industry is essential to important sectors of the economy.

The consequence of a supply disruption to an importing country will be more severe if that country is hit in isolation, while other importers can obtain their needs without problem, for then that country's international competitiveness will suffer.

The negative consequences of a commodity supply disruption will be strongest in the short run, but will subside in the longer term, even if the disruption continues. Economic forces will bring relief through substitution and other adjustments. Cobalt provides an illustrative example. It has been considered a strategically important metal for the production of indispensable steels and alloys. In 1978, the price of cobalt quintupled in consequence of political upheavals in Zaire where about half of world output is produced. The price level remained exceedingly high during a 4-year period. However, cobalt proved much more dispensable than had been generally believed. The force and speed of the substitution processes that were initiated by the price change took many observers by surprise. Demand in the United States fell by almost one-half between 1978 and 1982,[3] and developments in other industrialized countries ran more or less in parallel. Petroleum exhibits a somewhat similar, though more drawn-out pattern. The intensity of use of petroleum demand (consumption per constant dollar GDP) in the OECD economies declined by almost 40 percent between 1973 and 1986 as a result of substitution and other adjustments to the high price. The adjustments to high cobalt and petroleum prices were costly, and brought initial hardship both to the industries that relied heavily on their use and to the importing macroeconomies at large. This hardship gradually dwindled, as the affected economies reduced their dependence on the two commodities.

An assessment of the economic impact of a supply shortfall must proceed on the assumption of *ceteris paribus*. For this reason, it is hard to draw definite conclusions from the cases of cobalt and petroleum, since so many other forces were at work concurrently with the disruption of supply in these two commodity markets.

Attempts have been made to measure the economic costs of commodity supply disruptions on the basis of specific scenarios.[4] The outcomes, which may or may not be realistic, depend entirely on the assumptions underlying the scenario, viz.: how large and lasting will be the supply shortfall; how fast can alternative supply be mobilized; how, and at what speed will the national economies affected by the shortfall react?

The arbitrariness of the results is apparent from two studies on chromium. In the 1970s, a German study concluded that the country's GDP would fall by about a third as a result of a complete unavailability of chromium supply. This drastic result must be due to the extreme assumption about supply, and equally extreme suppositions about inflexibilities in the economic system. In 1986, a study in the United States assumed a 3-year loss of 100 percent of South Africa's chromium supply and a 90 percent loss of Zimbabwe's, and concluded that the impact would reduce the US GDP by 0.2 percent in the first year, by 0.1 percent in the second year, and by about 0.05 percent in the third year.[5]

There are also important non-economic aspects of commodity supply disruptions. For example, the military-strategic issues are paramount, and underlie many of the efforts to assure access to commodity imports. It is widely felt that a country may not be able to defend itself if there is a breakdown in the supply of commodities crucial for the armaments industry or otherwise for military operations.

5.3 Measures to alleviate the consequences of supply disruption

An extended menu of measures has been used by the major industrialized countries to alleviate the risks for and consequences of disruptions in important commodity imports. The menu can usefully be divided into (a) the measures intended to secure an uninterrupted import flow, and (b) those intended to assure a greater domestic availability that can be relied on in the event of an import breakdown. We will discuss them in this order.

Most of the measures to assure stable commodity imports concern the choice of suppliers, and the development of special relationships with them. At first, this may seem surprising. In a perfectly competitive international market, a sudden reduction of supply, caused by, say, a strike or civil unrest in an important exporting country, would lead to an immediate increase in price. This would cause demand to shrink until it equalled the reduced supply, so that all buyers could satisfy their demand in full. No special relationship between buyer and seller would be needed in such a market.

The realities of most international commodity markets differ significantly from the perfect competition paradigm. First, difficulties could arise because alternative suppliers may be unable to offer the precise grades required. Second, most of the physical trade is typically conducted on the basis of standing relationships that take time to develop. Quite often, the price at which transactions take place reacts to shifts in demand and supply with a lag. After a sudden reduction in supply, the buyers whose source had been knocked out would need time to establish new trading relations. In the meantime some of their demand would be unsatisfied, with price remaining below market clearing equilibrium.

In these circumstances it becomes important to avoid the disadvantage suffered by the commodity user who is left out in the cold. There is a benefit in stable relations with reliable suppliers, even though, in the end, the supply disruption will result in higher prices for all buyers.

Choice of suppliers

An obvious and straightforward measure in this regard is to diversify the importing country's sources of supply. The consequence of a breakdown of one source will never be critical if none of the suppliers accounts for a dominant share of the total. This explains why all major importing countries have spread their sources of bauxite, copper and iron ore over three continents, namely, Africa, Australia and South America.

The choice of suppliers could also favor the ones deemed to be stable and secure. After experiencing the OAPEC oil embargo in the early 1970s, the major oil importing countries made conscious efforts to reduce their reliance on the Arab Middle East suppliers. The shortlived embargo on soybean exports instituted by the US government in 1973, reduced confidence in the United States as a reliable supplier, and strengthened Brazil's position in the soybean market. Canada's refusal to honor its uranium supply commitments to some European countries in the 1970s encouraged the development and expansion of alternative supply, especially in Africa.

These efforts to assure imported supply security do carry a cost. The security aspects of current trade arrangements for high-volume products like oil, iron ore, bauxite and coal add considerably to transport costs. The preference for secure suppliers results in a distinct difference in delivered prices in some cases. A premium can be commanded by the supplier who has established a record of reliability. Suppliers with an uncertainty element, in contrast, have to accept a discount. South Africa has accepted lower prices for its coal in the late 1980s to compensate the buyers for the risk that their governments may embargo imports from that country. Similarly, the importing nations are providing costly encouragement to chromium suppliers outside South Africa, to assure some alternatives to the dominant and exceedingly competitive production in that country, because of the political risk surrounding South Africa's supply.[6]

Tighter relations with suppliers

These might involve anything from long-run contracts to complete backward integration, with the commodity user owning the commodity production facilities. Although each importing country has employed a wide array of arrangements, a distinct difference in emphasis between the United States and the former colonial powers of Western Europe on the one hand, and Japan on the other, has been noted.[7]

In the 1950s and 1960s, direct foreign ownership was commonly regarded by the resource-based enterprises in the United States and Europe as the most effective means to assure steady import flows. Obviously, direct investments to exploit foreign natural resources also had other strong motivations, for example, the improved profitability that followed from a wider use of these firms' superior managerial and technical endowments, or their desire to expand beyond the restrictions imposed by the size of the national economy. Nevertheless, backward integration was seen as an important tool to assure not only against disruption of physical availability when market disturbances occurred, but also against the fluctuations of market prices. Irrespective of what happened to prices, the owner could always count on the output at the cost of production.

As events turned out, the backward integration proved to be of doubtful value to the multinationals. Many of these investments were nationalized in the 1960s and 1970s by the newly independent administrations in developing countries, and the compensation was often inadequate, when it was paid at all (see chapter 7). More importantly, however, the nationalizations disintegrated the very foundations on which the policies of supply security had been based.

Foreign ownership of export oriented raw material production continues to exist, but it has become less significant as a result of the state takeovers. However, there have also been other developments diluting the role of ownership ties for supply security. In the most recent decades, many governments, and not only in the developing countries, have asserted their right to regulate foreign trade. One illustrative example concerns uranium exports from ventures with foreign ownership in Australia. On occasion, the government has decided against exports to particular countries, and over long periods of time it has imposed minimum export prices, without regard to the possible interest of the foreign owners.

In contrast to the US and European practices, Japanese supply security arrangements emphasized the establishment of long-term supply contracts with independent raw materials producers. Quite often, these contracts involved a Japanese provision of long-term capital with some concessional element as an inducement to establish raw material production, and technical assistance in a variety of fields, including exploration for minerals, but seldom managerial control.

The long-term contractual arrangements entered into in the 1960s could stretch over anything from a year to more than a decade. When long-term investment finance to develop the raw material project was provided, the supply obligations regularly lasted until the loans had been repaid. The standard contracts of the period specified both quantities and prices. The latter often contained escalation clauses, to compensate for cost increases or exchange rate movements. With the high inflation and greater volatility of commodity prices in the 1970s, most of the price provisions were deleted, so much of the assurance against varying prices was lost. The typical long-term contract in the 1980s is basically an agreement about quantities, with prices following current quotations, though often with some limited stabilization formula.

Long-term contracts do provide a shield against supply disruptions, so long as they last. The problem is that when they involve corporate parties in different countries, their enforcement is not easy. Hence, if changing circumstances create dissatisfaction with one of the parties, a renegotiation will be an essential prerequisite for the contract to survive. The supply assurance at predetermined conditions, therefore, becomes quite limited. In addition, supply under long-term contracts, such as from foreign owned facilities, is subject to the exporting government's intervention in foreign trade.

Tighter relationships with commodity suppliers also include treaties with political and/or economic content between the governments of the countries that trade. The importing government can offer political support, or an aid package, or a generous bilateral trade deal, or a long-term price guarantee, against a promise of first option on the raw material produced by the exporting country.

Other measures to assure imported supplies

Military power has long antecedents in its role as a guarantor of international commodity supplies. Both the Allied and the German and Japanese fleets provided protection to the commodity flows from overseas to Europe during the Second World War. The naval protection of petroleum shipping from the Persian Gulf in 1988 is a more recent example of this role.

Sharing arrangements among importers constitute yet another measure to alleviate the impact of supply shortfalls, especially when the buyers are unevenly hit. The petroleum sharing arrangements under the auspices of the International Energy Agency arose as a result of the Arab oil exporters selective embargo against Holland and the United States in 1973−4.

Barter arrangements can sometimes help in cementing bonds with foreign raw material suppliers. This is especially true when the primary commodities are swapped against tailor-made manufactures to suit the commodity exporting country's needs. Barter arrangements of this nature made Finland a priority customer of USSR petroleum during the two oil crises of the 1970s.

Promotion of domestic output

With greater domestic output, the impact of a foreign supply disruption will be less severe. The measures to promote production within the country can be dealt with very briefly, since they were discussed in some detail in chapter 2. As is apparent from that discussion, promotion of domestic output often has another, even stronger, motivation, i.e. to maintain employment and prevent capital destruction in the activities supported, irrespective of whether there is a threat to domestic supply.

Import restrictions commonly constitute a key element in the promotion of domestic output. These permit higher prices to be charged domestically than would be possible if there were a free import flow. Subsidies to domestic production can be a supplement or complement to protection. Domestic public procurement is another tool to encourage domestic production. This measure, too, would ordinarily involve the payment of prices above the world market level to the domestic producers.

Strategic stockpiling

The word "strategic" can have either or both of two connotations. It can mean that the stock consists of important and indispensable products. It can also mean that the stock is intended for strategic military situations. The first meaning is always applicable to strategic stockpiling. On the second, the stockpiling governments tend to be vague, leaving the decision about stockpile releases to their own discretion.

Government efforts to establish stockpiles of strategically important imported commodities have been launched in a number of countries, including Japan, Germany, France, Spain, Sweden, Switzerland and South Korea.[8] The efforts of the United States are, without comparison, the largest and most persevering. In fact the United States has continuously maintained stockpiles of a large number of imported commodities at least since the Korean war in the early 1950s, with the stocks sometimes representing very large quantities in relation to global use. In some cases, the inventory goals have represented several years of total US consumption.[9]

The stockpiling programs of the United States reveal some of the problems surrounding this kind of policy. One problem is to determine the events that would trigger a release from the stocks. The US programs have had a strategic-military objective. Releases have been envisaged only in the event of scarcities caused by a war involving the United States itself. Shortages or violent price increases caused by other circumstances, for example, the oil embargo in 1974, or the cobalt price explosion at the end of the same decade, did not warrant releases from the existing strategic stockpiles.

Another problem, discussed earlier in the present chapter, is the definition of commodities which require special action. The most recent strategic stockpiling rules in the United States list no less than 58 different commodities for the inventory program, selected by the dual rule of (a) import dependence and (b) importance for supporting the military effort during wartime.

The determination of stockholding size requires a delineation of possible war scenarios, of the ensuing import shortfalls and their durations, and of the shares of these shortfalls that it is strategically important to satisfy from the government inventories. In this regard, the US policies have been very unstable. For example, in 1973 the Nixon administration issued new assumptions for the determination of needed strategic stocks. This involved a reduction of the then existing inventory, worth some $6.7 billion, by about 90 percent.[10] However, subsequent administrations reverted to the earlier assumptions about stockpile needs.

The very large stockpile requirements for a number of commodities in the US programs have created serious procurement problems. A speedy inventory accumulation would increase world demand and push up prices, a development that the US authorities wanted to avoid. Even more serious have been the decisions to reduce stockpile goals, with their depressing influence on market prices. Tin is a commodity in which the United States initially accumulated a stockpile far above one year's global output. Later assessments have set the stockpile goals much lower, and the US administration has faced perennial conflicts with the international tin agreement and the major tin producing countries about the price-depressing impact of the proposed inventory disposals.[11]

Finally, the stockpile policies have involved a substantial net cost, despite the occasional profit earned from sales of commodities which were originally acquired at a lower price. No assessment of this cost has been undertaken. Apart from the interest on the capital tied up, one must reckon with a deterioration in quality due both to the passage of time and to the technical change which has altered the needed specifications, and made old stocks unsuitable for the most critical needs.[12] One would also have to assess the extent to which the existence of the government's strategic stock has involved a saving to society by reducing the needs of private inventories.

The functioning of the US strategic stockpiles has never been put to a fully fledged test, but complaints have been voiced about the great inflexibility in the procedure for inventory releases. This criticism hits a crucial point in the stockpiling programs. Several stockholding governments have on occasion exhibited a perverse inventory behavior. The development of a serious shortage has instigated not inventory releases, but efforts to increase existing public stockpiles, thereby further aggravating the physical shortage and price explosion. Such behavior was seen, for example, in some European countries in connection with the second oil price shock in 1979–80.

5.4 The economics of supply security policies

Some of the measures employed for reducing the impact of supply disruptions will always involve a cost. This is true of efforts to promote domestic production which would otherwise have been uncompetitive. It is also true of stockpiling, and of the maintenance of military installations to assure a free passage for commodity trade in the case of war. Other measures discussed in the preceding section often also carry a cost, although they need not necessarily do so. We indicated how the choice of a supplier network that aims at reducing the risk of supply disruption often involves an additional cost for transport from far-away sources, and for price premia to suppliers with a reliable record. Tighter relations with suppliers may or may not involve a cost to the importing countries. Profitability could be a sufficient motivation for backward integration into foreign raw materials production, so that no other inducements would be needed. Long-term contracts could be desirable to the commodity exporters too, and so not involve a cost to the importers. However, when supply security is an explicit consideration, a cost can clearly emerge from such arrangements, for example in the form of a government subsidy to encourage direct foreign investments, or though the provision of concessional finance or payment of higher prices, in exchange for long-term contracts. Sharing agreements, too, involve a cost if they require the parties to such pacts to carry inventories for use during crises.

The cost of measures to assure commodity supply can be regarded as a kind of insurance premium, and a rational decision-maker would try to determine whether the premium is worth the benefit it yields. The required benefit–cost analysis is exceedingly tricky, and seldom practicable. It is nevertheless worthwhile to point to the elements that are involved and the relationships that must hold for such expenditure decisions to be rational. In principle, each commodity of some critical importance to the importing economy would need a separate investigation.

The first point that has to be clarified is the cost of the measures. If they are costless, for example, because they automatically yield improved supply security as a byproduct in the pursuit of some other objective, then the investigation can be limited to establishing the existence of a supply security benefit. When the measures carry a cost, then the total cost and the share attributable to improved supply security must be determined.

An evaluation of the benefits would have to start out by considering the likelihood that supply disruptions of differing nature and of varying severity will in fact occur. It is necessary to consider disruptions of differing nature (e.g. war, cartels, selective embargoes), for only then will it be possible to gauge how well the different measures can alleviate the effects of each. It is also necessary to consider disruptions of differing severity (quantity lost, duration of disruption), for the next step in the analysis should be to determine their damage to the national economy. The assessment of the direct and indirect incidence of a supply disruption through an entire macroeconomy is indeed a herculanean task, with no generally accepted methodologies. After having established the damage, one would need to juxtapose the different supply security measures against the alternative disruption scenarios, to gauge their benefit, i.e. how they would reduce the damage. The measures would be worthwhile only when the present value of their cost is less than the present value of this benefit.

In practice, decisions to incur expenditures aimed at improving the security of commodity supply are mostly based on hunches and intuition, and on prodding by those who benefit from the measures as such, and not necessarily from their alleviating impact in times of crisis. This is not to say that measures to improve the security of critical commodity supply are not worthwhile, even when they carry high costs. In many cases they very well may be, even if their benefit−cost ratio cannot be determined. The survival of industries, or even nations, can be critically dependent on the access to particular commodities during a supply crisis. But in the absence of hard numbers, we conjecture that policies of supply security have been carried too far in many instances, so that their cost substantially exceeds any reasonable benefit, given the expected likelihood of disrupted supply. This would be most true in the case of the United States, where the actions to enhance supply security have been quite substantive even in cases where the share of imports in total use is not exceedingly high.

We base this conjecture on the historical evidence of the infrequency of severe supply disruptions, and of the very substantial flexibilities, both in supply arrangements and in needs, during periods of severe crisis.

The period since the Second World War has witnessed substantial and sometimes violent fluctuations in commodity prices, but very few critical disruptions of physical supply. The more important ones include the interruption of chrome exports from the USSR during the Korean war in the early 1950s, the embargo by the Arab petroleum producers in 1973–4, and the withdrawal from the market by the members of the uranium cartel in the mid-to-late 1970s.[13] On the whole, however, this long period has witnessed a very considerable stability in the global export supply, despite the many structural shifts that occurred in commodity production and use. For instance, over the period 1966–74, the Chilean copper industry went through several upsetting changes. In 1967, the government acquired joint venture interests in the large foreign-owned copper mines. In 1971, these mines were completely nationalized by the Marxist administration of Salvador Allende. Then, following the 1973 coup, the incoming military government adopted a strongly pro-capitalist copper policy. Yet, throughout this period of change, the size and direction of Chile's copper exports did not experience any drastic contraction or change.[14] With the benefit of hindsight, it is easy to point out that the damage of possible forthcoming crises would have to be truly monumental for its present value to exceed the present value costs of measures to assure supply security, maintained now for over 40 years.

Historical evidence also indicates that trade is fluid and usually finds ways around emergent obstacles. Selective embargoes against individual countries are hardly ever effective. The United States did obtain most of its petroleum import needs throughout the OAPEC embargo. Rhodesia overcame the UN sanctions imposed between 1966 and 1972, and succeeded in selling its chromium and tobacco in foreign markets. The sanctions against South Africa in the late 1980s do not prevent the country from procuring its imported raw materials needs, nor from finding markets for its exports.

Throughout the Second World War, the imports of Sweden could be maintained at about 50 percent of their pre-war volumes, despite the fact that the country was virtually surrounded by an intensive war activity. Only in one year towards the end of the war did the imports decline, to only one-third of their pre-war level.[15] The global production system usually contains considerable scope to compensate for the elimination of some important suppliers.

Similarly, there is a surprising flexibility in the needs for apparently indispensable materials. The ability to dispose of a substantial proportion of total cobalt usage when its price rose at the end of the 1970s is a succinct illustration.

The combined flexibility of procurement and savings in usage during difficult times is starkly illustrated by the finding that the stocks of a group of strategically important metals in Germany in 1945 at the end of the Second World War, were greater than when the war began,[16] despite the embargoes instituted by the Allied navies and the boost in the needs of these materials for the exceedingly intensive 6 years of war effort.

These observations suggest that the costs of some measures to secure imported commodity supply, for example, the US maintenance of a strategic stock of tin equal to about one year's global output, or the lasting Japanese habit of providing subsidized long-term finance in exchange for long-term supply contracts, may have been excessive.

NOTES

1 J. M. Keynes, "National Self-sufficiency," *Yale Review*, Summer 1933.
2 For a more detailed discussion of the characteristics of these metals and their markets, see M Radetzki, "Strategic Metal Markets; Prospects for Producer Cartels," *Resources Policy*, December 1984.
3 US Bureau of Mines, *Mineral Facts and Problems*, 1985 edition.
4 US Bureau of Mines, "Chromium, Effectiveness of Alternative US Policies in Reducing the Economic Costs of Supply Disruption," November 1981; and US Department of the Interior, "Cobalt, Effectiveness of Alternative US Policies in Reducing the Economic Costs of Supply Disruption," August 1981; US Bureau of Mines, *South Africa and Critical Materials*, July 1986.
5 US Bureau of Mines, *South Africa and Critical Materials*.
6 *Mining Annual Review*, 1987.
7 R. Vernon, *Two Hungry Giants, the United States and Japan in the Quest for Oil and Ores*, Harvard University Press, Cambridge, Mass., 1983.
8 R. Vernon, *Two Hungry Giants*; W. A. Vogley, "Materials Policy: Europe," in M. B. Beaver et al., (eds.), *Encyclopedia of Materials Science and Engineering*, Pergamon, New York, 1986; S. J. Warnecke, *Stockpiling of Critical Raw Materials*, Royal Institute of International Affairs, London, 1980.
9 US Bureau of Mines, *Mineral Commodity Summaries*, annual, several issues.
10 R. F. Mikesell, *Stockpiling Strategic Materials*, American Enterprise Institute for Public Policy Research, Washington DC, 1986.
11 C. Brown, *The Political and Social Economy of Commodity Control*, Macmillan, London, 1979.
12 Mikesell, *Stockpiling Strategic Materials*.
13 M. Radetzki, *Uranium, A Strategic Source of Energy*, Croom Helm, London, 1981.
14 S. Zorn, "Industrial Countries' Approaches to Security of Supply, and Effects on Developing Countries," *Primary Commodities: Security of Supply*, Friedrich Ebert Stiftung, Bonn and Washington, 1981.
15 M. Radetzki, *Sverige avskärmat*. SNS, Stockholm, 1981.
16 E. S. Mason, "Natural Resources and Environmental Restrictions to Growth," *Challenge*, January–February 1978.

6

Producer Cartels in International Commodity Markets

Producer cartels are about monopolistic coordination aimed at raising the suppliers' revenues. The developments in the oil market since the early 1970s instigated a large number of theoretical and modelling exercises to explain the functioning of commodity cartels in general and of OPEC in particular.[1] Despite these efforts, many of the key issues concerning commodity cartelization remain to be clarified. In the words of a recent survey: "There are a large number of alternative theories, but a much smaller number of sensible applied models."[2]

In the present chapter, I shall adopt a very simple approach. I will begin by studying the necessary preconditions in terms of elasticities and market shares, for successful cartel action and then go on to try to assess the producers' ability to exercise monopoly power in different commodity markets. Finally, some historical experiences of cartel action by commodity producers will be explored. What were the triggers? How did it go? How did the buyers react?

6.1 The formal preconditions for successful cartel action

Successful cartelization measures involve *either* a restriction of supply, *or* a rise in the price charged by the members of the collaborating group, leading to increased revenue for the group. With a given demand schedule, there is a unique relationship between the quantity supplied and the price at which the market is cleared, so the two measures would have equivalent consequences for the suppliers. Where the institutional market arrangements involve producer-set prices, cartel action would ordinarily take the

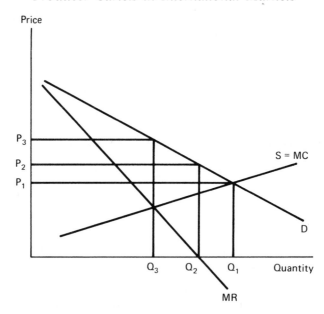

Figure 6.1   Maximization of profit and maximization of revenue

form of an increase in the producer quotations. Where prices are set by exchanges, the cartelized producers could achieve their aim by reducing supply until the desired price level is reached.

Under ideal conditions, a cartel should of course aim at maximizing the joint profits of its members. In terms of figure 6.1, this would be achieved by reducing supply from Q_1 the competitive equilibrium, to Q_3, given by the intersection between the cartel's marginal cost and marginal revenue. Any output above this level would be unprofitable, because the marginal cost of that output exceeds the marginal revenue. The criterion for successful cartelization used here involves the simpler rule of revenue maximization which disregards the costs saved by production cuts. Under this criterion, output would be reduced from Q_1 to Q_2, the latter determined by the marginal revenue of the cartel being equal to 0. I have adopted this simpler rule for the purpose of our analysis because I believe that this is about as much as a real world cartel could aim for. I know no cases of cartels that have defined their supply schedule with sufficient precision, and instituted income transfers between individual members, to make profit maximization a practicable policy.

The present analysis subsumes that the participants in the cartel can reach full agreement on a marketing policy that aims at increasing the group's sales revenue, and that they will adhere strictly to the policy rules. The possibility of increasing the group's revenue over that reaped in the absence of joint action will then be greater, *first*, the higher is its share in global supply, *secondly*, the lower is the (absolute) value of the price elasticity of global demand, and *thirdly*, the lower is the value of the price elasticity of supply outside the cartel.

In formal terms, successful market intervention by the cartel requires that initially the (absolute) value of the price elasticity of demand for its output, E_{DC}, should be less than 1. If E_{DC} is greater than one, the cartel's revenue will decline if the members jointly raise prices or cut supply. The value of E_{DC} is determined by the formula:

$$E_{DC} = (1/M)E_{DW} - (1/M)(1-M)E_{SR};$$

where M = the cartel's share of world supply;
    E_{DW} = the price elasticity of world demand; and
    E_{SR} = the price elasticity of supply outside the cartel.

An E_{DC} which is less than 1 implies that the marginal revenue from the cartel's aggregate supply is negative. Hence, the sales revenue will increase as supply is curtailed. A maximum will be reached when E_{DC} reaches a value of 1, and marginal revenue equals 0. This will happen when supply has been cut to Q_2 in figure 6.1. The smaller the (absolute) value of E_{DC}, the greater the potential for raising revenue through cartel action.

The success of the cartel has an important time dimension. This is because the (absolute) price elasticities of world demand and outsider supply (E_{DW} and E_{SR}) will tend to increase over time, as the final users and independent producers adjust to the conditions caused by the cartel's intervention. The higher prices resulting from cartel action can greatly increase the cartel members' revenue in year 1, over what they reaped in the competitive market that prevailed in year 0. If the higher price is maintained, their revenue in year 5 may prove substantially lower than in year 0, as a result of the gradual shrinkage of the total market and of the cartel's market share. Present value calculations of the revenue gains and losses over time will be needed to determine the benefit of such a course of events. But a cartel is unlikely to be judged a success unless it manages to keep the members' revenue above the competitive level for a period of at least several years.

It may be something of a paradox that a cartel which commands no credence in the outside world will have greater prospects to succeed in its market actions than one which does. This is because if no one believes a cartel will survive, there will be no adjustment to the higher prices resulting from its actions. With no adjustments, the short-run values of E_{DW} and E_{SR} will not increase over time.

Table 6.1 The price elasticities of demand for output from a cartel (E_{DC}) which controls 60 percent of world supply ($M=0.6$)

E_{SR}	0.1	0.2	0.4	0.7	1.0
E_{DW}					
−0.1	−0.23	−0.30	−0.43	−0.63	−0.88
−0.2	−0.40	−0.47	−0.60	−0.80	−1.00
−0.4	−0.73	−0.80	−0.93	−1.13	−1.33
−0.7	−1.23	−1.30	−1.43	−1.63	−1.83
−1.0	−1.73	−1.80	−1.93	−2.13	−2.33

The above formula can be used to determine the limiting combinations of the price elasticity of world demand, E_{DW}, and the price elasticity of supply outside the cartel, E_{SR}, that have to hold for the price elasticity of demand faced by the cartel, E_{DC}, to be less than (absolute) 1, and hence for cartel action to increase cartel revenue. Table 6.1 presents such limiting values for a cartel whose share of world supply, M, equals 60 percent. It will be seen that the potential for revenue-raising action exists in all cases where the (absolute) values of E_{DW} and E_{SR} are less than 0.4, but also for selected other value combinations.

The value of E_{DC} is also related to the range of commodities coverage under the cartel's control, but multicommodity cartels will gain additional market power (a lower E_{DC}) from their wider coverage only if the commodities are each others' substitutes. No synergies will be gained from launching a joint cartel by the coffee and copper producers. Since there is little relationship between the markets, price-raising supply restrictions in one will have no effect on the other. In contrast, the copper producers' market intervention will be reinforced by a simultaneous restriction in aluminum supply. When copper producers intervene in isolation, the higher copper price will induce substitution in favor of aluminum, and the reduced copper demand will dilute the benefit from intervention. If the copper producers coordinate their action with the aluminum producers so that the prices of both products rise in parallel, no substitution from one to the other will be induced by the price rise, and the producers of both metals will be better off than if each group had acted separately.

The increased market power follows from the fact that the (absolute) price elasticity of world demand, E_{DW}, is lower for copper-cum-aluminum, than for each metal in isolation. The greater the substitutability between the products, the higher will be the benefit of joint cartel action for both, and the lesser will be the possibility to establish a successful cartel for each product in isolation. However, market power is only one of several aspects that determine the prospects for launching successful cartels. Another is the ability to administer and coordinate the members' actions, and this is likely to be much harder when several commodities are involved.

6.2 Other preconditions for successful cartel action

The preceding section clarified why low price elasticities and the control of a large share of world supply are necessary preconditions for successful cartel action. That discussion, however, is far from adequate for determining the commodity markets in which cartelization is feasible.

A first problem arises because of the ambiguity and instability of the elasticity values. As already noted in chapter 2, price elasticity estimates can vary greatly, depending on precisely what is measured, the method used, and the time of measurement. It is not realistic to believe that exercises like that contained in table 6.1 could bring out neat distinctions between commodities that are amenable to successful cartel action and those that are not. The situation is much more blurred, and the best one could expect from the analysis of elasticities is a crude distinction between those commodities that might possibly meet the necessary conditions, and those that clearly do not.

A second problem concerns the practicalities of producer coordination intended to control a large share of world supply. Since cartel action is about cuts in supply, the initial issue that needs to be resolved is the overall size of the cut. Well-established producers and producers with above average cost levels are likely to be interested in greater cuts than new and low cost producers who are keen to expand their output. The need to assure the full collaboration from producers who jointly account for a large proportion of total supply will tend to result in agreements scaled down to suit the convenience of the parties which desire the least proportional output reduction.

Coincidental with the determination of the overall cut are decisions about its distribution among participating members. Optimally, only the high cost output ought to be cut, but to be acceptable, such policy would require income transfers from lower-cost producers who are allowed to continue their operations, to those who close down. Given the difficulty in implementing income transfers, the sharing of cuts would typically be in proportion to output before the cartel action.

After the joint supply cut has been implemented, each individual member will have a strong temptation to covertly increase his supply, and so benefit from the higher price while letting the other cartel members carry the burden of restriction. A close inspection of the participating members' adherence to the agreement will therefore be needed to prevent it from breaking apart.

A few important inferences for the practicability of international commodity cartels can be drawn from the above. *Ceteris paribus*, the smaller the group of participating producers needed to attain the required share of world supply, the simpler will it be to reach and maintain a supply-restricting agreement. Agreement will be much easier to reach and administer in a group of four than in a group of 12 or more. Similarity among the participants will also facilitate monopolistic coordination. If they are of equal size, have matching cost structures and levels, pursue similar goals and operate in comparable social and political environments, an agreement will be much easier to reach than when there are great differences within the group. The ease with which output and supply can be monitored will also affect cartel operation. The cohesion and trust within the collaborating group will benefit from transparency of the burden sharing.

Empirical studies of international cartel action in commodity markets have often regarded countries instead of producing corporations as participants in the market arrangements. This has greatly facilitated the analysis. Individual producers are not always easy to identify, and the volume of their exports may be hard to quantify. Identification and quantification are much easier to handle at the national level. There are also some more fundamental arguments in favor of treating national governments instead of corporations as cartel members. First, in many countries, corporations are subject to anti-trust legislation which makes their overt participation in cartel action difficult. Governments are not subject to such restrictions. Secondly, the governments have and often exercise sovereign powers to regulate exports as they deem fit. And thirdly, there has been a proliferation over the past decades of cases where the governments have taken over the ownership or control of the corporate units which generate the export supply. In the early 1980s, about one half of the productive capacity of metal mineral industries in developing countries is government owned.[3] The agricultural exports from many countries, both developing and industrialized, are handled by variously structured national marketing boards under public control. The general implications from this change are dealt with in chapter 8.

The growing government involvement in commodity production and trade has greatly increased the concentration of international commodity supply, and there is ample justification in such cases for regarding countries as the basic supply units. In other cases, where the international supply is dominated by many independent private firms, an assessment of country concentration will underestimate the number of agents that need to be involved in cartel collaboration.

The increasing role played by governments in international commodity supply raises another issue for the prospects of commodity cartels. Given that the governments pursue objectives other than profit maximization, will they be as interested and able as private corporations to seize existing opportunities for launching and operating price-raising international commodity cartels? Summarizing experiences from the inter-war period, Rowe[4] concluded that an effective international commodity control scheme could be secured only with the active participation of governments. Empirical evidence from petroleum, bauxite, phosphates, and uranium in the post-war period suggest an affirmative answer,[5] but there are other views:

> The divergent productive strategies often pursued at the national level have further increased the difficulties faced by producers in keeping an effective hold on the market. What probably used to be a game quietly and effectively played by a few decisionmakers has now become a semipublic international political affair. The case of copper is highly representative of this trend. The weakening of the real prices of metal that has become evident in the mid and late 1970s is in part the reflection of this reduced ability of metal suppliers to influence the markets.[6]

The characteristics of commodity markets that are amenable to successful price-raising actions by producers can now be summarized, and the potential candidate commodities which meet the required criteria picked out. The method used will be that of successive elimination.

Reasonable prospects for cartelization require a relatively low price elasticity of demand. The commodities must not be easily replaceable by close substitutes. This permits us to exclude the group of edible oils and their raw materials, which are easily interchangeable, and whose production is so dispersed that a joint product cartel would hardly be feasible. The same is true for fruits like bananas, apples and oranges. With some hesitation, we also exclude natural rubber, because of the growing importance of its petroleum-based synthetic substitute.

Another precondition for successful cartel action is that the price elasticity of outside supply should be low, at least in a perspective of 3–5 years. This would exclude quite a number of commodities, for example the cereals group and sugar, whose production could be speedily expanded in many places in response to higher prices that looked like staying high for a couple of years. The same is true for products like cotton, jute and possibly wool.

After these eliminations, we are left with timber, the tropical beverages and most minerals, all characterized by the long periods required to create new production capacity. One would now like to fine-tune the price elasticities of these commodities, to get a better grasp of the prospects for market control, but given the ambiguity of existing elasticity values, such an effort would probably be futile.

The level of supply concentration might throw at least some additional light on the issue under scrutiny. With all else equal, a high level of concentration among producers should facilitate supply coordination, and on this ground, prospects seem brighter for cocoa and tea than for coffee, given that in the early 1980s four countries accounted for two-thirds of cocoa and tea supply, but for only 46 percent in the case of coffee.[7] On the same ground, the prospects for successful mineral cartels would be greater for chromium, cobalt, manganese, niobium, platinum and vanadium, in all of which the output of the four largest producing countries exceeds 75 percent of the world total, than for cadmium, copper, lead, silver and zinc, where the corresponding share is 50 percent or below.[8]

Further insights would require analyses of the affinity of the producers, the structure of the export market, and the industrial organization of the buyers of each commodity. The prospects for successful cartel action would be more limited where the buyers are few, financially powerful and able to retaliate.

6.3   Actual experiences of commodity cartels

This section presents brief accounts of the cartels that operated in the petroleum, bauxite, phosphate, uranium and tin markets in the 1970s and 1980s. Among the cartels to be described, the one for petroleum has had by far the most important implications for the world economy. Before the actions leading to increased prices, world exports of petroleum amounted to $27.9 billion, almost 8 percent of world trade. At the time, the aggregate value of trade for the four other commodities were no more than some $2 billion. An increase in petroleum prices would have more than ten times larger repercussions than corresponding proportional rises for the other four commodities. Also, the ability of the petroleum producers to maintain the high monopoly price levels proved much more lasting than for the other products.

This account relates to minerals only, because in the post-war period, commodity cartel action has been limited by and large to the mineral products group. This has not always been so, and there are many examples from the 1920s and 1930s of more or less successful attempts to cartelize the markets for, for example, rubber, coffee and sugar.[9]

OPEC

The Organization of Petroleum Exporting Countries was brought into existence in 1960. Its major purpose was to form a united front in an attempt to arrest the fall in posted prices of oil.[10] These prices were used to determine the income tax imposed on the multinational corporations that exploited oil in the OPEC countries. Given the entry of new producers, particularly Libya, Nigeria and Abu Dhabi, and the ensuing excess supply of oil, OPEC was not successful in its endeavor, and the posted price of Saudi Marker Crude in 1970 was $1.8 per barrel, down from $1.9 in 1960. This corresponded to a decline of 17 percent when measured in real terms.[11] However, the period was extremely important for the oil producers in that it established a sense of cohesion and common purpose within the group.

By the early 1970s, the market situation had changed in view of the very fast growth of world oil consumption (8.3 percent compound annual growth between 1960 and 1972). The greatly increased reliance on OPEC supplies helped the organization to raise the posted price to $2.5 in 1972. The sellers' market became even more accentuated during the boom of 1973, when the prices of virtually all commodities rose sharply. Late in the year, the OPEC governments agreed to roughly triple the posted price, whereby they hugely increased their fiscal revenue. The oil companies had to pass the increase on to the final consumers. With the very low short-run price elasticity of demand for oil, and of supply outside OPEC, there arose little need for downward supply adjustments by the cartel, in response to the higher price.

During the 1970s the OPEC countries instituted additional increases in the posted price, but these mainly compensated for the ongoing inflation. Also, a large part of OPEC's production capacity was nationalized during this period.

In 1979–80 there was another upward explosion in prices resulting from the reduced Iranian supply after the religious revolution in that country, and later from the outbreak of the Iran–Iraq war. While this second price rise was not caused by OPEC's own actions, the cartel undertook to maintain the very high price that had resulted from these events.

In the 1980s OPEC experienced increasing difficulties in its efforts to control oil prices. The longer-run price elasticities of oil turned out much higher than the short-run ones. World demand for oil stagnated in response to the increasing price levels. Consumption[12] in the OECD area, which accounts for three-quarters of total non-socialist world consumption, fell by 13 percent between 1973 and 1986, despite an expansion of the area's GDP by 40 percent. Non-socialist world supply outside OPEC, which had

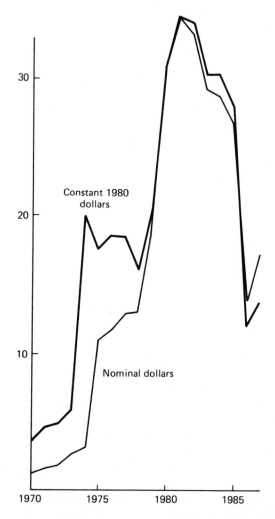

Figure 6.2 Petroleum prices: weighted average of OPEC crudes, US$/barrel (*Source*: World Bank, *Commodity Trade and Price Trends*, several issues)

been stagnant at 16−17 million barrels per day until 1977, rose in subsequent years, to reach 25.3 million in 1985. From a full capacity utilization output at 31.5 million barrels per day in 1979, OPEC had to reduce production to 17.2 million in 1985, in order to maintain the high prices. The cohesion within the cartel had been greatly eased by the preparedness of the Saudis to cut output from 10 million barrels per day in 1980 to only 3.5 million in 1985.

In 1986 the oil producers lost their tight grip over the price. After internal controversy, output was increased by 2.2 million barrels per day to 19.5 million, prices declined by almost half, and the cartel's revenue was sharply curtailed. There was a price recovery in 1987, as inventory demand was boosted by the war efforts in the Persian Gulf, and by a marginal reduction of OPEC's output.

Judged by its performance until 1988, the OPEC cartel has been a surprising success in terms of its ability to raise prices and revenues to its members. Few other conceivable scenarios could have yielded equally large present values for OPEC's oil exports. In comparison with most other cartels, the longevity of the monopolistic coordination is quite impressive. Even after the collapse in early 1986, the price maintained by OPEC's restrictive output was between two and three times higher than the purely competitive level.[13] In the absence of monopolistic coordination, OPEC would have had to produce in excess of 45 million barrels per day, more than 15 million above its current capacity, to secure the revenue that it actually obtained in that year.

The strong and lasting market power exercised by OPEC has been based on a combination of very low price elasticities for oil in the short and medium term, the preparedness of Saudi Arabia, the largest OPEC producer, to assume a major burden in cutting supply, and the exceptional concentration of economic oil reserves within the group. After 15 years of cartel intervention, the price sensitivity of demand and outsiders' supply has proved far higher than was expected in 1980, when OPEC decided to defend prices above $30 per barrel. In the late 1980s, Saudi Arabia's output has shrunk considerably, so the prospects for further cuts of its supply are limited. These two developments have weakened OPEC's market power. However, the group's central position in terms of reserves remains, and provides the underpinnings for less drastic, yet quite profitable monopolistic coordination over the coming decade.

Bauxite

In the late 1960s, Jamaica began to urge the governments of bauxite producing countries to form an association for the exchange of information, reduction of rivalries, the establishment of a joint front to the multinational aluminum companies, and coordinated increases of export taxes.[14] Enthused by the successful collaboration within OPEC, but also by the booming demand for their product, the bauxite producing countries founded the International Bauxite Association (IBA), early in 1974. By 1975, its members accounted for 85 percent of non-socialist world output.

Jamaica's government was also the first to raise its bauxite revenues. At the time, the country was the world's second largest producer, and, on account of transport distances, enjoyed a considerable cost advantage in the US market. As in the case of OPEC oil, the production units were largely owned by the vertically integrated aluminum companies, and there were hardly any market quotations for the product. In 1974 and 1975 the government instituted a very sharp increase of production levies and export taxes, to appropriate its locational monopoly. As a result, the import price from Jamaica to the United States roughly doubled[15] (see figure 6.3).

The government apparently expected that the other members of IBA would follow suit, whereby the relative loss of Jamaica's competitiveness would be abated. To some extent, this also occurred. Several Caribbean producers, e.g. Surinam and the Dominican Republic, instituted fiscal levies similar to Jamaica's. Guinea, too, raised its bauxite taxation, but by less than the Caribbean countries. Australia, the world's largest producer, and an IBA member, refused to join in these actions.

The increased bauxite costs had no perceptible impact on global demand for the product. The price elasticity of bauxite demand is close to zero. This raw material constitutes a very small share of overall aluminum production costs. Within a wide range of prices, there are no competitive substitutes for bauxite in aluminum production.

In retrospect, it appears that the Caribbean governments' action led to a substantial loss in the international competitiveness of their supply. The taxes resulted in a gradual, but very large shrinkage of the Caribbeans' market share, as is apparent from table 6.2. The main gainers were Australia and Guinea, members of the IBA who were more concerned about competitiveness, and Brazil, which never joined the IBA.

The weak development of aluminum demand after the second oil price rise (primary aluminum consumption in 1985 was no higher than in 1979) added to the cartel members' problems. The demand for bauxite is a derived demand, and the cartel had no control at all over the aluminum market. The falling shares of the world bauxite market would have been easier to accommodate in an expanding market. The stagnant total demand for bauxite speeded up the erosion of the cartel.

In terms of our formal analysis, the cartel action was not very successful in increasing members' revenue in the medium term, because E_{DC} was too high. The very low value of E_{DW} was overwhelmed by a low M (the initial market share of the Caribbean producers) and a high E_{SR}. In distinction from the case of OPEC, the advantage of the Caribbean countries' resource endowment was not pronounced enough to give them a more lasting market power. The frequent alterations of the Jamaican taxes and levies in the 1970s and 1980s, and the other concurrent changes

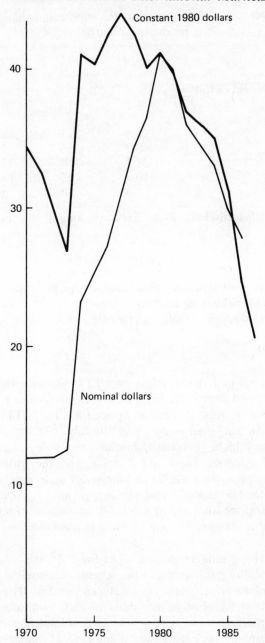

Figure 6.3 Bauxite "prices": US import reference price based on imports from Jamaica, US$/ton (*Source*: World Bank, *Commodity Trade and Price Trends*, several issues)

Table 6.2 Non-socialist world bauxite output, and shares of leading
producing countries

	1974	1978	1982	1986
Non-socialist world output (million tons)	71.3	73.4	66.7	79.2
Country shares (%)				
Jamaica	21.5	15.9	12.4	8.8
Surinam	9.7	6.9	4.7	4.7
Australia	28.1	33.1	35.4	40.9
Guinea	10.7	17.3	17.7	18.6
Brazil	1.3	1.5	6.3	8.2

Source: Metallgesellschaft, *Metal Statistics*, annual, several issues

implemented in its bauxite/alumina industry (e.g. production controls, nationalizations) make it difficult to isolate the impact of cartel action on the government's revenue from the bauxite levies.

Phosphate rock

Booming demand and the example of OPEC led to a decision by the wholly state owned Moroccan phosphate rock producer Office Chérifien des phosphates,[16] to raise its producer price f.a.s. from $14 to $42 per ton in January 1974, and then again to $63 in July.[17] In the short run, this intervention was highly effective, because the state owned phosphate enterprises of Algeria, Togo and Tunisia, and the mixed-owned Cie Sénégalaise des phosphates de Taiba followed it up by similar action. The members of the US export cartel, Phosrock, also acted in concert, by raising their list price from $13 to $55.[18] US legislation does permit export oriented cartel measures, so long as there is no impact on the domestic market.

The price-raising scheme proved short-lived. In the year 1974 itself, exports from all the participants in the scheme increased significantly. In 1975, however, the world depression reduced demand. The higher prices also resulted in deferral of farmer demand and substitution in favor of other fertilizers. The cartel was unable to withstand these strains. The Moroccan phosphate rock price was reduced to $49 in 1976, and $40 in 1977. As is apparent from figure 6.4, by 1977 the real price was already at par with levels in pre-cartel days.

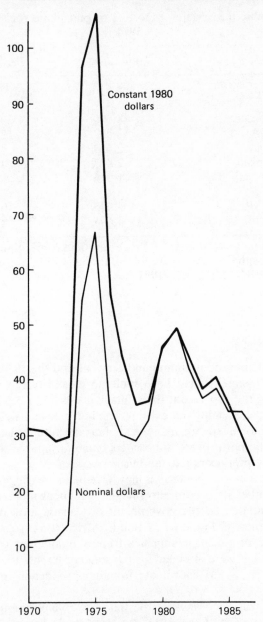

Figure 6.4   Phosphate rock prices: (Moroccan Fas Casablanca), US$/ton
(*Source*: World Bank, *Commodity Trade and Price Trends*, several
issues)

Table 6.3   Major exporters of phosphate rock in
1974

	Thousand tons	*Percent*
World	55,016	100.0
Morocco	18,690	34.0
USA	12,407	22.6
Togo	2,633	4.8
Tunisia	2,407	4.4
Senegal	1,916	3.5
USSR	5,945	10.8
Pacific Islands	4,695	8.5

Source: UNCTAD, "Processing and Marketing of
Phosphates: Areas for International Cooperation,"
TD/B/C.1/PSC/22, 1981

Uranium

The international uranium mining industry entered the 1970s in a state of
profound depression. It had been built up to satisfy the huge military
demand during the 1960s. But the military needs had been fully satisfied
by the end of the decade, and existing uranium capacity was far in excess
of nuclear reactor needs for many years into the future. The prices were
very low and did not provide full cost coverage for a large segment of the
industry. Many producers left the business.

The depressed market conditions may have been the trigger that brought
producers together in an effort to safeguard their own survival. A series
of meetings initiated by the government of Canada took place in 1971.
The governments of France and South Africa were represented, and
leading private producing companies from a number of countries took
part. The meetings were intended to "put some order into the international
uranium market ... to coordinate uranium production and marketing
policies."[19]

The market was very weak at the time the collaboration started, and
the bargaining power of the cartel remained frail. The most it could do
was to reduce rivalry among members, and to issue directives aimed at
preventing further price falls. At the end of 1973, however, a number of
independent but coincidental factors completely reversed the market
situation.[20] The most important of these was probably a decision by the

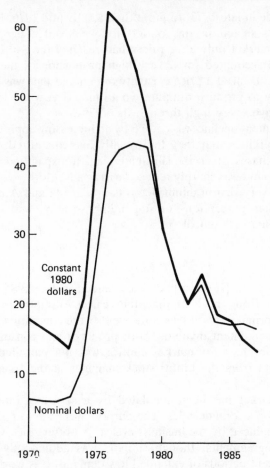

Figure 6.5 Uranium prices: uranium oxide spot US$/lb. (*Source*: Nuexco, *Market Report*, several issues)

US enrichment agency to change the rules under which it provided enrichment services. At the time, this agency held a virtual world enrichment monopoly. According to the new rules, enrichment services had to be commissioned decades in advance, and there were high penalties for cancellation. Existing and planned nuclear utilities signed up excessive enrichment contracts, and then went on a buying spree to secure their future uranium needs.

Having institutionalized their collaboration, the uranium producers responded by withdrawing from the market, and the prices exploded. As figure 6.5 reveals, spot quotations went up from less than $7 per lb of uranium oxide in late 1973, to more than $40 by mid-1976. Prices in long-run contracts signed in this period followed suit. The producers re-entered the market only after prices had reached the $40 level.[21]

The cartel accounted for a very high proportion of the non-socialist world supply. It faced a price elasticity of demand that was close to zero. New capacity to produce uranium would take 5 years to implement. So the prices stayed very high through the 1970s.

The subsequent decline was caused by an increasing appreciation among the nuclear utilities that they had greatly overcommitted themselves to uranium purchases, given the shrinking plans to expand nuclear capacity. Uranium demand was sharply reduced as a result. More recent discoveries of large and very rich uranium deposits in Canada and Australia helped to alter earlier perceptions of impending scarcity, and added to the problems of market control.

Tin

The tin episode to be described below ended in late 1985. The circumstances differ from those of the other cartel examples in at least two respects. In formal terms at least, the events were conditioned by the international tin agreement involving both producer and consumer interests. And the major tool for market control was not curtailed supply, but added demand from the buffer stock manager of the International Tin Agreement.

The tin market has been regulated by a series of international tin agreements for several decades. The purpose has been to reduce the price fluctuations induced by the business cycles. A buffer stock was the major tool in the agreements, though support was additionally provided by export quotas in periods of extended low demand. It is worth noting that the importance of tin is much more vital to the producing member countries' governments than to the members on the consuming side. This asymmetry may explain the following events.

The first half of the 1980s was characterized by stagnant demand and very depressed prices for virtually all commodities (see figure 2.6), and these tendencies affected tin in equal measure. In 1981, in anticipation of a new decision about floor prices to be defended by the tin agreement, a "mystery" buyer, later revealed to have been the commodity trading firm Marc Rich acting on behalf of the government of Malaysia, the world's leading tin producer, entered the market, and made very large purchases. This led to substantial price increases, and influenced the level of the floor price determined by the Agreement in October of that year. Early in 1982, the "mystery" buyer became a seller, and the burden of defending the "artificially" high floor price was transferred to the buffer stock manager.[22] Despite the introduction of export quotas in April 1982, the buffer stock manager's task proved excessive, as is amply demonstrated by the events a few years later.

The high prices maintained by the International Tin Agreement encouraged non-members to expand supply. For instance, the output of Brazil, a non-member, rose from 6,900 tons in 1980 to 26,500 tons in 1985, the latter representing almost 17 percent of non-socialist output. The export quotas of member countries were breached by sizable smuggling. Tin of "unspecified origin" reached over 16,500 tons in 1983, most of it from South-East Asia.[23] An additional difficulty arose from the decline in non-socialist tin demand. Consumption levels in the first half of the 1980s were some 15 percent below those of the late 1970s.

The buffer stock manager bought most of the time between 1982 and 1985, in an effort to defend the agreed price. In 1985 he is reported to have held physical stocks of over 60,000 tons, in excess of 4 months' non-socialist production at the time. To stretch his resources, he used these stocks as collateral for loans spent on forward purchases in the defence of price. Forward transactions were much more economical than physical purchases, since they required margins of no more than 10 percent of the purchase value.

In October 1985, the buffer stock manager's resources had been completely exhausted. As a result, he ceased operations, defaulting on his futures purchase commitments and leaving behind a total debt far in excess of $1 billion. Tin trade on the LME was suspended, and when free market transactions opened in London in the spring of 1986, the prices quoted were about 60 percent below those that prevailed before the crisis (figure 6.6).

The monopolistic coordination implemented through stock purchases by the International Tin Agreement clearly succeeded in maintaining prices far above market equilibrium between late 1981 and late 1985. But it is an open question whether this yielded a net benefit to the producing participants in the scheme.

The tin events resemble the attempts of the Hunt Brothers in the late 1970s to corner the silver market by massive forward purchases. The price of silver was pushed up to historically unprecedented levels in 1980, but the scheme collapsed in the early 1980s as supply, especially of old silver scrap, increased to such an extent that it exhausted the resources available for market control.

Conclusions

The above examples provide only a very limited sample of commodity cartel experiences, and one must be cautious about generalizations based

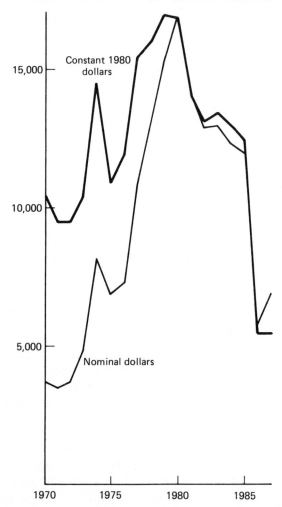

Figure 6.6   Tin prices: LME (1985–7, London free market), US$/ton
(*Source*: UNCTAD, *Monthly Commodity Price Bulletin*, several issues)

on this material. A different set of examples might lead to quite different conclusions. A few findings are nevertheless in order.

The cases of oil and uranium support the thesis that the establishment and consolidation of producer organizations often occurs in response to very depressed market conditions, which threaten the survival of many participants.

The examples of oil, bauxite, phosphate rock and uranium suggest that periods of booming demand greatly facilitate price-raising producer action. Obversely, market management by producers is likely to have little price impact in recessions when there exists considerable excess capacity. The efforts to cartelize these four markets occurred simultaneously, and the generally high level of commodity demand is certainly an important explanation of their timing. We have also alluded to the possibly contagious effect of OPEC's success on the producers of the other three commodities.

The examples given have demonstrated the limited durability typical of price-raising cartel arrangements and have pointed to the exceptional natural endowments of the OPEC countries as the major explanation for the surprising lasting power of the petroleum cartel.

In all the cases surveyed, the governments played instrumental roles in the market rigging exercises. This evidence suggests that there is little validity in the claim that governments are unable to operate monopolistic interventions in commodity markets.

NOTES

1 For an illustrative example of such works, see J. M. Griffin and D. J. Teece (eds), *OPEC Behavior and World Oil Prices*, Allen and Unwin, London, 1982.
2 D. Gately, "A Ten-year Retrospective: OPEC and the World Oil Market," *Journal of Economic Literature*, September 1984.
3 M. Radetzki, *State Mineral Enterprises: Their Impact on the International Mineral Markets*, Resources for the Future, Washington DC, 1985.
4 J. W. F. Rowe, *Primary Commodities in International Trade*, Cambridge University Press, Cambridge, 1965, p. 137.
5 See next section.
6 E. R. Grilli and Maw Cheng Yang, "Primary Commodity Prices, Manufactured Goods Prices and the Terms of Trade of Developing Countries: What the Long Run Shows," *World Bank Economic Review*, January 1988.
7 World Bank, *Commodity Trade and Price Trends*, 1986 edition.
8 Metallgesellschaft, *Metal Statistics*, 1986.
9 Rowe, *Primary Commodities in International Trade*, chapter 10.
10 E. F. Penrose, *The Large International Firm in Developing Countries; The International Petroleum Industry*, Allen and Unwin, London, 1968.
11 World Bank, *Commodity Trade and Price Trends*, 1985 edition.
12 Oil consumption and production figures from BP, *Statistical Review of World Energy*, June 1987.
13 M. Radetzki, "Outlook for Oil and Coal Prices in International Trade," *Skandinaviska Enskilda Banken Quarterly Review*, No. 4, 1986.
14 C. P. Brown, *The Political and Social Economy of Commodity Control*, Macmillan, London, 1980.
15 R. Vedavalli, "Market Structure of Bauxite/Alumina/Aluminum, and Prospects for Developing Countries," *World Bank Commodity Paper No. 24*, 1977.

16   Brown, *Economy of Commodity Control*; UNCTAD, "Processing and Marketing of Phosphates: Areas for International Cooperation," TD/B/C.1/PSC/22, 1981.

17   UNCTAD, *Monthly Commodity Price Bulletin*, 1960–84 Supplement.

18   Brown, *Economy of Commodity Control*; UNCTAD, "Processing and Marketing of Phosphates."

19   "Canada, Australia Move Forward Uranium Price, Processing Collaboration," *Nucleonics Week*, May 13, 1971, quoted in T. Neff, *The International Uranium Market*, Ballinger, Cambridge, Mass., 1984.

20   M. Radetzki, *Uranium, A Strategic Source of Energy*, Croom Helm, London, 1981.

21   Ibid.

22   *Mining Annual Review*, 1983.

23   A. I. MacBean and D. T. Nguyen, *Commodity Policies, Problems and Prospects*, Croom Helm, London, 1987.

7

Public Ownership of Commodity Production

Why should we devote special attention to the issue of public ownership in a book that deals with international commodity markets? The answer is that state owned enterprises have assumed very important positions among the suppliers in many important commodity markets during recent decades. There is a widespread belief that these enterprises behave in some ways differently from privately owned supply agents, and particularly that they do not aim at maximizing profits. Especially in the period of depressed commodity prices in the 1980s, there have been animated exhortations about the perverse economic behavior of state owned commodity producers.[1] If these beliefs are correct, we would risk being seriously wrong by analyzing the international commodity markets on the assumption that all supply agents are profit maximizers. Hence, a special scrutiny of the state owned enterprises' role in international commodity supply is warranted.

There are two important limitations to the subject treatment in the present chapter. First, it deals only with the non-socialist countries. In the socialist nations most production is in public hands as a matter of course. Hence, there is little other entrepreneurship with which the state owned enterprise activities could be contrasted.

Secondly, the subject is limited, by and large, to the mineral industries. Many countries, especially developing ones, have a large proportion of their mineral sector activities owned and operated by state owned corporations. In agricultural production, in contrast, public enterprises are regularly of minor importance. In the developing countries, the limited government presence in agriculture mainly reflects the dominance of small scale operations which have always remained in private national hands. The virtual absence of government as an agricultural producer should not be taken to mean that it does not have a major impact on the agricultural sector. But rather than being involved in agricultural production as such, government influence is exerted by control of domestic supply through ownership in agro-based industries such as sugar refining, maintenance of fiscal monopolies for beverages and tobacco, or by marketing boards that regulate producer prices for exported commodities. In many countries, public involvement in agriculture also takes the form of agricultural development corporations that provide finance or supply agricultural inputs.[2] As discussed in the preceding chapter, international trade policies, too, have a very profound influence on agriculture, both in industrialized and developing countries.

Table 7.1 provides rough measures of the unimportance of state ownership in agriculture, and the much greater importance of the government in the mineral sector, in a group of industrialized and developing countries.

Even in the minerals area, public ownership of production on a large scale is a relatively recent phenomenon. Observing the case of copper, Sir Ronald Prain noted that production in which the government held any sort of interest in the early 1960s was a mere 2.5 percent of the non-socialist world total. By 1970 this figure had risen to more than 40 percent.[3] Broadly, the same picture emerges for the metal mineral industries in general. In the mid-1950s state involvement in the world outside the socialist countries was insignificant. At that time the metal mineral industries of Africa, Asia and Latin America were completely dominated by privately owned multinationals from the leading industrialized market economies. In the early 1980s state ownership in metal minerals comprised something like one-third of overall capacity. The emergent state enterprise phenomenon is heavily concentrated in the developing countries, where it accounts for about one-half of the total. In the industrialized market economies, its share is more like 10 percent.[4] Since the share of the developing countries in the non-socialist world output of metal minerals amounts to about 40 percent, it follows that these countries account for some three-quarters of the global state owned capacity in these industries, in absolute terms.

In petroleum, the emergence of state ownership on a large scale is even younger. As late as 1966, the share of state owned production in the world outside the socialist countries was negligible. In 1970 it represented a mere 7 percent, but by 1979 it had risen to 55 percent.[5]

This chapter continues by clarifying a few methodological issues. How precisely is state enterprise defined? And what do the percentage shares quoted above represent? We subsequently explore the motivations for establishing public ownership in the mineral industries, in industrialized as well as developing countries. Then, after pointing to the features that

Table 7.1   State owned enterprises' share of sectoral GDP (percent)

	< 5	5–25	25–50	50–75	> 75
Austria (1970–5)	A	M			
Greece (1979)	A			M	
France (1981)	A		M		
Italy (1975)	A		M		
Portugal (1976)	A M				
United Kingdom (1975)	A				M
Congo (1980)	A M				
Ivory Coast (1979)	A	M			
Kenya (1980)	A M				
Senegal (1980)	A				M
Sierra Leone (1979)	A	M			
Tanzania (1980–1)	A				M
Tunisia (1976)	A		M		
Bangladesh (1980)	A				M
Burma (1980)	A				M
India (1978)	A				M
South Korea (1974–7)	A	M			
Nepal (1978–9)	A M				
Pakistan (1980)	A	M			
Sri Lanka (1974)	A M				
Argentina (1980)	A	M			
Mexico (1980)	A				M
Nicaragua (1980)		A			M
Uruguay (1979)	A M				

A = Agriculture; M = Mining.

Source: World Bank, *World Development Report*, 1983 edition, p. 50

characterize state owned mineral firms, we discuss the likely impact of a large state owned sector in a commodity, both on the domestic economy, and on the international market for that commodity.

7.1   How to define and quantify the state enterprise sector

The concerns about publicly owned firms are based on the belief that in some way these enterprises behave differently from the privately owned firms. If differential behavior is in the focus of interest, then the state enterprise sector should be defined not by equity ownership, but by the extent of government control, since control, rather than equity holdings, will determine behavior. In practice, the state sector is invariably measured by looking at the state equity holding, with the underlying presumption that public equity and control go hand in hand. This is by no means always true. The practice of using equity ownership as a differentiating rod between the private and state sectors is explained by the impracticability of establishing and measuring the degree of government control in a uniform way.

Even when equity ownership is employed, there are some tricky issues that must be resolved. Some analysts comprise within the state owned universe all enterprises in which the public equity holding is 5 percent or more, on the presumption that an important minority holding is enough for the government to exert its influence. Others include in the state owned group only the firms that are majority owned by government. The two measures will obviously yield very different quantitative results. Yet a third approach is to assume state owned capacity to be proportional to the government's equity holding in each firm. Though it avoids the arbitrary border lines of the above methods, the measure has a distinct disadvantage in not permitting a clear-cut identification of individual enterprises as either state or private.

The proportional rod was applied in deriving the state owned shares in metal mineral industries quoted above. The sources for the petroleum industry figures, and for table 7.1 above, do not state the method used for quantifying the public enterprise share. The latter appears to be based on individual country submissions, so in all likelihood, a variety of methods has been involved.

7.2 Motivations for public ownership in mineral industries

The mineral sector throughout the world has been a favorite area for government intervention in a variety of forms, including the taking up of direct equity positions. The authorities' desire to be involved and to control has a variety of explanations. First, the widespread perception of mineral wealth as a national patrimony has often been used to sanction public involvement, for instance to prevent appropriation by private interests, or to assure adequate mineral supplies for future generations. Secondly, the immobility of mineral deposits under exploitation facilitates far-reaching public intervention in such exploitation without any risk that the activity may escape beyond the government's reach. Thirdly, the frequent generation of high rents in mineral endeavors, coupled with the difficulty of appropriating such rents through fiscal measures, provides the temptation for a greater degree of public involvement. And fourthly, the extraction and processing of minerals is often regarded as strategically important, either because of the very large size of many mineral ventures, or because such activities assure a domestic supply of key inputs into manufacturing, including the defense industries.

Arguments such as these explain many of the public ownership positions in mineral industries in the industrialized market economies. The more important ones include all stages of aluminum production in France, aluminum smelting in Germany, Italy, Norway and Spain, copper mining through refining in Finland, iron ore production in France and Sweden, coal mining in Germany and the United Kingdom, parts of the petroleum industry in Norway and the United Kingdom, and steel manufacturing in several Western European countries. The modes for establishing these ownership positions have varied. In a few cases they resulted from confiscation of enemy property at the end of the Second World War. In some instances, the state acquired its ownership stake by bailing out bankrupt private enterprise. In others, the government purchased the equity at a price agreed through negotiations (Swedish iron ore), or determined unilaterally through a government decree (French aluminum).

However, as noted, a major proportion of the state owned mineral enterprises outside the socialist economies is found in the developing countries. Although the arguments enumerated above are certainly valid in explaining the existence of state ownership in the developing country group too, an additional perspective is required for a fuller understanding of the emergence and growth of the publicly owned mineral sector in the Third World.

The 1960s and 1970s involved a historically unique economic emancipation process for a majority of the developing countries, following the severance of formal or informal colonial bonds. With gradually improving administrative, technical and managerial capabilities in the post-colonial period, the ambitions and abilities of the authorities to promote development through control and direction of the national economy were expanded. The great importance of the mineral sector in many cases, its predominantly foreign ownership and secluded enclave character *vis-à-vis* the rest of the economy, made it a major target for public policy initiatives.

These initiatives took a variety of forms. The ultimate and most far-reaching measure in the developing countries heavily dependent on mineral exports was to nationalize the industry, in part or completely. The motivation to nationalize was usually based on the view that other intervention measures, like taxation or specific regulation pertaining to, for example, investment, employment or exports, were inadequate, and that only direct equity ownership could provide the means for extracting a major proportion of the mineral rent, and for establishing effective control over this key industry. The practice of compensation payments to previous owners varied, from none at all, to sums that might appear as adequate to impartial observers. However, the former owners invariably complained about the compensation received.

Several factors suggest that the phase of fast growth of the publicly owned universe in the mineral industry came to an end in the early 1980s, and that the share of the industry owned by the state will not increase further. The post-colonial push for economic emancipation, which was a major force behind many nationalizations, has been completed in a majority of developing countries. The most conspicuous foreign ownership positions have already been taken over by the national authorities. Relations between governments in developing countries and multinational mining firms have improved. The value and uniqueness of the inputs provided by the multinationals is better recognized by the governments. Constructive collaboration has replaced the political demagoguery that usually preceded nationalization actions in earlier years. Amicable joint venture arrangements for the development of new projects, with management responsibilities regularly entrusted to the private partner, have become common.

Equally important, during the 1980s a worldwide resentment against excessive public involvement in industry has led to many privatizations of state enterprises, both in industrialized and developing countries. The critics claim that state owned enterprises have not delivered according to expectations, and that in many cases they have become national liabilities.[6]

By the late 1980s, very few state owned firms in the mineral sector have been sold off. Examples of completed deals include British Petroleum in the United Kingdom. In Cananea, one of Mexico's major copper producers, the government equity, 52 percent of the total, valued at $910 million, was put up for bidding late in 1988, to private Mexican groups.[7] In the same year, Caraiba Metais, Brazil's only copper mine and smelter, wholly owned by the government, was offered for sale to domestic copper users.[8] Though others may follow, my view is that state owned enterprises will account for a substantial but relatively static proportion of the non-socialist world mineral supply through the rest of the present century.

7.3 The distinguishing characteristics of state owned mineral firms

Ideally, we would have liked to establish a clear-cut distinction between the private profit-seeking mineral firms on the one hand, and the state owned mineral enterprises, characterized by their social pursuits, on the other. In the real world, the distinction between the two types of enterprise is blurred. Private firms seldom conform to the pure microeconomic paradigm. Over time, the privately owned mineral enterprises in many countries have been increasingly conditioned, by law or convention, to assume many functions other than profit maximization. The state owned mineral enterprises come in many different shapes. Their characteristics range between forms quite akin to private corporations at one extreme, and ones where social considerations predominate over concerns with return on capital, at the other. But although the line is blurred, there does appear to be a significant difference in goals, characteristics and behavioral patterns between the average private and state owned mineral firm.

The emphasis in the following characterization is on the state owned mineral firms in developing countries. After all, this group has experienced the fastest growth, and it currently accounts for a dominant share of the total state owned universe in the mineral industry world wide. We begin by considering distinctive behavior in current operations, and continue by scrutinizing how investment behavior may differ between the public and private mineral firms.

In an analysis of state owned firms in the minerals industries, a crucial distinction is that between the newly established, inexperienced, and hence inefficient corporations, on the one hand, and the mature ones which have been there for some time and have acquired the necessary expertise to run their operations with reasonable proficiency, on the other. The relevance of this distinction is predicated on the fact that a large part of the existing state owned universe has been set up through successive waves of nationalizations of foreign owned positions in developing countries. Hence, throughout the past three decades, a considerable proportion of the state owned enterprise group has belonged to the new, inexperienced, and inefficient category.

Nationalizations frequently involved extended and heavy setting-up costs. The national firms established to manage the operations that were taken over from the foreigners usually had a difficult start. The old owners, dissatisfied with the compensation offered, were often unwilling to provide assistance. The new managers regularly lacked the appropriate experience, but were compelled to take on wide-ranging responsibilities long before they had a chance to acquire the necessary skills.

The result was almost invariably a disruption in operations that reached a maximum soon after takeover, and then gradually subsided over a long period of time. Initially, the inexperienced management was often unable to maintain production at full capacity levels, and the cost of output tended to rise. The ability to undertake investments in new capacity, probably the most complex task faced by the managements of mineral firms, usually took the longest time to master.

Available evidence suggests a wide variation in the time needed for overcoming the disruptions and inefficiencies due to managerial inexperience after nationalization. The speed of results in this respect appears to be related to the level of economic development of the country, the extent of earlier exposure of the national managers to the problems of the industry, and the ability to strike constructive arrangements with outside specialists for managerial support and training. Overcoming the loss of efficiency due to inexperience at the time of nationalization took no more than 5 years in the case of Venezuela's iron ore operations. In Indonesia's tin, more than 20 years were needed to develop a national management cadre of international quality standards, after the industry was taken over from the Dutch in the 1950s. In Zambia, where the government took a majority holding of the copper industry in 1969, the process has not yet been completed.[9]

The inefficiency due to inexperience that has characterized a substantial part of the state owned enterprise group through the past decades, is a transient feature. Since the process of nationalizations came to an end, the state owned universe is becoming increasingly mature. With time, the firms still suffering from managerial inexperience and related inefficiencies will overcome these predicaments.

Other characteristics of state mineral firms have a more permanent nature. For instance, these enterprises regularly have a more complex and diversified goal structure than privately owned firms. In addition to the requirement that a return on capital should be earned, the publicly owned corporations often pursue objectives with regard to employment, foreign exchange generation, regional development or skill creation and technological progress at the national level.

The suppression of the profit goal and the influence exerted by the government make the state owned enterprises more amenable to considering social benefit, including externalities that they will not reap, as a guiding criterion for their actions. For example, unemployment is a common problem in mineral exporting developing countries, and so the shadow wage would be lower than the actual wage. At least during periods of mineral price depression, the current account of such countries would often show a deficit, and so the shadow rate of exchange for their currency would be lower than the official one.[10] An application of these shadow rates will lower the supply curve and raise the demand curve in relation to the curves that would prevail if the market rates were used.

The addition of non-profit objectives to the goals of the state owned firm is bound to involve a cost to the firm, and so to result in permanently higher costs of mineral production. The requirement that the activity should result not only in mineral output, but also in the output of one or other social good, is akin to the requirement that byproducts be extracted from the ore, along with the main product. There is a cost in obtaining the byproducts, whether mineral or social. In the case of the state enterprise, the social byproducts do not yield a revenue to the firm, so the additional cost must be allocated in its entirety to the mineral output. We must add that though the cost of the social byproducts will reduce profits, the outcome may be desirable from society's point of view, and need not involve any inefficiency.

There is another reason, however, why the subordination of the profit motive to a set of social goals will often result in inefficiency, and will tend to increase production costs even further. Multiple goals will make it harder to measure managerial performance, and so are likely to lessen the pressure to minimize costs.[11] Where several goals are pursued at the same time, a high cost to produce the mineral will be easier to justify by the pursuit of some social objective than it would be in a firm where profit maximization is the sole yardstick for measuring the quality of management.

The three arguments just spelled out, namely a transient inefficiency due to inexperience, the costs involved in pursuing social goals, and a permanent inefficiency due to lesser pressure to minimize costs, should lead, on average, to higher costs of mineral production in state owned mineral enterprises than in private firms exploiting mineral deposits of a corresponding quality.

The owner governments often endow their mineral corporations with an implicit guarantee for financial survival. State enterprises are rarely allowed to go bankrupt. Undercapitalization resulting from unprofitable operation is remedied through new financial infusions.[12] Through their owners, such firms also have better access to subsidized capital, for example, from the international development agencies, than do private mineral corporations.

The impact of such guarantees and subsidies for the state owned firms' relative competitiveness should not be overemphasized. The benefits can be regarded as part-compensation for the costly social obligations that the state owned firms are forced to assume. Furthermore, the governments of countries heavily dependent on the mineral industry could not possibly find the means to provide subsidies to that industry over the long run. Excepting periods of severe mineral price depression, a majority of the large state mineral firms reap significant Ricardian rents which assure financial comfort and a significant revenue for the government budget, even after their social obligations have been paid for.

Is it possible to identify any systematic differences in the investment behavior between state owned firms and private multinational corporations in the mineral industry? State enterprises, like private ones, would ordinarily develop new production units only when it is commercially justifiable to do so. The capital invested has to yield sufficient return to service the loans, and to provide some return on equity after the costs have been covered. The easier access to low-cost finance from international development agencies is unlikely to alter behavior in this respect. The World Bank and the Regional Development Banks typically require careful feasibility studies proving commercial viability of the projects to be financed.

State owned mineral enterprises exhibit a wide variety of behavior with regard to developments in market share, and it is hard to draw any general conclusions about distinctive behavior in this respect. Some, like ZCCM in Zambia (copper) and Ferrominera in Venezuela (iron ore) have not invested very aggressively and have been losing market shares ever since nationalization. Others, like Brazil's CVRD, have been expanding their relative market positions at very fast rates (in iron ore), but then, so have some private multinationals, e.g. RTZ (in copper). Yet other state owned mineral firms, such as PT Timah in Indonesia (tin) and Codelco in Chile (copper), have experienced extended periods of market stagnation or even contraction after they became state owned, followed by periods of very fast growth that permitted them to resume their former market shares.

In some cases, the governments have induced state enterprise investments in uncommercial ventures, for example, to promote regional development or to satisfy national strategic needs of the output. Ownership is not a unique means to achieve such public ends. Support of private firms through subsidies or tariffs has accomplished identical objectives in countries where the government has abstained from owning the mineral industry.

In countries where private foreign investors feel exposed to political risk, we are likely to find a large difference in the rate of return on investments required by state owned and private mineral firms. If private foreign investors are to be attracted at all, the expected return on their projects has to be increased sufficiently to provide an adequate risk premium. State owned enterprises, by definition, are not exposed to the risk of expropriation or to milder forms of nationalization. For this reason, in the circumstances just described, their rate of return requirements will be lower.

The nationalizations of the 1960s and 1970s frequently involved a rupture of the international vertical integration chains maintained by the private multinationals. The downstream processing facilities located in the mineral importing countries were out of reach for the nationalization efforts.

In metal minerals, the sharp reduction of vertical integration that resulted from the state takeovers has not been followed by a recovery. A distinguishing characteristic of the state enterprises in these industries has been their unwillingness to invest abroad. Exceptions, like the investments

of Chilean Codelco and Zambian ZCCM in European downstream processing of copper, only underline the rule. The markets for unprocessed
and semiprocessed metal minerals have widened and become more competitive as a result of the increasing importance of transactions between
independent parties that has ensued (bauxite and iron ore provide illustrative examples).

The metal mineral experience contrasts with that in petroleum. After a
period of hesitation, the state owned oil enterprises from Norway, Kuwait,
Venezuela and other OPEC countries have energetically integrated forward by buying up refineries, distribution chains and other downstream
facilities in the industrialized importing nations.

In contrast to private multinationals, both the metal mineral and petroleum firms owned by the state rely almost exclusively on the natural
resource base of their home country. Furthermore, they exhibit a parochial
attitude *vis-à-vis* exploration for new deposits outside their national
boundaries. It has been claimed that the efficiency of their exploration
effort has suffered in consequence of the limited spread of exploration
risks.[13]

7.4 The impact of state ownership on the national economy

This section briefly reviews how the establishment and operations of state
owned mineral enterprises have impacted on the national economies of
their home countries. In turn, I shall assess whether the public takeover
has really contributed to improved government control, to greater national
revenue, and to other goal fulfillments. This review will help in illuminat-
ing some of the disappointments about public ownership expressed in
recent times.

As noted, many of the state owned units in the mineral industry were
taken over from foreign owners, and an important motivation for the
state action was that the foreign control over these important industries
compromised national sovereignty. State ownership, it was felt, would
provide the government with a crucial tool for directing national development. The outcome has not been entirely up to expectations. At least two
problems are involved. Both have to do with the generally unclear relationship between state enterprise managers and their owners.[14]

The first problem, involving too much and poorly coordinated owner
intervention, tends to make successful performance difficult.[15] A recent
example to demonstrate the damaging effects of excessive government
interference is that of ZCCM in Zambia. This corporation is the dominant
foreign exchange earner in the country. Since the late 1970s, it has not
been able to retain the foreign currency needed for its own operations.

The result has been deterioration of plant and machinery, increasing operating costs and falling output levels.[16] In many cases, the owners cannot be clearly identified, and certainly do not speak with one voice. The state commonly exerts its ownership rights through a variety of individuals and institutions. There is bound to be a tendency for the owner representatives who happen to have the greatest influence at a particular time, to extract economic or political benefit to themselves, by pressuring the enterprise to interpret its objectives and operating rules in a particular way.

The second problem is that the blurred nature of the principal—agent relationship has allowed a number of state mineral enterprises to grow into powerful political and economic empires, unrestrained by government control and public accountability. Influential politicians were often put in charge as presidents of the large corporate structures taken over at nationalization. Their political clout permitted them to act with a much greater independence from, say, the ministry of finance, than was possible for the former foreign owners who could always be threatened by nationalization. The specialized ministry often became the spokesman of, rather than the instrument for government control over, the enterprises.[17]

Pertamina, the Indonesian state petroleum firm, provides perhaps the most striking example of lost government control. Its management undertook international borrowing on a very large scale, and implemented unwieldy diversification into transport and tourism, all on its own initiative. The government regained control only after it rescued this corporation from an impending bankruptcy. In Latin America, a large proportion of the foreign borrowing during the 1970s, that eventually resulted in the international debt crisis, was incurred by the state owned enterprises, without proper monitoring by the government.

Hence, quite contrary to the original intentions, the nationalizations and the establishment of state enterprises in many cases led to a reduction, rather than an increase, of effective government control.

Another very important motivation for nationalization has been governments' desire to reap the entire mineral rent. Under foreign ownership, a substantial part of that rent was dissipated abroad. The share of rent accruing to the nation did indeed increase strongly when firms were taken over from foreigners. Some dissipation abroad continued, because the newly established state owned firms often had to rely on foreign management contracts and a variety of consulting services, whose providers could extract monopolistic profits. More important, however, was the fact that the partly temporary, partly permanent inefficiencies typical of the state owned firms reduced the total amount of rent. Thus, although there was an increase in the share of the rent accruing to the government, this did not always involve a rise in public revenue in absolute terms.

Another cause for disappointments, at least in metal minerals, was the downward shift in real price levels that occurred about the mid-1970s. With the lower prices that have generally prevailed since that time, the ability to generate rent by the metal mineral industries in general shrank considerably. The return on the investments that the governments made when they compensated the former owners at takeover has turned out to be much below original expectations. In petroleum, of course, the OPEC cartel assured exceedingly remunerative price levels for more than one decade longer.

Zambia provides a drastic example of reduced public revenue after the nationalization of its copper industry. In the period of private ownership, 1965−70, the average copper price was $1.92/lb, and the annual government revenue amounted to $758 million on average (all money is expressed in constant 1980 dollars). In 1971−4, after government had taken over as the majority owner, copper price was $1.49/lb, but the public revenue declined to $438 million per year. Between 1975 and 1980 copper prices were quite low in a historical perspective, averaging out at $0.90/lb, and the income reaped by the government was no more than $30 million per year.[18] We have not attempted to ascribe the falling government revenue to declining copper prices and public ownership, respectively.

How has state ownership contributed to the non-commercial goals that the public enterprises were set to pursue? The evidence as well as the measure of comparison are not very clear on this count. Nationalization of most of the managerial functions after takeover has indubitably speeded up skill creation among the indigenes by giving them a broader exposure to managerial responsibilities than would likely have occurred with continued foreign ownership.

The state owned mineral enterprises have clearly also pursued a variety of social goals more energetically than could be expected from the private multinationals. Given the cost incurred by the firms in the pursuit of the non-commercial objectives, the net benefit to society of these endeavors is somewhat uncertain. Employment creation and regional development are certainly worthy social pursuits, but the question is whether the state mineral enterprises are suitable tools to use. For example, serious doubts can be expressed about the suitability of highly capital intensive and commercially oriented corporate organizations for increasing employment in poor societies. Asking the mineral firms simply to maximize profits, and creating more appropriate institutions for the work towards social goals, might well yield greater benefit to society than is attained under the prevailing arrangements.

Before ending this somewhat disillusioned assessment of the impact of state owned mineral enterprises on the national economy, it is worth repeating that we are dealing with an average, and that state owned firms come in many different shapes. For instance, CODELCO, the Chilean state owned copper corporation, has been given a clear-cut mandate by the government to maximize profits, and to leave the pursuit of social goals to others.

7.5 Implications for the international mineral markets

The explosive growth of the state enterprise universe in the mineral industries, and the trauma with which many of the state owned firms came into being, have given rise to widespread concerns, and a variety of claims and exhortations about the likely impact that this new supply agent may have on the international mineral markets.

One important worry has been that the widespread nationalizations in developing countries will result in inadequate mineral supply, with harmful consequences for user industries in importing countries.[19] The underlying argument is that state owned firms are so inefficient and so heavily taxed that their profits are not sufficient even for capacity maintenance.[20] An opposite concern has been that the excessive investments and inflexible response to price changes, characteristic of state mineral enterprises, will result in lower average prices and greater price variations, with severely detrimental consequences to the privately owned mineral industries.[21] No convincing empirical support has been provided to back up these claims.

Recent empirical research has delineated the behavioral features typical of state owned mineral firms, and the environment in which they operate, in a more systematic way. A gist of these findings was provided earlier in the chapter. These findings permit us to make inferences about the actual or potential impact that the public enterprises may have on the international mineral markets. These inferences are summarized in the following paragraphs.

The waves of nationalizations through the past decades had a strongly negative impact on the privately owned mineral industry. This impact was felt both at the micro-level of the individual firm, and at the industry-wide level. Decisions about state takeover were usually preceded by periods of very tense relations between the foreign mineral investor and the host government. Impressed by the impending risk of drastic government intervention, the foreign enterprises sometimes resorted to actions that hurt their own long-run interest. When they were implemented, nationalizations often involved painful amputations of the traditional sources of corporate raw material supply. At the industry-wide level, the nationalizations implied a substantial shrinkage of the market share of the private sector. With the virtual cessation of nationalizations since about 1980, this detrimental impact is no longer in force.

The rupture of the international vertical integration chains at the time of nationalization, and the unwillingness of the state owned firms to invest abroad has clearly reduced the extent of vertical integration, at least in the metal mineral industries. This has considerably widened the markets for commodities like bauxite and iron ore, where formerly a very high proportion of trade involved transactions within the vertically integrated firms. Many multinationals now have to rely much more on raw materials supply from independent sources. To these firms, the raw material supply conditions have become less predictable, but on the whole not necessarily inferior to what they were before. The price of raw materials purchased from independent producers varies much more than did the cost of output in wholly owned mines. Also, a much more active procurement effort is now required. But it is hard to find evidence that ruptured vertical integration has reduced the reliability of supply. And the greater degree of competition following from an expansion of trade between independent parties may well have reduced the cost of mineral raw materials. Nevertheless, in more recent years, many private mineral firms have taken up equity participation in predominantly state owned mining projects in developing countries, primarily to assure and stabilize their raw material supply needs.

We noted above that the setting up of state enterprise in the mineral industries carried a heavy cost. Throughout the past 30 years, the state owned enterprises, on average, suffered from increased operating cost levels, difficulties in utilizing existing capacity in full, and inability to expand capacity. Because of their inexperience and ensuing inefficiency, these firms cannot have represented any formidable competitive threat to the private mineral industry. As the state owned universe is becoming increasingly mature in the 1980s, its competitive disadvantage on this count is being reduced.

Because of the multiple goals that they often pursue, state owned mineral firms will tend to have permanently higher costs of production than equally endowed private companies. These higher costs are compensated in part by the availability of public financial guarantees and concessions, and importantly by the rich resource base possessed by many of the developing countries in which state ownership predominates. Only if the state owned firms represented the marginal supply of the industry would their inflated cost levels lead to higher mineral prices. Normally, the cost conditions would not impact on price, but just reduce the competitiveness of the state owned group.

The tendency to consider social benefit instead of corporate profit will often lower the marginal cost schedule and raise the demand schedule of state mineral firms. This will provide economic justification for higher capacity utilization at each level of mineral prices, and a lesser degree of output adjustment to varying market price levels. The lesser flexibility of supply, in turn, ought to lead to greater variation in price than would occur in the absence of state enterprises.

We have been unable to find important differences in investment behavior that might result in excessive supply, or general tendencies to shifts in, say, industry concentration, or the degree of competitiveness, in consequence of the emergence of the state enterprise group.

While our conjectures are firmly based on casual empiricism and are supported by economic logic, it is difficult to provide a definitive empirical vindication to any of them. The major problem is that reliable data are not available, but it may also be that the tendencies are not strong enough to be borne out unambiguously in formal tests. For instance, a detailed econometric analysis of the copper industry failed to confirm a lesser price sensitivity of supply in state owned than in privately owned industries, though it indicated that such sensitivity was lower in poor countries and especially in countries heavily dependent on copper exports.[22]

The emergent picture suggests that the state owned enterprises are somewhat pedestrian institutions. The claim that their inefficiency is so severe as to endanger the global mineral supply is clearly exaggerated. So is the opposite claim that these firms are dangerous predators whose perverse actions threaten the viability of the private mineral industry.

NOTES

1 M. Radetzki, *State Mineral Enterprises. An Investigation into Their Impact on the International Mineral Markets*, Resources for the Future, Washington DC, 1985.
2 R. H. Floyd, C. S. Gray and R. P. Short, *Public Enterprise in Mixed Economies, Some Macroeconomic Aspects*, IMF, Washington DC, 1984.
3 R. Prain, *Copper, the Anatomy of an Industry*, Mining Journal Books Ltd, London, 1975.
4 Radetzki, *State Mineral Enterprises*.
5 R. Vernon, *Two Hungry Giants, The United States and Japan in the Quest for Oil and Ores*, Harvard University Press, Cambridge, Mass., 1983, table 2.1; BP, *Statistical Review of World Energy*, annual, several issues.
6 World Bank, *World Development Report*, 1983 edition.
7 *Financial Times*, October 18, 1988.
8 Metallgesellschaft, "Pressmeldungen über die Metallmärkte", April 1988.
9 Radetzki, *State Mineral Enterprises*.
10 Shadow wage rates and rates of exchange are defined as those rates at which full employment and a balanced current account would be attained.
11 H. Leibenstein, "X-Efficiency and the Analysis of State Enterprise," paper presented at the Second BAPEG Conference on Public Enterprises in Mixed Economy LDCs, Boston, Mass., April 1980.
12 M. Gillis, "The Role of State Enterprises in Economic Development," *Social Research*, vol. 47, summer 1980.

13 R. Mikesell, *New Patterns of World Mineral Development*, British-North American Committee, London, 1979.
14 Y. Aharoni, "The State Owned Enterprise: An Agent Without a Principal," in L. Jones et al., *Public Enterprises in Developing Countries*, Cambridge University Press, Cambridge, 1982.
15 T. Wälde, "Third World Mineral Development: Current Issues," *Columbia Journal of World Business*, spring 1984.
16 I. Dobozi, "Emergence, Performance and World Market Impact of the State Mining Companies in Developing Countries," *Studies on Developing Economies*, No. 123, Institute for World Economics, Budapest, 1987.
17 Floyd, Gray and Short, *Public Enterprise in Mixed Economies*.
18 *Zambia Mining Yearbook*, Kitwe, Zimbabwe, various issues; World Bank, *Commodity Trade and Price Trends*, 1986 edition; IMF, *Financial Statistics*, yearbook, 1982.
19 Mikesell, *New Patterns of World Mineral Development*; *North—South, A Program for Survival* (The Brandt Report), Pan Books, London, 1980.
20 P. N. Giraud, *Géopolitique des ressources minières*, Economica, Paris, 1983.
21 Summaries of these views are found, for instance, in *Mining Journal*, December 9, 1983; or in Metallgesellschaft, "Pressmeldungen über die Metall-märkte", January 1984.
22 A. Markowski and M. Radetzki, "State Ownership and the Price Sensitivity of Supply: the Case of the Copper Mining Industry," *Resources Policy*, March 1987.

8

The Problems of Heavy National Dependence on Commodity Production and Exports

8.1 Measurement of commodity dependence

The degree of national dependence on primary commodities can be measured in a variety of ways. One can alternatively try to establish the share of the commodity sector in GDP, investments, employment, government income or exports. The nature of the production and consumption of a specific commodity will influence the level of the alternative measures. Among commodities accounting for an equal share of GDP, one that is capital intensive (petroleum extraction) will normally account for a higher share of investments and a lower share of employment than another that is labor intensive (coffee). All else alike, the share of government revenue will vary with the generation of rent in the production of a specific commodity. Even when dependence measured by the share of GDP or of employment is high, the export dependence could be limited if most of the commodity is consumed at home (rice).

The difficulties in defining commodities in a uniform way, discussed in chapter 1, also blur the assessments of commodity dependence. Such dependence is sometimes measured by considering the raw material extraction exclusively. This is the practice when the share of agriculture or minerals in GDP is measured.[1] In other cases the processing activity is also comprised. The export share measurements usually consider processed commodities like metals or butter and flour, along with their raw materials.[2] The inclusion of processed products will obviously increase the dependence figures.

These ambiguities notwithstanding, it is generally agreed that the developing countries are far more dependent on commodity production

Table 8.1 Share of major commodity groups in total exports in 1984 (percent)

	Manufactures	*Non-fuel*	*Fuels*
Industrialized market economies	68.3	22.1	7.8
Developing countries excl. OPEC	45.2	33.7	19.1
OPEC	3.6	4.2	91.9
Socialist countries excl China	43.4	14.6	32.9

Source: UNCTAD, *Handbook of International Trade and Development Statistics*, 1986

and trade than are the industrialized economies. Table 8.1 reveals that non-fuel primary commodities constituted more than one-third of the non-OPEC developing countries' exports, compared to only one-fifth in the industrialized market economies. The averages for the country aggregates, reflected in these figures, of course hide a much higher non-fuel commodity dependence of individual developing countries.

Another aspect of dependence, not revealed by the figures of table 8.1, is the degree of commodity concentration. In Malaysia, commodity exports dominate total exports, but the commodity basket comprises both food, agricultural raw materials, metals and minerals and fuels, so the economic prospects of the country cannot be seriously dented by the developments in any one commodity market. In Niger, in contrast, a single commodity, uranium, dominates total exports. That nation is therefore heavily exposed to the fortunes of that commodity.

Niger belongs to a group of so-called "monoeconomies", defined as countries whose national economies depend very heavily on the production and exports of a single commodity.

Uniform and systematic inter-country comparisons of the dependence on an individual commodity are hard to come by, except in the case of export shares. Table 8.2 lists 19 monoeconomies, defined as countries in which a single non-fuel commodity accounted for 50 percent or more of total exports in 1982–3.

The degree of export dependence measured in the table will vary over time, with the price of the commodity. The higher the relative price of the leading commodity, the greater will be its dominance in total exports. A larger number of sugar exporters would have been included in table 8.2

Table 8.2   Non-fuel monoeconomies: countries in which one commodity accounted for 50% or more of total 1982−3 exports

	Product	Export share (%)
Burundi	Coffee	82
Chad	Cotton	69
Cuba	Sugar	76
El Salvador	Coffee	54
Ethiopia	Coffee	62
Guinea	Baux./alumina	91
Iceland	Fish	66
Jamaica	Baux./alumina	64
Liberia	Iron ore	65
Malawi	Tobacco	57
Mauritania	Iron ore	50
Mauritius	Sugar	65
Niger	Uranium	74
Rwanda	Coffee	81
Somalia	Live animals	77
South Africa	Gold	50
Surinam	Baux./alumina	53
Uganda	Coffee	95
Zambia	Copper	90

Source: UNCTAD, *Handbook of International Trade and Development Statistics*, 1986

if the 1980−1 exports had been considered, for sugar prices were then more than twice as high as in the subsequent 2-year period.

With the exception of two somewhat special cases, Iceland and South Africa, all the non-fuel monoeconomies in table 8.2 are developing countries. All of them are also small. At higher levels of economic development, or with a large size of GDP, a single commodity will seldom dominate any important aspect of the national economy. The leading raw material exports from Australia (coal) and Canada (natural gas) in 1982−3 accounted for 14 and 6 percent only of the two countries' exports. The leading exports from two large developing economies, Brazil (coffee) and Thailand (rice) constituted no more than 11 and 14 percent of total exports.

Oil is exceptional among commodities. Because of its market size and the very high petroleum prices that prevailed in 1982−3, all OPEC countries are classed as monoeconomies on our definition. In these years, petroleum and petroleum products accounted for between 50 and 75 percent of total exports also in several non-OPEC countries, namely Brunei, Egypt, Mexico and Syria.[3]

The leading commodity will not only dominate exports, but will also play other important roles in monoeconomies. Thus, its share of GDP or employment will often exceed 10 percent, and it will easily account for 25 percent or more of government revenue.

A heavy dependence on commodities creates special complications − sometimes also opportunities − for national development. The resolution of these complications will require special policy actions, to avoid the traps that a one-sided commodity reliance could involve, but also to help realize the opportunities inherent in commodity production and trade. Problems of commodity dependence will emerge particularly stark in monoeconomies. In studying these problems and their policy solutions, we will therefore make many references to these economies.

The rest of this chapter is devoted to considering the major issues raised by high dependence on commodities in the exporting countries. Sections 2 through 5 discuss, in turn, the problems raised by commodity instability, extraction of fiscal revenue from commodity production and trade, the Dutch disease, and the exchange rate policies needed to maintain a balanced current account in the face of commodity price variations.

8.2 Export instability

We noted in chapter 3 on price formation that primary commodity prices tend to fluctuate much more than manufactures prices. Unless there are compensating variations in the quantities traded, we should therefore expect a greater variation in the export revenues of countries with a heavy commodity component in their exports.

This deduction is indeed corroborated by empirical evidence, at least at a high level of aggregation. Analyzing exports for the 1950s, 1960s, and 1970s for different country groups, MacBean and Nguyen conclude that instability, measured as the mean absolute deviation from the trend value of export revenue, was much lower in the 19 industrialized countries than in the 89 developing countries included in their sample, both for the period as a whole and for each decade separately. They also notice a persistently higher instability among poorer countries, when the LDC sample is divided into two sub-groups.[4]

A priori one would have expected to find an increasing instability with rising commodity concentration, on the assumption that fluctuations in individual commodity markets have a tendency to cancel out. A number of studies trying to explore the inferred relationship, have failed to confirm such a connection.[5] For example, MacBean's and Nguyen's measures of export revenue instability for a total of 108 countries, just quoted above, comprises 16 of the 19 monoeconomies listed in table 8.2, but the rank of these during the 1970s varies between 15 and 98, with an average of 50. This suggests that the monoeconomies did not experience a greater instability in export earnings than the sample average.

These counter-intuitive results are puzzling. The reason could be that the proceeds from commodities exported by countries with a high degree of commodity concentration tend to move in an offsetting fashion, but this argument has no bearing on monoeconomies, where only one commodity is involved. Another explanation could be that the commodity dependent countries tend to specialize in products with relatively stable export revenue flows. For instance, these could be commodities whose prices vary due to unstable supply (annual crops); at least for the major exporters, a reduced supply will tend to be compensated by higher prices, and so to even out the export proceeds.

To get a feel for the national significance of the instability in export revenue that can occur in monoeconomies, we can consider a case where the leading commodity accounts for 75 percent of exports and where total exports correspond to 25 percent of GDP. Then, if price doubles from one year to another, a not unusual development in commodity markets, the increase in export revenue will correspond to 19 percent of GDP. If price then falls again to the old level, the decline in the export revenue will correspond to 16 percent of GDP, on the assumption that the entire initial increase in export revenue was added to GDP, and more if the assumption does not hold. The impact will be even greater if export supply responds to the price changes.

These are not unrealistic numbers. Mainly as a result of coffee price changes, the total export proceeds of Burundi exploded in 1977 and collapsed in 1978. The shifts corresponded to about 12 percent and 14 percent of GDP. For similar reasons, the annual export proceeds in Niger and Zambia rose between 1978 and 1980 by amounts corresponding to 25 percent and 17 percent of GDP, but fell by almost the same percentage shares of GDP between 1980 and 1984.[6]

Even for countries that are not monoeconomies on our definition, the export revenue changes due to commodity dependence can be quite important in relation to the national economy. These changes, caused predominantly by international price variations, are unpredictable and, in the main, outside the control of the exporting countries. UNCTAD has recently assessed the impact on export revenue from the extended depression in non-fuel commodity markets in the early 1980s.[7] The UNCTAD study measures the difference between actual non-fuel commodity export revenue in 1980–4, and projections of that revenue, based on an extension of the actual 1970–80 trend. The average annual shortfalls in the 5-year period correspond to 2.6 percent of GDP in Chile, 5.8 percent in Costa Rica, 7.3 percent in Ghana, 8.4 percent in Guyana, 7.0 percent in Honduras, 8.9 percent in Ivory Coast, 4.2 percent in Jamaica, 10.1 percent in Liberia, 10.6 percent in Niger, 9.9 percent in Papua New Guinea, and 2.7 percent in Thailand. The shortfalls in individual years are of course substantially larger.

Are the numbers presented here big or small? An impression of their significance is obtained by comparing with the rise of the OECD countries' aggregate import bill in consequence of the oil price increases in 1973 and 1979. On each occasion, this rise corresponded to between 2 and 3 percent of the area's GDP, though of course the numbers were higher for individual OECD countries. In this perspective, the export instability experienced by many commodity dependent countries is extremely high.

Not only have existing studies been unable to confirm a positive relationship between commodity concentration and export instability; an equally counter-intuitive result of numerous research efforts is the failure to establish the negative effects of such instability on national development.

A priori, there are a number of strong grounds for the belief that such a relationship does exist. Most of these were spelled out succinctly in a now famous memorandum written in 1942 by Keynes.[8] When producer incomes vary in an irregular and unpredictable way, they will hamper a rational investment pattern in the commodity producing industry. What may seem a very good investment opportunity while prices are high, can turn out to be a loss-making venture when the price level drops. Such experiences will tend to discourage total investments. Export instability can also be expected to have a negative impact on the macroeconomy, through such variables as imports, savings, employment and government revenue. By creating uncertainty, instability will also impede national planning, and require the maintenance of higher exchange reserves which could otherwise have been put to alternative use. The painful and extended adjustments in the OECD economies in response to the changing petroleum prices in the 1970s, involving a sharp drop in productivity increase, and a sizable decline in economic growth rates, suggest the nature of difficulties confronting commodity exporting countries in consequence of the violent fluctuations of their export revenue.

Yet, research on the subject has not confirmed these a priori suppositions. Quoting ten studies published between 1962 and 1983, Behrman notes that only five yield a significant negative association between export instability and GDP growth, while one finds a positive connection between the two. The author concludes that the studies do not provide a robust relationship, either negative or positive, between primary commodity export instability on the one hand, and growth or growth related variables like investments, investment income or savings, on the other.[9] It could be that the research approaches have not been perceptive enough to reveal the relationship, or, as Behrman suggests, that the problems in empirical estimates have obscured the negative effects.

Despite the inconclusive analytical results, export instability has since long been an important policy issue. At the international level, it has aroused two responses, namely the establishment of commodity agreements and compensatory finance schemes. At the national level, several commodity dependent countries have created financial buffer institutions to help overcome some of the difficulties raised by export instability. Each will be discussed in turn.

International commodity agreements have a long parentage.[10] In his 1942 memorandum, Keynes proposed the establishment of a series of interlinked buffer stocks for the main internationally traded commodities, with finance to be provided from what eventually became the International Monetary Fund.[11] These ideas were never implemented, but in 1976, UNCTAD launched a proposal for an Integrated Program for Commodities,[12] much along the lines of Keynes's ideas. It was felt that the links would save on the financial resources needed for buffer stock operation. Given the lack of synchronization in commodity price movements, the financial resources used to prop up coffee prices could be shifted, for instance towards the defence of a falling copper price, when coffee quotations strengthened. Like Keynes's ideas, the UNCTAD proposal has so far not been put to practical use.

In fact, only a handful of individual commodities have been covered by international agreements in the period since the Second World War. In the most recent decades, all the agreements have had several common features. Thus, they have all operated under the auspices of UNCTAD. They have had an equal representation of producing and consuming interests. The proclaimed aim has been to stabilize prices. Buffer stocks and/or export restrictions have been the tools used.

The problems of commodity dependent countries arise from excessive export revenue fluctuations, not from unstable raw materials prices *per se*, and international commodity agreements that aim at stabilizing prices will not necessarily contribute to a steadier export revenue flow. Price stabilization will normally reduce export revenue volatility only when the instability is induced by fluctuating demand. This would usually be the case for minerals and metals whose demand depends on business cycle variations. In figure 8.1, stabilization of price at P_2 will even out the revenue variation between P_3Q_3 during boom and P_1Q_1 during recession, to P_2Q_2 throughout the cycle. When price instability is caused by shifts in supply, as is true for most food products whose output depends on weather variations, stabilization of prices may in fact destabilize export earnings. In figure 8.2, prices move inversely to quantities, and variations

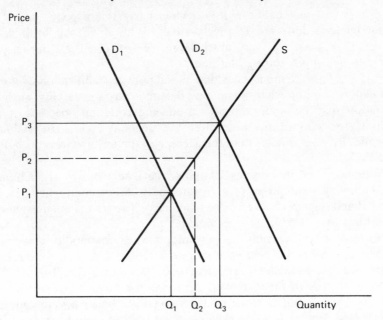

Figure 8.1   Price stabilization with variable demand

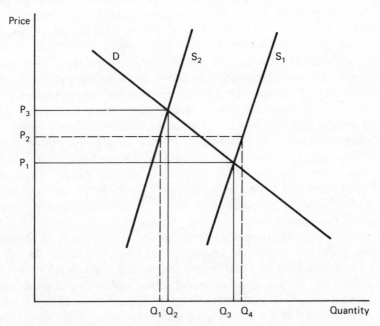

Figure 8.2   Price stabilization with variable supply

in export revenue, between P_1Q_3, when harvests are good, and P_3Q_2, when harvests fail, are relatively small. With price stabilized at P_2, however, revenue will vary much more, or between P_2Q_4 during good harvests, and P_2Q_1 during bad ones.

Figure 8.1 also demonstrates that although price stabilization does even out export revenue when fluctuating demand causes instability, such stabilization may be undesirable to producing countries, because it also reduces the sum of revenues over the demand cycle. The stabilized revenue, P_2Q_2, is smaller than the average of the unstable revenues, P_3Q_3 and P_1Q_1.

Note, however, that figures 8.1 and 8.2 have been drawn with a number of simplifying assumptions (e.g. linear supply and demand schedules, and parallel and regular shifts of these schedules). The results obtained above, therefore, do not have general validity.[13]

No more than five fully fledged international commodity agreements with binding economic clauses, i.e. those for cocoa, coffee, natural rubber, sugar and tin, have been operative since the mid-1970s. Two of them became defunct in the mid-1980s, the one for tin because of the 1985 debacle when its buffer stock manager could not honor his commitments to buy (see chapter 6 on producer cartels), and the one for sugar which was not renewed on expiry in 1984. All five agreements have aimed at keeping the price within a predetermined band which was adjusted at irregular intervals. The cocoa and rubber agreements have been operating with the help of buffer stocks whose purchases added to demand to boost low prices, and whose sales added to supply to depress high prices. The coffee and sugar agreements tried to keep prices within the band by regulating supply through export quotas. The tin agreement used export restrictions as a reinforcement to its buffer stock operations.[14]

Several factors explain the limited enthusiasm for establishing and operating international commodity agreements. Quota allocations in the case of export restrictions have often involved controversies among the producing countries. They have also tended to conserve the historical production pattern, to the detriment of new, low-cost producers. A fundamental reason for the weak support by the commodity dependent developing countries is probably that the operations of the agreements have had only an indirect, and highly uncertain impact on export revenue instability, the major concern of these countries.

The consuming and producing interests in the agreements have obviously had divergent views about the level of prices to be defended. The agreements were intended to stabilize prices around some kind of market equilibrium, but there are genuine and severe difficulties in establishing and forecasting that equilibrium. Despite occasional gains from buffer stock transactions, the schemes have regularly incurred net operational costs. The importing/consuming countries' willingness to share these costs, and to provide part of the finance needed for buffer stock operations, has been lukewarm.

The consuming side claimed, correctly, that the agreements, as structured, had no means to prevent price rises above the band, after the buffer had been depleted, or all export quotas removed. Representatives of the importing countries have also expressed concern that the agreements sometimes had a tendency to raise, rather than stabilize prices. This was undoubtedly true for the tin agreement in the years before its collapse. It has also been claimed to be true of the coffee agreement, where the politically motivated acceptance of higher prices by the United States, the most important consumer member, made the agreement a vehicle for income transfers to the producing countries.[15]

Looking at the history of the agreements, it is also clear that they have not been particularly successful even in their limited objective of maintaining prices within the predetermined bands.[16] The resources in the hands of the agreements, and the preparedness of the member nations to take necessary action, have apparently been inadequate, given the strength of the market forces at play.

In contrast to commodity agreements, the existing **compensatory finance schemes** respond much more pointedly to the problem of export revenue instability. Their aim is precisely to compensate for shortfalls in the export revenues of individual countries. Two such schemes are in operation in the late 1980s.

The Compensatory Finance Facility of the International Monetary Fund was established in 1963, but its activities became quantitatively important only after 1975.[17] Though lending is not directly related to commodity trade, in practice a large part of the financial flow is directed to developing countries whose exports are dominated by commodities. IMF's member countries can obtain bridging finance under this facility, to cover temporary shortfalls in overall export earnings, largely due to factors beyond their control. To be eligible for drawings under this facility, member countries have to satisfy IMF's criteria on policy cooperation. The maximum borrowing has always been related to the borrowing country's quota in the IMF.[18] In the mid-1980s, the limit amounted to 83 percent of the quota. The global potentially available financial resources exceed $20 billion.

The export shortfalls to be covered under this facility are calculated in SDR (Special Drawing Rights), as the negative difference between the exports in a given year, and the geometric average export proceeds in the 5-year period centered on that year. To assess the shortfall, therefore, forecasts have to be made of the exports 2 years into the future. Interest is paid on the loans received, and repayment is ordinarily required in the third to fifth year after drawing, or earlier if the country's export revenues improve substantially.

In 1980–6, 69 countries borrowed a total of about $10 billion under this facility. Of these countries, 52 had a non-fuel commodities share in total exports of 50 percent or more. These countries accounted for 65 percent of the total drawings.[19]

Studies of the IMF's compensatory finance facility suggests that the impact of its operations on the actual export instability of client countries, though statistically significant, has been so small that it hardly warrants the economic costs involved in such lending.[20] Two problems seem to be involved. The first is the calculation of shortfalls from the 5-year average trend. The 2-year forecast on which this trend is based, often contains large errors. The estimated shortfalls on which payments are made, therefore, deviate from actual shortfalls. The second, and probably more serious problem is that years of shortfall can well coincide with repayment obligations. This will occur if the export revenue falls for a number of years, for then the formula used will yield a shortfall in every year. For instance, in 1986, a number of countries drew on the facility to compensate for shortfalls in export revenue, but at the same time their repayment obligations due to earlier drawings absorbed even larger sums.[21]

The second scheme for stabilization of export earnings, STABEX, is operated by the European Economic Community. It is much smaller, has a more narrow geographical reach, and works according to rules that differ considerably from those of the IMF facility. STABEX was established in the mid-1970s. The beneficiaries are more than 60 developing countries associated with the EEC under the Lomé conventions. Nearly all of them are former colonies of some EEC countries. Compensation payments are tied in most cases to shortfalls in the revenue from exports to the EEC of individual agricultural products. The shortfall is measured as the difference between export earnings in the actual year, and the average of exports during the preceding 4 years. The concessionary element in STABEX payments is much greater than in the IMF facility. No interest is charged. Reimbursements are conditional on the recovery of prices, volumes, and export earnings for the commodity, and are made in five annual installments following a 2-year grace period. Requirements to repay may be waived if the market recovery does not materialize. The STABEX transfers to 23 "least developed" countries participating in the scheme are made as grants without repayment obligations.

Since the inception of the scheme, three commodity groups, groundnuts, coffee and cocoa at different levels of processing, have accounted for almost two-thirds of the amounts transferred. The amounts set aside for STABEX payments in the 1980–4 period amounted to less than $1 billion. Actual payments exhausted all the available resources.[22]

It is clear from the above descriptions of the IMF and EEC schemes that the existing international compensatory finance facilities provide a highly incomplete and not always very effective insurance against export revenue instabil:ty in commodity dependent countries. This is why some developing courtries which rely heavily on commodity exports have instituted **domestic arrangements** to shield the commodity producers or the government from the instability of international commodity markets.

State marketing boards were set up decades ago in many developing countries with the objective to protect domestic producers of agricultural commodities from excessive price variations in the international markets. Many of these agencies became statutory monopsonies, and developed into fiscal instruments to extract public revenue from the agricultural sector, with stabilization evolving into an unimportant side objective. Examples of wide wedges between the international price at which the produce is sold, and the prices offered by the boards to agricultural producers include groundnuts and cocoa in Nigeria, coffee in Tanzania and Uganda, and, until recently, a number of staple foods in Zaire.[23]

In the 1980s there has been a marked policy shift in the activities of many state marketing boards back to the objective of price stabilization. An interesting instance is the change in the policies of Papua New Guinea's "buffer funds" for cocoa and coffee.[24] From having acted mainly as the government's tax collector, the funds are more recently intended to function mainly as price stabilizers. The cocoa fund does so by taxing or subsidizing exports by an amount equal to half the difference between the actual international price and the 10-year moving average of that price. Producer price fluctuations thus split the difference between fast-changing world prices and slower changes in the moving average. The rules for the coffee fund are somewhat more complex, since it is also responsible for Papua New Guinea's export controls and stock holding obligations under the International Coffee Agreement.

Both funds are supposed to be self-financing, with subsidies cancelled out by export taxes. This, of course, presupposes a stagnant long-run international price trend. If, in fact, the price trends turn out to be downward-sloping, for instance on account of productivity improvements in the two industries, the policies will involve continuous producer subsidizations. This is not a feasible government policy where the commodity holds a dominant position in the national economy.

Other domestic arrangements adopted by some countries have the purpose of stabilizing the government revenue from commodity production. Again, an example from Papua New Guinea is illustrative.[25] In 1974, when the country became strongly dependent on the exports of copper and gold, the government decided to establish a Mineral Resources Stabilization Fund, and decreed that all government revenue from ongoing mining activity, including income tax, dividend withholding tax and dividend on government equity, be paid into the fund. Withdrawals, to be credited to the government budget, were to be set at stable levels which at the same time ensured the long-run financial viability of the fund.

The withdrawal rules required forecasts of the fund's revenue, to show that the actual withdrawals made in each year did not exceed a maximum that could be continued unchanged in real terms for 5 years into the future, without exhausting the fund. The forecasts needed before withdrawal levels could be established included not only the metal prices, but also anticipated operating results of the mining companies, changes in the taxation regime, and the interest earnings of the fund.

The fund's actual performance has had a moderately stabilizing impact on the government budget. Between 1978 and 1987, the instability of the outflows was about one-third less than that of the inflows. But the problems of establishing a mean around which to stabilize are amply illustrated by the fact that the maximum allowable withdrawals calculated each year have varied as much as the inflows to the fund.

Another fundamental problem of stabilization is demonstrated by the older attempts in Zambia at the time of its independence in the mid-1960s, to stabilize the government revenue from copper, the dominant commodity in its national economy. Copper prices were exceedingly high in these years, and the amounts set aside for use in more meager years grew at explosive rates. There quickly evolved a perception that the current prices were perhaps not excessive, but rather represented a sustainable long-run average. From this perception followed extremely strong political pressures that the funds put aside be immediately used for the many urgent development tasks. The Finance Ministry, which operated the scheme, was unable to resist the pressures, and when prices fell and government revenues from copper contracted in the late 1960s, there were no reserves to even out the government budget.

The key problems of national instability caused by high commodity dependence are as old as Joseph's advice to the Pharaohs, and simple to summarize: when harvests vary, set aside from fat years for consumption in meager years. High reliance on commodities with unstable supply, demand and price can seriously destabilize the national economy. Efforts to even out prices and revenues may therefore often be appropriate and worthwhile. If the stabilization actions are to gain credibility, however, considerable resources have to be put aside. Historical evidence suggests that stabilization schemes typically involve a cost that can often be substantial. Furthermore, the averages and trends of the series to be stabilized are extremely hard to forecast. Actions which *ex ante* may appear as purposeful for the attainment of stabilization, can easily turn out to have effects quite opposite to their intentions. The costs, difficulties and disappointing results probably explain the somewhat limited enthusiasm for efforts to stabilize commodity markets and commodity revenues, both at the international and national level.

8.3 Extraction of fiscal revenue

An economy which is heavily dependent on the production and trade of a particular commodity will ordinarily have to rely on that commodity for a large part of its fiscal revenue. The two issues that have to be resolved are (a) how much revenue can be obtained, and (b) what should be the form of taxation, in order not to kill nor weaken the milking cow.

The public sector share of GDP in most developing countries, including the major commodity producers, was quite low in the early 1960s. It experienced a very substantial expansion during the following two decades, as the increasingly emancipated government administrations of these countries enhanced their ambitions to establish physical and social infrastructure facilities, promote national entrepreneurship, and contribute to development in other ways. The public expenditure expansion had to be financed by increased tax revenues. Where the commodity sector was dominant, it was seen as a natural source for a large part of the revenue needs. The overall fiscal burden became so onerous in many countries, that it led to a stagnation or decline of commodity production and trade, in absolute or relative terms. The extractable fiscal revenue ceased to grow or contracted in consequence.

The maximum fiscal extraction policy compatible with unchanged output is one where all revenue above the variable cost of production is creamed away, leaving no return at all to the invested capital. So long as the variable costs are covered, it will be economical to maintain production in existing facilities. This policy is feasible only in the short run, however. Its consequence would be a complete cessation of capacity expansion and capacity maintenance, and so output would soon start to contract.

In the long run, the resource rent is an important determinant for how much revenue the taxman can take from commodity production, without harming the tax base. The resource rent is that part of profit which is attributable to the superior quality of the land, climate or mineral deposit, over the marginal quality of these resources used in the production of a commodity. Superior resource bases, consisting of conveniently located fertile soils which enjoy a favorable climate and rich mineral deposits, have provided a strong comparative advantage to a number of countries in the production of various commodities. The resource rents generated by these activities have made them by far the most important sources for tax in many nations.

In principle, the entire resource rent can be taxed away without impairing the long-run viability of commodity production. If the costly North Sea oil deposits represent the marginal oil production, then any cost advantage due to the superior deposits in, say, Saudi Arabia or Indonesia, can be taxed away, leaving the investors in these countries with no more than the normal return on capital investments, i.e. about the same as that obtained by the North Sea investors. A moral argument in favor of appropriating the entire resource rent through tax has often been forwarded. This is that the resource rent represents the superior natural endowment of the nation. The state, as the representative of the nation, should therefore have a first right to this rent.

In practice, the determination and extraction of resource rents raises many difficulties. For instance, a reduction in global demand, or technical progress, which result in price declines, will normally lead to closure of the highest cost units, and so reduce the size of rent throughout the industry. High profitability could be due not to a superior resource base, but to the monopolistic supply of superior management or technology which may cease to be available unless it is allowed to keep its returns. Extraction of the full resource rent also requires that the costs of each production unit are analyzed in detail, which is a difficult undertaking. Partial extraction of the rent is therefore the most that can be accomplished, if one wants to avoid causing long-run harm to the industry.

The fiscal regimes applicable to commodities in monoeconomies and other commodity dependent countries tend to give an impression of complex and confusing structures which are difficult to disentangle and hard to compare. On closer scrutiny, however, most of the fiscal provisions can be categorized as variations of three alternative measures used by governments to obtain revenue from the commodity sectors.[26]

The first measure, **the royalty**, extracts the fiscal dues on the basis of production, or sales or exports. Royalties come in many different forms. They can be shaped as a levy per ton produced, or per dollar sold. Especially for agricultural products, they are often imposed by state marketing boards to which the farmers are compelled to sell, in the form of a difference between the export price obtained by the board, and the price offered to the producers. In the case of minerals, royalties often have the more straightforward form of export taxes. Royalties are regularly regarded as the prime tool for extracting the resource rent. This provides the rationale for differentiating royalty rates between products and production units, depending on the quality of the resources that are being exploited.

Royalties have the important advantage of easy assessment and application. They also afford the government with a relatively stable revenue, since production and sales ordinarily vary much less than profits. This advantage must be weighed against the harmful consequences of this fiscal tool. To producers, royalties constitute additions to cost, which have to be paid irrespective of profit levels. A high royalty can easily wipe out the entire profit, or even impose losses, when pre-tax profits are low. Producers will therefore avoid ventures with less than exceptional profits prospects, or with cyclical price and profit patterns, since the viability of such projects will be continuously or recurrently impaired by high royalties. The less outstanding resource endowments which could support commodity production with only normal profitability will not be developed at all when royalties are high.

Although we deal here with the imposition of royalties by individual countries on their own, it is important to note that royalties have been used on several occasions to implement international monopolistic co-ordination, most notably in the case of OPEC. Prior to the nationalization of the oil producing installations, sales taxes were predominantly used by the OPEC countries to raise export prices. The same was true of the monopolistic effort by the Caribbean countries to raise bauxite prices in the mid-1970s (see chapter 6 on producer cartels).

The second measure, the **profits tax**, extracts the fiscal dues on the basis of profits, i.e. on the income that remains after deducting all costs of production. Withholding taxes (e.g. on dividends, or on professional fees, paid abroad) are usually regarded as part of the profits tax system. A major variation among profits taxes concerns the specification of allowable costs. Another variation is between proportional and progressive profits taxes. One approach in designing a progressive profits tax is through an "additional profits tax." By creaming off a substantial proportion of profits that are considered "above normal," the additional profits tax can be employed as a substitute to royalties for appropriating resource rents.

While avoiding some of the problems with royalties, profits taxes are much more difficult to impose and assess, especially when producers are many and small. Profits taxes also yield a far greater variation in public revenue than royalties, notably when an additional profits tax forms part of the fiscal structure.

The third measure for fiscal extraction is through provisions affording **public ownership positions** in the production activity, for free or on concessional terms. Public ownership for fiscal extraction is often employed when it is felt that neither royalties nor profits taxes provide adequate tools for capturing the resource rent.

The extent of fiscal extraction through public ownership depends entirely on the degree of concessionality through which that ownership was ac-quired. Ownership participation resembles the profits tax in that it assures the government of a share of the profit, so long as a profit is earned. But although public ownership may be desired on other grounds, it is an opaque tool for fiscal extraction, especially because of the costly legal or moral obligations that may arise with an ownership role. Furthermore, as noted in the preceding chapter, because of the inefficiencies characteristic of many state enterprises, the involvement of government as owner often leads to a reduction of the size of the overall resource rent.

Private investors have had varying attitudes to public ownership acquisitions on concessional terms. In the 1950s and 1960s they regularly regarded such government involvement as undesirable in principle, because of the perceived dilution of managerial control. More recently, many investors have been favorably inclined to a degree of government participation, because they saw such partnership as an assurance of fair treatment to themselves.

Parenthetically it may be noted that the production sharing agreements practised, among others, by Indonesia in its relation with financiers and managers from Japan or the USSR are akin to concessional ownership positions. Under these, the government remained the sole owner, while the foreigners financed the investment and ran the operations in return for a share of the output.

There is a tradeoff between the size and form of the fiscal burden. While the producers may prefer one fiscal tool to another, a fiscal package using unpopular tools may nevertheless appear preferable if it involves a lesser overall tax burden.

Royalties, frequently imposed in the shape of price controls or overvalued exchange rates, have dominated the taxation of agricultural commodities. The primary reason is the administrative difficulties in imposing profits taxes on large groups of small-scale agricultural producers. The small scale and predominantly national ownership also explains why public ownership in agricultural production has been quite limited.

In many cases, the government impositions on agricultural commodity production have been excessive in the sense that they resulted in a shrinkage in the relative or even absolute levels of output, especially if other countries provided the producers with less onerous fiscal regimes. From the early 1960s to the early 1980s, Ghana's share of the world cocoa market shrank from 40 percent to 14 percent, that of Nigeria from 18 percent to 11 percent, as a result of heavy export taxes. At the same time, Ivory Coast, with much more favorable fiscal treatment of its cocoa producers, expanded its share from 9 percent to 26 percent. Admittedly, part of this increase was accomplished through the exports of cocoa that had been smuggled out of Ghana. Differences in fiscal treatment also explain why in the same years the share of Nigeria and Zaire in the world palm oil market shrank from 48 percent to virtually zero, while that of Malaysia expanded from 18 percent to 71 percent. Overtaxing lost Egypt half its international market share in cotton, while Sri Lanka saw its world market share of tea dwindle from one-third to one-fifth. Kenya, which treated its tea producers more fairly, saw its share triple to 9 percent during the same period.[27] The declines in fiscal bases undoubtedly came as disappointments to the governments of the high-tax countries.

In the case of minerals, the fiscal menu has been much more varied, but, for historical or other reasons, the emphasis on the respective tools has varied considerably among countries.[28] Royalties have been applied in some measure by most mineral exporting countries. Concessionally acquired public ownership positions have been quite common, though the reasons for these acquisitions usually went beyond fiscal concerns (see chapter 7). The administrative sophistication of the mineral enterprises made the application of profits taxes reasonably practical.

Excessive fiscal ambitions slowed down or arrested the expansion of the mineral industries in some countries. This was true, for instance, of Zambia and Peru, though other factors also contributed. Very high royalty impositions by some Canadian provinces in the early 1970s virtually arrested all mineral exploration efforts in these territories, but there was no visible impact on mineral output because the royalties were soon withdrawn. The internationally coordinated efforts of the oil and bauxite producers to increase prices through export taxes substantially reduced the demand for their output, with a lag. In the weak mineral markets of the 1980s, there has been a reversal of earlier fiscal trends. Some of the leading mineral exporting countries have attempted to attract foreign investments by offering internationally more competitive fiscal arrangements.

Monoeconomies and other countries heavily dependent on commodity production and exports have to tread a difficult balance in designing their fiscal systems. On the one hand the governments need fiscal revenue to cover public recurrent and investment expenditures, and the commodity sector is their major revenue source. Lax taxation of oil in the Middle East and bauxite in the Caribbean in the 1960s resulted in very meager national benefit to the countries producing these commodities. On the other hand, they have to be cautious in the determination of the overall fiscal burden, and in the selection of fiscal instruments. The instances of agricultural shrinkage, listed above, point to the potential dangers. Faulty decisions in these two respects have proved counterproductive in many cases.

Most of the instances of overtaxed and shrinking commodity production quoted above were the result of misconceived expectations about the primary sector's ability to generate public revenue. However, there may be cases where excessive fiscal burdens are imposed precisely for the purpose of diminishing what is considered an excessive commodity dependence of the national economy. The market instability of the dominant commodity may be felt overly onerous. The country's competitive advantage in the commodity may have contracted, or the commodity market may be in a structural depression, so that there is little likelihood for large and sustainable private or public revenue generation. In such circumstances, the policy could have the explicit purpose of reducing the importance of the sector through fiscal squeeze, and of encouraging diversification by an expenditure policy that promotes, say, manufacturing, or other commodities with more dynamic market prospects.

Surprisingly, fiscal squeeze aimed at reducing commodity dominance and at promoting diversification is sometimes urged for precisely the opposite reason, i.e. when the commodity sector has an outstanding ability to generate resource rent and fiscal revenue. This is the subject of the next section.

8.4   The "Dutch disease"

The term "Dutch disease" was coined in the late 1970s, to describe the economic dislocations, and especially the deindustrialization that tend to afflict countries which hit a resource-based bonanza. This may be through opening up large-scale, export oriented and highly profitable resource projects, or through a rise in the profitability of existing production because of a strong and lasting price increase caused by a boost in demand, or by monopolistic supply intervention. Though it normally involves mineral commodities, the Dutch disease can equally be based on booming agricultural products like sugar, coffee or rubber.

In a way, the concept is a misnomer. For although the Netherlands did experience some economic dislocation in consequence of the country's large income from the export of gas through the 1970s, the syndrom occurred earlier, and had a much greater impact on several other national economies. Long ago, the booms in guano and sugar caused serious dislocation in the Chilean and Cuban economies. More recently, the cases of Zambia (copper), Niger (uranium), Colombia (coffee) and Nigeria, Saudi Arabia and Norway (oil) come to mind. One may also object to the term "disease," since the additional income provides a potential for increased national welfare, as well as the means for overcoming any undesirable consequences that may arise.

To explore the macroeconomics of the Dutch disease,[29] it is instructive to subdivide the national economy into three sectors, namely, (a) the booming commodity sector, (b) the sector where other tradables are produced, whether for export markets, or as substitutes for imports, to satisfy domestic demand, and (c) the sector for non-tradables, goods and services that are not amenable to international trade.

The earnings from the commodity boom invariably result in a substantial increase in the demand for tradable as well as non-tradable goods and services. The price of tradable goods is basically determined outside the country, and so is not affected by the commodity boom. Increases in demand will be satisfied by expanded supply through imports which are perfectly price elastic (the booming country is assumed to account for a small share of world imports). By contrast, the supply of non-tradables is limited by the domestic production capacity, so their price will tend to be pushed up by the expanding domestic demand. The shift in relative prices between tradables and non-tradables makes domestic production of tradables less attractive. Hence, their output declines, and a greater proportion of domestic demand is satisfied through imports.

The shrinkage of the tradables sector is reinforced as the booming commodity activity attracts labor and other inputs by bidding up their price. The high profits in the booming commodity production permit it to absorb the higher costs and yet remain internationally competitive. The tradable sector, in contrast, has no excess profits which could absorb the input cost increase. Hence, its international competitiveness is weakened.

In more normal circumstances, the rising prices of non-tradables and the increased costs throughout the economy would weaken the current account and force through a devaluation. This in turn would restore the international competitiveness of the tradables sector. With the booming commodity, exports and the current account develop strongly, with no need to devalue. The result is an increasing overvaluation of the domestic currency.

The ultimate consequence of the disease is a withering of manufacturing and the non-booming commodity output, an increasing dependence on imports, and an expanded dominance of the booming commodity in the national economy.

Nigeria provides an interesting case study. Before the oil price increases of the early 1970s, the country was self-sufficient in food, and a sizable exporter of agricultural commodities. The high petroleum prices and export incomes in the late 1970s and early 1980s led to an inflationary boom that resulted in an increasing overvaluation of the country's currency. The agricultural sector lost much of its international competitiveness. Agricultural exports dwindled. Food imports substituted increasingly for a shrinking domestic food production. There was no pressure to restore competitiveness through devaluation, because the booming petroleum export revenue assured a positive current account. Neither was there any urgency to arrest the Dutch disease. Petroleum prices were believed to follow a permanent upward path in real terms, and the petroleum industry was seen as a lasting generator of high and rising income for Nigerian society. There was little anticipation of, and preparation for, the oil price collapse of the mid-1980s.

Why is it that the comfortable life afforded by the booming commodity often raises concerns and proposals for policies to restore a more balanced economic structure? Most, but not all, of the reasons rest on the fear that the booming conditions may not last. Some economic or technical change in market conditions could reduce demand and so end the commodity boom. For example, the producers' monopolistic power could be weakened by forthcoming new production, with an ensuing price collapse. The emergence of substitute materials might undermine the profitability of the booming commodity. Or, in the case of minerals, the resource base could be exhausted, leading to declining output. When the boom comes to an end, there will be little else on which to support the national economy, and the tradable sector that was destroyed in the first place, may take a long time to rebuild, especially under the depressed conditions that will ensue.

Other reasons for concern about the Dutch disease have to do with the dualism that often follows in the wake of the commodity boom. Where the booming commodity is produced by capital intensive means, for example, the extraction of petroleum or the production of nickel, the withering of the tradable sector will often result in unemployment problems, because of the limited ability of the booming sector to absorb the labor that becomes redundant. Unless forceful measures for income redistribution are implemented, the national economy risks becoming highly dualist, with a poor hinterland existing besides the booming and rich commodity sector.

In an initial step, the policy remedies all involve the removal of a substantial part of the profits from the booming sector. This reduces its expansion. It also limits the conspicuous consumption and waste that is often connected with new riches.

A follow-up policy step involves the use of the resources extracted from the booming sector. There are basically two options. First, the resources can be employed for subsidizing the uncompetitive tradable sector, so as to assure its survival. And secondly, they may be employed for the build-up of reserves to carry the nation through after the boom has ended.

Interesting tradeoffs that go beyond economics and have no self-evident right or wrong answers present themselves in the efforts to tackle the Dutch disease. What additional income is the country willing to forfeit in the effort to restrict the booming sector expansion? And what criteria should be used when investing the booming sector revenues in other tradable activities? Most would agree that subsidization of wheat production in the desert of Saudi Arabia to an extent that yields export surpluses is going a bit too far. That is easy. In other cases, the borderline between appropriate and inappropriate action in this area may be much harder to agree upon.

8.5   Exchange rate policies in commodity dependent economies

It was noted in the preceding section that there is a tendency for countries with a booming commodity sector to experience currency overvaluation. That overvaluation could come about without any nominal exchange rate change, simply because inflation is faster than inflation in the rest of the world.

A change in a country's real exchange rate, against the US dollar to be precise, measures the change in the cost level of that country, expressed in dollars, against the change in the cost level in the United States. This can be illustrated by considering a hypothetical case. Suppose that in 1984 it cost 10,500 Chilean pesos to produce one ton of copper. At an exchange rate of 10 pesos to the dollar, this corresponded to 1,050 dollars. Since the cost to produce copper in the United States was only 1,000 dollars, the Chilean competitive position was somewhat weak.

Suppose further that between 1984 and 1986 the peso costs in Chile increased by 40 percent while the dollar costs in the United States rose by 10 percent, but that Chile devalued, with 15 pesos equal to one dollar at the new exchange rate.

After these changes the cost to produce copper in Chile in 1986 will be 14,700 pesos, equal to 980 dollars, while in the United States the cost will be 1,100 dollars, with Chilean competitiveness substantially strengthened. The real Chilean devaluation equals the change in the ratio of Chilean/ US costs, expressed in dollars. As is apparent from the numerical tabulation below, the ratio will have fallen from 1.05 to 0.89, implying a real devaluation of 15.2 percent.

	Chile	USA	Chile/USA$ ratio
1984	10,500 P = $1,050	$1,000	1.05
1986	14,700 P = $980	$1,100	0.89

The primary rationale for real devaluation is to reduce a current account deficit. This is accomplished through strengthened competitiveness of exports as well as of the import competing output sold in the domestic market. A real devaluation will therefore normally have the effect of stimulating exports and discouraging imports at the same time.

Monoeconomies and other countries heavily dependent on the production and export of commodities whose prices vary in a synchronized manner, are likely to record current account surpluses during the high price periods, and deficits when prices are low. If prices and export revenues moved according to a reasonably regular cycle, the current account instability could be countered with the help of exchange reserves, international borrowing, or with the IMFs compensatory finance facility.

This, however, is generally not the case. Many commodity dependent countries did employ these stabilization tools in the early 1980s, in the belief that the low commodity prices in those years constituted a temporary trough. However, as time passed, and after they became heavily indebted to the rest of the world, it became clear that the commodity price depression was so durable that temporary stabilization measures were of little help.

Since then, many of the commodity dependent nations have implemented sizable real devaluations in an effort to come to grips with the swelling current account deficits resulting not only from low commodity prices, but increasingly also from the expanding service costs for their foreign debt. For example, between 1980 and the first half of 1987, the real devaluation against the US dollar was, in round numbers, 25 percent in Brazil, 30 percent in the Philippines, 40 percent in Turkey and Colombia, 50 percent in Chile, and even more in Zaire and Zambia.[30]

The exchange rate policies implemented by the commodity dependent countries in the 1980s raise a number of issues to which there are no clear-cut answers.

First, what are the prospects that the improvement in competitiveness gained through real devaluation can be maintained over time? One effect of devaluation is that all import prices, including the prices of imported inputs in commodity production, will rise. The change in competitiveness is dependent on reduced dollar payments to the domestic factors of production. The domestic share in total production cost is often limited, especially in small underdeveloped countries. Devaluation must then be quite sizable to have a perceptible impact on competitiveness. A further problem is that devaluation will tend to speed up the inflation process. Domestic factors will require compensation for the increased cost of imports, again, most forcefully in small economies where trade has a heavy weight. If compensation is granted, the initial improvement will be depleted. It is then of course possible to implement new devaluation rounds, but the development may become explosive, unless the government succeeds in containing the upward price pressure by domestic labor and capital.

The second issue that needs clarifying is what will happen to the volume sold by the country that devalues. The exchange rate change will result in a downward shift in that country's supply curve, measured in dollars, from S_1 to S_2 in figure 8.3, so if the country had unutilized capacity prior to devaluation, its supply will rise in the short run. When the country is a price-taker in the international market, the initial price, P_1 will remain unchanged, and the quantity supplied will rise from Q_1 to Q_3, with an unambiguous increase in dollar revenue. If, on the other hand, the country accounts for a significant share of the world market, its

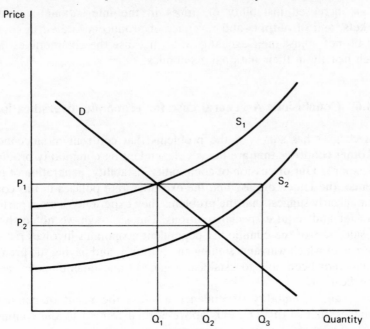

Figure 8.3 The impact of devaluation on output and price

demand curve will be downward-sloping like D, so devaluation will cause price to fall, and the quantity will only rise to Q_2. The change in the price-maker's revenue following from devaluation can be both positive and negative, and will depend on the price elasticities of his demand and supply.[31] The price-maker analysis applies also in the case of a number of small exporting countries devaluing in unison. In the longer run one will also have to consider the impact of improved competitiveness on capacity expansion.

The series of devaluations implemented by a number of commodity dependent countries in the 1980s expanded these countries' shares in many commodity markets, at the expense of less commodity dependent nations which did not devalue. The devaluation policies quite likely also led to an extension and further aggravation of the commodity price depression.

A third intriguing issue is whether symmetrical exchange rate policy responses can be expected from the commodity dependent economies, when there is a recovery in commodity price and demand. If adjustments of exchange rates are regularly implemented by the commodity dependent countries in response to commodity price movements, the implication will be an increased instability of prices in the international commodity markets, and of outputs and revenues of producers located in countries that do not adjust their exchange rates because the commodities do not weigh heavily in their national economies.

8.6 Conclusion: A general case for economic diversification?

This chapter has surveyed the problems that confront monoeconomies and other countries that are heavily dependent on commodity production and exports. Our discussion of commodity instability, generation of public revenue, the Dutch disease and the exchange rate policies in this country group, clearly suggest that the problems they experience have a particular character and require special solutions. But although we noted that the one-sidedness of the commodity dependent economies involves risks, the coverage of which warrants signing an insurance, and paying the premium, we have not been able to establish a general and unambiguous case for diversification.

After all, commodity dependence is often the result of competitive advantage that normally yields above-normal returns to the commodity sector. These may well be more than adequate to cover the cost of instability. Obversely, part of the resource rents contained in the above-normal returns will be forgone when the country diversifies out of its reliance on commodities.

It is true that the global demand for many commodities has trend growth rates that are slower than for the aggregate of manufactures. Slow demand growth *per se* need not involve disadvantage. The market for the output of a monoeconomy can expand briskly if the supply from other sources stagnates. Besides, high profits can well be earned even when demand does not expand.

We showed in an earlier chapter that the aggregate price index for commodities has tended to lag behind that for manufactures. This, too, does not by itself constitute a case against commodity specialization. There may be many exceptions from the aggregate commodity price trend. Besides, the profitability from commodity production can well be maintained in the face of falling prices, if technical advancement reduces the cost of production in equal or greater measure.

Commodity dependence need not necessarily trap a country in technical or other backwardness. Contrary to some perceptions, commodity production often requires as much advanced technology and human skills as manufacturing. Modern agriculture and mining make heavy use of microbiology, electronics and the highly qualified labor that goes with these techniques.

Large and profitable primary commodity production, both agricultural and mineral, holds a prominent place in the economies of advanced nations like Australia, Canada and the United States. This production would be even greater if the resource base permitted. The markets or governments would force a contraction of the raw materials industries if they were unprofitable or otherwise socially undesirable.

On these grounds we conclude that a heavy concentration on commodity production in a national economy is not detrimental *per se*. Certainly, cases can be found where heavy dependence on production of raw materials based on competitive advantage that has since been lost can damage social and economic development. Diversification out of such dependence is then strongly warranted. But it is much harder to find tenable arguments for a recommendation to, say, Malaysia, or Venezuela, both heavily dependent on the exports of a few commodities, that they should reduce their commodity dependence by a greater emphasis on manufacturing.

NOTES

1 See for instance the UN, *Yearbook of International Accounts Statistics, annual*.
2 This is the case in GATT's *International Trade*, annual.
3 UNCTAD, *Handbook of International Trade and Development Statistics*, 1986.
4 A. I. MacBean and D. T. Nguyen, *Commodity Policies: Problems and Prospects*, Croom Helm, London, 1987.
5 One of the more recent attempts yielding inconclusive results is by P. Brundell, H. Horn and P. Svedberg, "On the Causes of Instability of Export Earnings," *Oxford Bulletin of Economics and Statistics*, No. 3, 1981.
6 UNCTAD, *Handbook of International Trade and Development Statistics*, 1979 and 1986; *World Bank, World Development Report*, annual, several issues.
7 UNCTAD, "Commodity Export Earnings Shortfalls, Existing Financial Mechanisms, and the Effects of Shortfalls on the Economic Development of Developing Countries," TD/B/AC.43/5, July 1987.
8 J. M. Keynes, "The International Control of Raw Materials (A UK Treasury Memorandum dated 1942)," *Journal of International Economics*, No. 4, 1974.
9 J. R. Behrman, "Commodity Price Instability and Economic Goal Attainment in Developing Countries," *World Development*, May 1987.
10 For a description of the stabilization arrangements between the two world wars, see J. W. F. Rowe, *Primary Commodities in International Trade*, Cambridge University Press, Cambridge, 1965. The commodity agreements operating in the first decades after the Second World War are described in M. Radetzki, *International Commodity Market Arrangements*, C. Hurst, London, 1970.
11 Keynes, "International Control of Raw Materials."
12 For a description see for instance D. L. McNicol, *Commodity Agreements and Price Stabilization*, Lexington Books, Lexington, Mass., 1978.

13 See A. Maizels, "Commodity Instability and Developing Countries: The Debate," *Wider Working Paper*, No. 34, World Institute for Development of Economic Research of the UN University (Wider), Helsinki, January 1988, for a fuller discussion of the relationship between stabilization of price and revenue.

14 The detailed mode of operation of the five agreements is described in C. L. Gilbert, "International Commodity Agreements: Design and Performance," *World Development*, May 1987.

15 A. D. Law, *International Commodity Agreements*, Lexington Books, Lexington, Mass., 1975.

16 Gilbert, "International Commodity Agreements."

17 In August 1988, the scheme was renamed the "Compensatory and Contingency Financing Facility."

18 IMF quotas are financial commitments by member countries to this international organization. A country's quota is related to the size of its GDP.

19 UNCTAD, "Commodity Export Earnings Shortfalls."

20 M. Finger and D. DeRosa, "The Compensatory Finance Facility and Export Instability," *Journal of World Trade Law*, No. 1, 1980; D. DeRosa, "Stabilizing LDC Export Earnings: A Cost Benefit Analysis of the Compensatory Financing Facility," IMF, Revised Draft Paper, Washington, DC, May 1988.

21 UNCTAD, "Commodity Export Earnings Shortfalls."

22 Ibid.

23 UNCTAD, "The Processing and Marketing of Coffee," TD/B/C.1/PSC/31/ Rev.1, 1984; World Bank, "Groundnut Handbook," 1984; World Bank, *Price Prospects for Major Primary Commodities*, Report No. 814/86, vol. II, 1986; FAO, *The State of Food and Agriculture 1985*, 1986.

24 World Bank, *World Development Report*, 1986 edition.

25 J. Guest, "Problems in Managing the Mineral Resources Stabilization Fund," *CIPEC Quarterly Review*, October/December 1987.

26 R. Kumar and M. Radetzki, "Alternative Fiscal Regimes for Mining in Developing Countries," *World Development*, May 1987.

27 World Bank, *World Development Report*, 1986 edition.

28 M. Faber, "Some Old and New Devices in Mineral Royalties and taxation," in *Legal and Institutional Arrangements in Mineral Development*, Mining Journal Books, London, 1982.

29 For a fuller treatment of the subject, see J. P. Neary and S. Van Wijnbergen (eds), *Natural Resources and the Macroeconomy*, MIT Press, Cambridge, Mass., 1986, chapter 1.

30 IMF, *International Financial Statistics*, monthly, several issues.

31 For a formal analysis of this problem see M. Wattleeworth, "The Effects of Collective Devaluation on Commodity Prices and Exports," International Monetary Fund DM/87/1, January 1987.

Appendix: World Exports of Major Primary Commodities 1974–1987

	1974	1975	1976	1977	1978	1979	1980	1981	1982	1983	1984	1985	1986	1987
Crude petroleum (SITC 333)														
Volume (million tons)	1,387	1,273	1,715	1,740	1,700	1,770	1,600	1,430	1,280	1,220	1,240	1,210	1,313	1,225
Value ($ billion)	114	102	148	164	162	241	358	360	311	260	259	237	131	165
Aluminum metal (SITC 684.1)														
Volume (million tons)	3.7	3.3	3.6	3.9	4.3	4.1	4.9	4.8	5.3	6.2	5.8	6.5	6.8	7.1
Value ($ billion)	2.7	2.5	3.2	3.8	4.7	5.6	8.0	7.0	6.4	8.1	7.9	7.5	8.5	12.0
Copper														
Volume (million tons metal content)														
Concentrates (SITC 287.11, 287.12)	1.2	1.1	1.2	1.2	1.2	1.2	1.3	1.5	1.6	1.4	1.4	1.8	1.9	n.a.
Blister (SITC 682.11)	0.8	0.7	0.8	0.9	0.8	0.8	0.7	0.7	0.8	0.8	0.8	0.8	0.8	n.a.
Refined (SITC 682.12)	3.1	2.7	2.9	3.0	3.1	3.0	3.3	2.9	3.0	3.4	3.3	3.3	3.3	3.6
Total	5.1	4.5	4.9	5.1	5.1	5.0	5.3	5.1	5.4	5.6	5.5	5.9	6.0	n.a.
Value ($ billion)														
Concentrates	2.0	1.1	1.3	1.3	1.2	1.9	2.5	2.1	2.0	1.9	1.6	1.5	1.6	n.a.
Blister	1.5	0.8	1.1	1.2	1.0	1.2	1.3	1.1	1.1	1.2	1.0	0.8	0.7	n.a.
Refined	6.1	3.4	3.9	3.9	4.2	5.6	7.1	5.0	4.6	5.4	4.5	4.2	4.5	6.1
Total	9.7	5.3	6.4	6.4	6.4	8.7	10.9	8.2	7.7	8.5	7.1	6.5	6.8	n.a.
Iron ore (SITC 281.5, 281.6)														
Volume (million tons iron content)	250	234	232	220	218	247	241	234	213	197	232	233	235	237
Value ($ billion)	4.4	5.2	5.6	5.4	5.3	6.6	7.4	7.6	7.2	6.5	7.0	7.0	6.9	6.8

Appendix: *(con't)*

	1974	1975	1976	1977	1978	1979	1980	1981	1982	1983	1984	1985	1986	1987
Cotton (SITC 263.1)														
Volume (million tons)	3.8	4.0	4.1	3.9	4.5	4.4	4.8	4.3	4.4	4.3	4.3	4.3	4.7	5.2
Value ($ billion)	4.9	4.5	5.2	6.1	6.1	6.7	7.8	7.3	6.4	6.5	7.0	6.1	5.2	8.6
Natural rubber (SITC 232)														
Volume (million tons)	3.2	3.0	3.3	3.3	3.3	3.4	3.3	3.2	3.1	3.5	3.6	3.6	3.7	3.7
Value ($ billion)	2.3	1.7	2.4	2.6	3.1	4.1	4.4	3.4	2.5	3.3	3.5	2.7	2.9	3.6
Tobacco (SITC 121)														
Volume (million tons)	1.4	1.3	1.3	1.3	1.4	1.4	1.4	1.5	1.4	1.4	1.4	1.4	1.3	1.3
Value ($ billion)	2.5	2.6	2.9	3.0	3.8	3.8	3.8	4.4	4.6	4.2	4.2	4.1	3.9	3.9
Coffee (SITC 071.1)														
Volume (million tons)	3.4	3.6	3.7	2.9	3.4	3.8	3.7	3.7	3.9	4.0	4.1	4.3	3.9	4.4
Value ($ billion)	4.3	4.3	8.3	12.5	11.0	12.1	12.5	8.5	9.3	9.6	10.6	10.8	14.2	10.0
Sugar (SITC 061.1, 061.2)														
Volume (million tons)	22.9	21.6	22.9	28.4	25.7	26.1	26.9	28.8	30.2	28.9	28.7	28.3	28.2	27.9
Value ($ billion)	7.3	9.1	6.3	6.0	6.1	6.8	9.8	9.1	8.0	8.1	10.1	8.9	9.4	9.8
Wheat and wheat flour (SITC 041, 046)														
Volume (million tons)	65.5	73.8	69.1	74.5	84.9	81.6	99.5	105.5	105.2	111.8	116.1	105.3	95.7	102.9
Value ($ billion)	11.1	12.5	10.6	9.4	11.3	13.3	18.7	20.1	18.2	17.9	18.2	15.3	13.0	13.7

Source: BP, *Statistical Review of World Energy*, annual, several issues; World Bank, *Commodity, Trade and Price Trends*, 1986 edition; UNCTAD, *Commodity Yearbook 1986, 1987*; *Commodity Yearbook 1987, 1988*; IMF, *Primary Commodities, Market Developments and Outlook*, May 1988.

Bibliography

Aharoni, Y., "The State Owned Enterprise: An Agent Without a Principal," in L. Jones et al., *Public Enterprises in Developing Countries*, Cambridge University Press, Cambridge, 1982.

Améen, U., R. Gyllenram and A. Holmström, draft working papers on commodity exchanges, Royal Institute of Technology, Stockholm, 1988.

Anthony Bird Associates, *Aluminum Analysis*, No. 29, April 1986; No. 33, April 1987.

Association of Iron Ore Exporting Countries, *Iron Ore Statistics*, 2, 1987.

Bairoch, P., "La baisse des couts des transports et le développement économique," *Revue de l'Institut de Sociologie*, Brussels, 1965.

Behrman, J. R., "Commodity Price Instability and Economic Goal Attainment in Developing Countries," *World Development*, May 1987.

Black, D., *Success and Failure of Futures Contracts: Theory and Empirical Evidence*, Monograph Series in Finance and Economics, New York University, 1986.

Bosworth, B. P. and R. Z. Lawrence, *Commodity Prices and the New Inflation*, Brookings Institution, Washington, DC, 1982.

BP, *Statistical Review of World Energy*, London, annual.

Brown, C. P., *The Political and Social Economy of Commodity Control*, Macmillan, London, 1980.

Brundell, P., H. Horn and P. Svedberg, "On the Causes of Instability of Export Earnings," *Oxford Bulletin of Economics and Statistics*, No. 3, 1981.

Crowson, P., "The Global Distribution and Availability of Mineral Resources," paper presented to a symposium on mining and petroleum at the Delft University of Technology, 3–4 November 1987.

Cyert, R. M. and J. G. March, *A Behavioral Theory of the Firm*, Prentice-Hall, Englewood Cliffs, NJ, 1963.

Darmstadter, J. et al., *Energy in the World Economy*, Resources for the Future, Washington, DC, 1971.

DeRosa, D., "Stabilizing LDC Export Earnings: A Cost Benefit Analysis of the Compensatory Financing Facility," IMF, Revised Draft Paper, Washington, DC, May 1988.

DeRosa, D., "Agricultural Trade and Protection in Asia," IMF Working Paper/ 88/63, Washington, DC, July 1988.

Dobozi, I., "Emergence, Performance and World Market Impact of the State Mining Companies in Developing Countries," *Studies in Developing Economies*, No. 123, Institute for World Economics, Budapest, 1987.

Drexel, Burnham, Lambert, *Fine Tuning the Options Instrument – Synthetic Options for Metals Hedgers and Traders*, New York, 1986.

Drexel, Burnham, Lambert, *Managing Basis Risk Using Futures and Options, Framework for Analysis and Simulation*, New York, 1986.

Drexel, Burnham, Lambert, *Options Hedging and Trading Techniques in the Metals Industries*, New York, 1986.

Drexel, Burnham, Lambert, *Understanding the Delta or Hedge Ratio in Options Trading and Hedging*, New York, 1986.

Drexel, Burnham, Lambert, *An Introduction to Technical Analysis of the Futures Markets*, New York, 1987.

Drexel, Burnham, Lambert, *Futures and Options Monthly Report* (New York), January 15, 1988.

Edwards, F. R., "The Clearing Association in Futures Markets: Guarantor and Regulator," in R. W. Anderson (ed.), *The Industrial Organization of Futures Markets*, Lexington Books, Lexington, Mass., 1984.

Energy in Profile, Shell Briefing Service No. 4, 1985 and No. 4, London, 1987.

Erzan, R. and G. Karsenty, "Products Facing High Tariffs in Major Developed Market Economy Countries: An area of priority for developing countries in the Uruguay Round?," Seminar Paper No. 401, Institute for International Economic Studies, University of Stockholm, December 1987.

Faber, M., "Some Old and New Devices in Mineral Royalties and Taxation," in *Legal and Institutional Arrangements in Mineral Development*, Mining Journal Books, London, 1982.

FAO, *The State of Food and Agriculture 1985*, Rome, 1986.

Financial Times, October 18, 1988.

Finger, M. and D. DeRosa, "The Compensatory Finance Facility and Export Instability," *Journal of World Trade Law*, No. 1, 1980.

Fliessing, H. and S. Van Wijnbergen, "Primary Commodity Prices, the Business Cycle, and the Real Exchange Rate of the Dollar," World Bank Background Paper WDR–1985, Washington, DC, 1985.

Floyd, R. H., C. S. Gray and R. P. Short, *Public Enterprise in Mixed Economies, Some Macroeconomic Aspects*, IMF, Washington, DC, 1984.

Friedman, M., "In Defence of Destabilizing Speculation," in *The Optimum Quantity of Money and Other Essays*, Macmillan, London, 1969.

Gately, D., "A Ten-year Retrospective: OPEC and the World Oil Market," *Journal of Economic Literature*, September 1984.

GATT, *International Trade*, Geneva, annual.

Ghosh, S., C. L. Gilbert and A. J. Hughes Hallet, *Stabilizing Speculative Commodity Markets*, Clarendon Press, Oxford, 1987.

Gilbert, C. L., "International Commodity Agreements: Design and Performance," *World Development*, May 1987.

Gillis, M., "The Role of State Enterprises in Economic Development," *Social Research*, vol. 47, summer 1980.

Giraud, P. N., *Géopolitique des ressources minières*, Economica, Paris, 1983.

Gordon, R. L., *World Coal, Economics, Policies and Prospects*, Cambridge University Press, Cambridge, 1987.

Granger, C. W. J., "The Purpose and Working of Commodity Markets," in C. W. J. Granger (ed.), *Trading in Commodities*, Woodhead Faulkner, Cambridge, 1974.

Griffin, J. M. and D. J. Teece (eds.), *OPEC Behavior and World Oil Prices*, Allen and Unwin, London, 1982.

Grilli, E. R. and Maw Cheng Yang, "Primary Commodity Prices, Manufactured Goods Prices and the Terms of Trade of Developing Countries: What the Long Run Shows," *World Bank Economic Review*, January 1988.

Guest, J., "Problems in Managing the Mineral Resources Stabilization Fund (in Papua New Guinea)," *CIPEC Quarterly Review*, October–December 1987.

Hotelling, H., "The Economics of Exhaustible Resources," *Journal of Political Economy*, April 1931.

IMF, *International Financial Statistics*, Washington, DC, monthly.

IMF, *Financial Statistics*, yearbook, Washington, DC, 1982.

IMF, *Primary Commodities, Market Developments and Outlook*, Washington, DC, May 1988.

Keynes, J. M., "National Self-sufficiency," *Yale Review*, summer 1933.

Keynes, J. M., *The General Theory of Employment, Interest and Money*, Harcourt, New York, 1936.

Keynes, J. M., "The International Control of Raw Materials (A UK Treasury Memorandum dated 1942)," *Journal of International Economics*, No. 4, 1974.

Ke-Young Chu and T. K. Morrison, "The 1981–1982 Recession and Non-oil Primary Commodity Prices," *IMF Staff Papers*, March 1984.

Kindleberger, C., *The Terms of Trade, A European Case Study*, John Wiley, New York, 1956.

Kumar, R. and M. Radetzki, "Alternative Fiscal Regimes for Mining in Developing Countries," *World Development*, May 1987.

Labys, W. C., and H. C. Thomas, "Speculation, Hedging and Commodity Price Behavior: An International Comparison," *Applied Economics*, No. 7, 1975.

Laird, S. and A. J. Yeats, "Empirical Evidence Concerning the Magnitude and Effects of Developing Country Tariff Escalation," UNCTAD Discussion Paper, Geneva, 1986.

Landes, D. S., "The Great Drain and Industrialisation: Commodity Flows from Periphery to Centre in Historical Perspective," in R. C. O. Matthews (ed.), *Economic Growth and Resources*, vol. 2, *Trends and Factors*, Macmillan, London, 1980.

Langhammer, R. J. and A. Sapir, *Economic Impact of Generalized Tariff Preferences*, Trade Policy Research Centre, London, 1987.

Law, A. D., *International Commodity Agreements*, Lexington Books, Lexington, Mass., 1975.

Layard, P. R. G. and A. A. Walters, *Microeconomic Theory*, McGraw-Hill, New York, 1978.

Leibenstein, H., "X-Efficiency and the Analysis of State Enterprise," paper presented at the Second BAPEG Conference on Public Enterprises in Mixed Economy LDCs, Boston, Mass., April 1980.

Lewis, W. A., "World Production, Prices and Trade 1870–1960," *Manchester School of Social and Economic Studies*, May 1952.

Loo, T. and E. Tower, "Agricultural Protectionism and the Less Developed Countries," Center for International Economics, Canberra, 1988, as reported in *The Economist*, June 4, 1988.

MacBean, A. I. and D. T. Nguyen, *Commodity Policies, Problems and Prospects*,

Croom Helm, London, 1987.

McNicol, D. L., *Commodity Agreements and Price Stabilization*, Lexington Books, Lexington, Mass., 1978.

Maizels, A., "Commodity Instability and Developing Countries: The Debate," *Wider Working Paper*, No. 34, World Institute for Development of Economic Research of the UN University (Wider), Helsinki, January 1988.

Manners, G., *The Changing World Market for Iron Ore 1950–1980*, Resources for the Future, Washington, DC, 1971.

Markowski, A., and M. Radetzki, "State Ownership and the Price Sensitivity of Supply: the Case of the Copper Mining Industry," *Resources Policy*, March 1987.

Mason, E. S., "Natural Resources and Environmental Restrictions to Growth," *Challenge*, January–February 1978.

Metallgesellschaft, *Metal Statistics*, Frankfurt am Main, annual.

Metallgesellschaft, "Pressmeldungen über die Metallmärkte," Frankfurt am Main, monthly.

Metals Analysis and Outlook, quarterly.

Metals Analysis and Outlook, Five Year Outlook 1987–1991, August 1987.

Mikesell, R. F., *New Patterns of World Mineral Development*, British–North American Committee, London, 1979.

Mikesell, R. F., *Stockpiling Strategic Materials*, American Enterprise Institute for Public Policy Research, Washington, DC, 1986.

Mill, J. S., *Principles of Political Economy*, John W. Parker, London, 1848.

Mining Annual Review, annual.

Mining Journal, December 9, 1983.

Morton, K. and P. Tulloch, *Trade and Developing Countries*, Croom Helm, London, 1977.

Neary, J. P. and S. Van Wijnbergen (eds.), *Natural Resources and the Macro-economy*, MIT Press, Cambridge, Mass., 1986.

Neff, T., *The International Uranium Market*, Ballinger, Cambridge, Mass., 1984.

North–South, A Program for Survival (The Brandt Report), Pan Books, London, 1980.

Nuexco (Nuclear Exchange Corporation), *Market Report*, Merlo Park, California, monthly.

Penrose, E. F., *The Large International Firm in Developing Countries; The International Petroleum Industry*, Allen and Unwin, London, 1968.

Prain, R., *Copper, the Anatomy of an Industry*, Mining Journal Books Ltd, London, 1975.

Prebish, R., "The Economic Development of Latin America and Its Principal Problems," *Economic Bulletin for Latin America*, 1962, pp. 1–22.

Priovolos, T., "Commodity Bonds: A Risk Management Instrument for Developing Countries," World Bank Commodity Markets Division, Working Paper No. 1987–12, Washington, DC, 1987.

Radetzki, M., *International Commodity Market Arrangements*, C. Hurst, London, 1970.

Radetzki, M., "Commodity Prices during Two Booms, 1950 and 1973," *Skandinaviska Enskilda Banken Quarterly Review*, No. 4, 1974.

Radetzki, M., "The Rising Costs of Base Materials – the Case of Copper," *Mining Magazine*, April 1979.

Radetzki, M., *Sverige avskärmat*, SNS, Stockholm, 1981.

Radetzki, M., *Uranium, A Strategic Source of Energy*, Croom Helm, London, 1981.

Radetzki, M., "Regional Development Benefits of Mineral Projects," *Resources Policy*, September 1982.

Radetzki, M., "Strategic Metal Markets; Prospects for Producer Cartels," *Resources Policy*, December 1984.

Radetzki, M., *State Mineral Enterprises: An Investigation into Their Impact on the International Mineral Markets*, Resources for the Future, Washington, DC, 1985.

Radetzki, M., "Outlook for Oil and Coal Prices in International Trade," *Skandinaviska Enskilda Banken Quarterly Review*, No. 4, 1986.

Radetzki, M., "Developing Countries: The New Growth Markets," in J. E. Tilton (ed.), *World Metal Demand: Past Trends and Future Prospects*, Resources for the Future, Washington, DC, (forthcoming).

Radetzki, M. and K. Takeuchi, "Growth Patterns in Copper Consumption in Industrializing Countries," *World Bank Staff Commodity Working Paper*, No. 21, Washington, DC, 1989.

Ridler, D. and C. A. Yandle, "A Simplified Method for Analyzing the Effects of Exchange Rate Changes on Exports of Primary Commodities," *IMF Staff Papers*, November 1972.

Rowe, J. W. F., *Primary Commodities in International Trade*, Cambridge University Press, Cambridge, 1965.

Sapsford, D., "The Statistical Debate on the Net Barter Terms of Trade between Primary Commodities and Manufactures: A Comment and Some Additional Evidence," *Economic Journal*, 1985, pp. 781−8.

Scitovsky, T., *Welfare and Competition*, Unwin, London, 1952.

Shearson Lehman Brothers, *Futures Facts*, undated, circa 1985.

Sherer, F. M., *Industrial Market Structure and Economic Performance*, Rand McNally, Chicago, 1980.

Singer, H., "The Distribution of Gains between Investing and Borrowing Countries," *American Economic Review*, 1950, pp. 473−85.

Stein, J. L., "Destabilizing Speculative Activity Can Be Profitable," *Review of Economics and Statistics*, vol. 43, 1981.

Stewart, B., "An Analysis of Speculative Trading in Grain Futures," US Department of Agriculture Technical Bulletin 1001, 1949.

Streit, M. E. (ed.), *Futures Markets, Modelling, Managing and Monitoring Futures Trading*, Basil Blackwell, Oxford, 1983.

Telser, L. G., "Why There Are Organized Futures Markets," *Journal of Law and Economics*, April 1981.

Tilton, J., "Comparative Advantage in Mining," IIASA Working Paper WP 83−91, September 1983.

Tyers, R. and K. Anderson, "Liberalising OECD Agricultural Policies in the Uruguay Round: Effects on Trade and Welfare," *Journal of Agricultural Economics*, May 1988.

UN, *International Trade Statistics Yearbook*, New York, annual.

UN, *Monthly Bulletin of Statistics*, New York, June 1987.

UN, *Yearbook of International Accounts Statistics*, New York, annual.

UNCTAD, *Handbook of International Trade and Development Statistics*, New York, annual.

UNCTAD, *Monthly Commodity Price Bulletin*, New York, 1960−1984 Supplement.

UNCTAD, "The Processing and Marketing of Manganese: Areas for International Cooperation," TD/B/C.1/PSC/20, Geneva, August 1981.

UNCTAD, "Processing and Marketing of Phosphates: Areas for International Cooperation," TD/B/C.1/PSC/22, Geneva, 1981.

UNCTAD, "The Processing and Marketing of Primary Commodities," TD/B/C.1/PSC/23, Geneva, 24 November 1981.

UNCTAD, "The Processing and Marketing of Coffee," TD/B/C.1/PSC/31/Rev.1, Geneva, 1984.

UNCTAD, "Marketing and Processing of Tea: Areas for International Cooperation," TD/B/C.1/PSC/28/Rev.1, Geneva, 1984.

UNCTAD, "Commodity Export Earning Shortfalls, Existing Financial Mechanisms, and the Effects of Shortfalls on the Economic Development of Developing Countries." TD/B/AC.43/5, Geneva, July 1987.

UNCTAD, "Review of the Current Market Situation and Outlook for Iron Ore," TD/B/IBC/IRON ORE/AC.1/8, Geneva, September 1987.

UNCTAD, *Revitalizing Development, Growth and International Trade*, New York, 1987.

UNCTAD, *Commodity Yearbook 1986*, New York, 1987.

UNCTAD, *Commodity Yearbook 1987*, New York, 1988.

US Bureau of Mines, "Chromium, Effectiveness of Alternative US Policies in Reducing the Economic Costs of Supply Disruption," Washington, DC, November 1981.

US Bureau of Mines, *Mineral Commodity Summaries*, Washington, DC, annual.

US Bureau of Mines, *Mineral Facts and Problems*, Washington, DC, 1985 edition.

US Bureau of Mines, *South Africa and Critical Materials*, Washington, DC, July 1986.

US Department of Interior, "Cobalt, Effectiveness of Alternative US Policies in Reducing the Economic Costs of Supply Disruption," Washington, DC, August 1981.

Vedavalli, R., "Market Structure of Bauxite/Alumina/Aluminum, and Prospects for Developing Countries," World Bank Commodity Paper No. 24, Washington, DC, 1977.

Vernon, R., *Two Hungry Giants, the United States and Japan in the Quest for Oil and Ores*, Harvard University Press, Cambridge, Mass., 1983.

Vogley, W. A., "Materials Policy: Europe," in M. B. Beaver et al. (eds.), *Encyclopedia of Materials Science and Engineering*, Pergamon, New York, 1986.

Wälde, T., "Third World Mineral Development: Current Issues," *Columbia Journal of World Business*, Spring 1984.

Warnecke, S. J., *Stockpiling of Critical Raw Materials*, Royal Institute of International Affairs, London, 1980.

Wattleeworth, M., "The Effects of Collective Devaluation on Commodity Prices and Exports," *International Monetary Fund* DM/87/1, January 1987.

World Bank, *Commodity Trade and Price Trends*, Washington, DC, annual.

World Bank, *World Development Report*, Washington, DC, annual.

World Bank, *Price Prospects for Major Primary Commodities*, Report No. 814, Washington, DC, 1975 and 1986.

World Bank, *World Tables 1976*, Washington, DC, 1976.

World Bank, "Export Oriented Processing of Primary Commodities in Developing Countries," Commodity Note No. 14, September 1979.

World Bank, "Rice Handbook," Washington, DC, 1981.

World Bank, "Rubber Handbook," Washington, DC, 1981.

World Bank, "Tea Handbook," Washington, DC, 1982.

World Bank, " Groundnut Handbook," Washington, DC, 1984.

World Bank, "Banana Handbook," Washington, DC, 1985.

World Bank, "Coffee Handbook," Washington, DC, 1985.

Yeats, A. J., "Do International Transport Costs Increase with Fabrication? Some Empirical Evidence," *Oxford Economic Papers*, November 1977.

Zambia Mining Yearbook, Kitwe, Zimbabwe, annual.

Zorn, S., "Industrial Countries' Approaches to Security of Supply, and Effects on Developing Countries," *Primary Commodities: Security of Supply*, Friedrich Ebert Stiftung, Bonn and Washington, 1981.

Index